WHEN LIFE GIVES YOU LEMONS . . .
DRINK COCONUT MILK

Life-Changing Stories from
Twenty-Two Amazing Women

SEASON 1

Jana Danielson

Published by
Hybrid Global Publishing
333 E 14th Street
#3C
New York, NY 10003

Manufactured in the United States of America, or in the United Kingdom when distributed elsewhere.

Danielson, Jana.
When Life Gives You Lemons . . . Drink Coconut Milk: Life-Changing Stories from Twenty-Two Amazing Women
     ISBN: 978-1-957013-59-6
     eBook: 978-1-957013-60-2

Cover design by: Tyler Danielson
Copyediting by: Jake Williams/Jana Danielson
Interior design by: Claudia Volkman
Author photo by: Lisa Bissonnette

DEDICATION

This book is dedicated to my boys. My high school sweetheart turned husband of over 25 years, Jason. You are my soulmate, my best friend and the love of my life. Thank you for seeing the things in me that I have yet not seen and encouraging me to reach higher and think bigger than I ever thought possible. Tyler, Will and Tommy—thank you for choosing me to be your mom. You bring me the juiciest lemons so that I can drink the sweetest, most nutritious coconut milk from them. I love you!

CONTENTS

INTRODUCTION

We have all heard the saying, when life gives you lemons, make lemonade. In fact, that was one of my mantras that I would say in my mind over and over and over. It reminded me that even on those days where little hiccups or little bumps happened that there was still lots of magic to be learned in those instances. Well, the title of this book is *When Life Gives You Lemons . . . Drink Coconut Milk*. Now that's a total pattern interrupt to what we have known to be, when life gives you lemons, make lemonade.

First of all, lemonade is packed with sugar and you can have that crash coming down on the other side. Now, why coconut milk? This title of my book is really rooted in an experience that my family and I had very recently. Toward the end of 2021, my husband, Jason, came home from work and asked the question, what do you think about moving to Mexico? It was a cold, dreary day, at our then home in Saskatoon, Canada. I immediately responded, yeah, of course, I'd like to move to Mexico. And he said to me, well, I'm not joking. And I responded back, well, I'm not joking, either, when actually, I was joking. He wanted to tell me that there was a new opportunity in Mexico that our family could take advantage of if we chose. During this time, he was building a new company, and we had this opportunity presented to us.

So you need to understand we are two Saskatchewan born, small town, farm kids. We went to the same preschool program together right through elementary and high school. We moved to the same city to go to university. We got married and had our three amazing boys. We had great careers in the corporate world, which we left behind to open up our own businesses. We are your typical Saskatchewan people who in many cases set down roots and stay. So the idea of uprooting and moving two countries away sent a whole bunch of emotion through me. As the mom, I kept asking myself, was I doing right by my family? Jason and I have spent time apart for different business reasons. And now, after 25 and a half years of marriage, I didn't want to do it anymore. So yeah, he could have flown back and forth from Mexico to Canada or the boys and I could have flown back and forth to see him, but this sparked an interest that maybe we should go on this adventure as a family.

The other consideration was my bricks and mortar business, my Pilates studio and my integrated health therapies clinic (and yes, I do have an online business called the Metta District, which is my lifestyle community, and I do have a product in the e-commerce space, the Cooch Ball for women and the Gooch Ball for men). This beautiful business that I grew because of my own health journey, which you will learn more about in my chapter, was like my fourth baby. It started out in my basement, and grew into a beautiful 2,000-square-foot Pilates studio, which then grew into a beautiful 9,000-square-foot integrated health therapies clinic and Pilates studio with a team of amazing beating hearts that believed in the same philosophy as I did, that the body is a system of systems and therefore needs different things at different times. I decided that I was going to put my family first. And I was going to trust in the years of building a team, of building processes, and building systems to be able to say yes to this adventure. That's exactly what we did.

In getting ready to move to Mexico, there were a lot of unknowns. We ended up with our dishwasher flooding our home just before we left. There were lots of little taps on the shoulder that allowed me to surrender into the more spiritual side of my being and really believe that this move was what we were meant to be doing. I didn't quite understand all the aspects of it. But we were going to do it. One night as I was packing, a wave of emotion that I could feel in my toes worked its way up through my body and I just cried and cried and cried. Jason walked into our bedroom and there I was, amongst all this clutter of boxes - some boxes that were going to my parents' place, some boxes that were going to his parents' place, some boxes that were going to be donated. And he asked the question, what's wrong? And I just said, what are we doing? What are we doing? This isn't what we do. He said, what do you mean? I said, we are the deeply rooted, high school sweethearts who have three boys we are raising with really solid, foundational values. He took my hands, and he looked right in my eyes, which felt like he was looking into my soul. And he said, we have given this family the deepest roots that two people who love each other can give. And it's now time for us to give this family wings and go on this adventure together to live in a different country, in a different culture, where different languages are spoken. We get to trade in snow for sand. He said to me, home is where you choose it to be. You don't only need to have one home. And he was right. So, I just surrendered. I surrendered into his arms, I surrendered into trusting that we were doing the right thing.

When we got to Mexico, it was like a roller coaster. First of all, it felt eerily comfortable for me. And I was thinking, isn't it supposed to feel weird? Is it supposed to feel foreign? But I fell in love with the people, I fell in love with their value system of family first. We would hear these beautiful people come together at the beach and laugh and laugh and laugh and be with their extended family and just be so joyful. They weren't sitting on their phones, they were just being with each other in the moment. I fell in love with it.

At the end of our very first week in Nuevo Vallarta, where we live, Jason and I went for a walk in our new neighborhood. We came around a corner on this one street and we saw a gardening maintenance truck and some workers. One of the gentlemen was way up high in a tree cutting down coconuts. This other gentleman picked up two coconuts that had just fallen to the ground. He took his machete and he cut the top of the coconut off. As we came around the corner, he handed one of those coconuts to Jason and one of those coconuts to me. In that exact moment where his hands and my hands were on that coconut, there was this sense of calm and confidence that I had not felt in months and months and months, even before Jason came home that day in late of 2021 and asked the question, do you want to move to Mexico? Way before then. When I looked into the worker's eyes, I immediately started crying. I think maybe he thought he hurt me somehow. Because he was responding, lo siento, lo siento, which is I'm sorry in Spanish. I said, no, no, no, I'm okay, I'm fine. We continued walking, and Jason looked at me and asked, are you okay? What happened? In the moment, when that sense of calm and confidence draped over me like a warm, fuzzy blanket, I knew that for this moment we were exactly where we were meant to be, hence the symbolism of the coconut milk part of this book title.

That moment is the inspiration for what you're about to experience in this collaborative book, where I have invited women who have been planted in my life for many different reasons, and who have impacted me radically. When the idea for this project came into my head, I heard the voice of my almost 103-year-old Baba. So, Baba is grandmother in Ukrainian, and I do have Ukrainian roots. Before my Baba passed away in the fall of 2021, one of the last times I visited her, she grabbed my hand and she looked me in the eye. Her nickname for me was Janzy. And she said, Janzy, you are destined for things greater than you could ever imagine. And she said, I never ever want you to forget that if God gave you the ability to think of an idea, any idea, then he also gave you the ability to see it through to fruition. When I got the idea for this book, I felt her presence, I felt her hand in mine, I felt the warmth of it, and I could hear her voice.

The women you are about to meet in these chapters have all experienced some pretty sour lemons, those moments where they were brought to their knees. In most cases, some people would think of surrender - wave the white flag, I'm done. And yet, something beautiful about the resiliency of the divine feminine, in the darkest moments, a little flicker of light, a little tiny sparkle shines through. And that was their coconut milk. I am so excited for you to connect with these women, to connect with their stories.

Many of these women you would look at face value and think oh my gosh, she is so lucky. Look at her career, look at her family, look at her relationship, look at her lifestyle. You might judge or have this feeling of, that's what I want. This book is about peeling back the layers and let me tell you, we peeled them waaay back. These women got raw in their interviews. They are baring their hearts and their souls. My dream for this book, as you hold it in your hands, or read it on your tablet, is that at least one story connects with you in such a deeply fundamental way, that you are changed as a person forever.

Each chapter is titled the name of the woman who you are about to meet. Twenty-one amazing beating hearts answered my invitation to be a part of this project. After each shares her 'lemons to coconut milk story' there is a Q&A section where she and I go a bit deeper into some of the journey that she shared with us. Then, you will find her bio and contact info so that you'll be able to connect with her if that feels right. This book is in your hands for a reason. There is no coincidence that you were called to have this resource in your life. Be humbled. Be inspired. Let the adventure of turning your lemons into coconut milk begin!

—Jana

CHRISTINE

Throughout my life, I've had several occasions where I could say we've turned lemons into coconut milk, but the one that is the most significant is the health crisis that both my daughter and I have faced. My daughter, Sophie, was only six years old when she was diagnosed with Acute Lymphoblastic Leukemia, and gosh, that was a really rough time. Originally, they said to us that because her organs had started shutting down, she may have had as little as two weeks to live.

It was such a shock when she was actually diagnosed. We had a blood test, and four hours later, our general practitioner phoned us in a panic. That was unusual in itself! I've never had a GP reach out and phone me before! She said, "You have to take her to the Children's Hospital right now. Literally, drop whatever you're doing and get there."

And a million things were running through my mind at the time, and none of them were cancer. I thought, gosh, is she contagious? What is this? Why would we need to go? It turns out that it was such an urgent matter because she had zero platelets. That effectively meant that even a paper cut would have led to her bleeding out within a few minutes. It literally would have been impossible to save her. That was a shock! She'd been at school the day before. All the "what if" scenarios go through your mind. Fortunately, she got through that. We were able to save her organs with blood transfusions. And then she went through the toughest two and a half years, hopefully of her life, but definitely the toughest two and a half years of my life. There were several occasions where I wasn't sure she was going to make it through the night.

I had an experience in the hospital with Sophie one night. It was actually Christmas Eve. I don't think I will ever fully recover from seeing an emergency crash team racing into the room to revive your child. There is no amount of therapy that can overcome seeing that. I also have an incredible amount of gratitude for the fact that if you're going to go through that, you want to go through that in a hospital. We had the people on hand who were there to save her life and to keep her with us. If we hadn't experienced that horrendous moment, we wouldn't have experienced the incredible amount of love and gratitude that got us through that tough time. I have two incredible memories to take out of that experience. One of them was a music therapist sitting with her. Her heart was beating, but it was too fast. The nurse was saying that she's not in a safe zone, her heart is racing, we need to get it into a safe zone. But the drugs were doing nothing. One of the nurses said, "I'm going to call in the music therapist."

It was Christmas Morning! What kind of human being gives up a part of his Christmas Day to come and help a child in need? A very special kind! I'll be forever grateful that he sat with her. It felt like a really long time, but it was probably only an hour. His playing was fast, like he was matching the beat to her heart rate. And I could tell that she was engaged with it, even though she was quite out of it, because she moved her head towards him and towards the music as if she was aware. And gradually over the period of time, the pace that he was playing music gradually slowed down, and so did her heart, and she got back into a safe zone. It was like witnessing a miracle. It felt like an eternity... I was holding my breath, just watching every heartbeat. I wish I had the wherewithal about me at the time to film what I was witnessing because I think that would be incredibly powerful.

The next major turning point for Sophie was just a few hours later. We were in Melbourne at the time. It wasn't even our local hospital. Sophie had been doing really well with her treatment. We'd been given clearance to go and spend Christmas with my husband's family in

Melbourne. So it meant that we were in a hospital with doctors and nurses who didn't know her, didn't know us. And so, we felt really uncomfortable. But one of the things that turned into quite a blessing through that tough time was that one of the big things they do in Melbourne is the local firefighters run a big Christmas Day media frenzy. They go into the Children's Hospital. I was in my pajamas, Sophie was in her undies, barely conscious. We were definitely not media ready. There were only three children who were too sick to leave the hospital. They had sent everybody else to a Christmas function at the charity house next door. Sophie couldn't leave. So, having this media turn up, they could see the look of horror on my face. But the firefighter who was dressed up as Santa still said, "I don't care about the media, I'm not here just for the cameras, I'm here for the children."

So, he kicked the cameras out. And he came in dressed up as Santa. Sophie, to this day, believes it was Santa who came to see her. He had presents that had been donated, and at that particular point, when he came in, Sophie was too sick to do much. She couldn't even open the present. But it was such a turning point that Santa had come to visit. He told her, this fireman told her, "You're going to be better in no time. In a couple of hours, you're going to be able to sit up and open these presents." And to everyone's amazement, she did! A couple of hours later, she sat up and she opened her present. I don't even know who that fireman was. His generosity to give up his time, despite the fact that it couldn't even be filmed, was wonderful. I have so much gratitude.

And since that, I have been so passionate about giving back to charities. It was the Redkite charity that provided the music therapist and I'm now a very big advocate for them. I also donate as many Christmas gifts as I can possibly get my hands on to our local children's hospital. I have donated several hundred gifts every year since. You just don't know when the right gift at the right time might spark another miracle. We were able to drag so many positives out of that horrendous day because we've been focused on paying it forward and making a difference to other people. And if we hadn't experienced that incredibly bitter lemon, then we might not have been able to make a difference now to thousands of other families. Who knows what we've sparked as a result.

That music therapist wasn't from our local hospitals. I've never seen him again, I didn't even get his name. Same with the firefighter. I've got no idea who he was, other than an incredibly good-looking Santa! But what he said to Sophie carried so much weight. She was six. The magic of Santa at six is so powerful, so very powerful, and what a blessing he gave us. These people are giving up their time to make a difference, and they made SUCH a difference for us that I've been inspired to do as much as I can. I've done so many charity talks. I've spoken to, now, tens of thousands of people in audiences around Australia. I've been incredibly passionate about talking to potential donors, big donors, people who have millions to contribute. I think my passion and heart and story of the difference that their money could potentially make has been so critical to helping charities to secure the extra funding that they need to make that kind of difference. And until my dying day, I will be giving back to charities. Because of that incredibly bitter lemon, who knows what I'm helping to spark for someone else.

That was the most memorable day of Sophie's journey. And about a year and a half into her two-and-a-half-year marathon, I suffered my own health crisis. I experienced a series of what turned out to be strokes and pseudoaneurysms on the brain. I experienced a whole range of strange symptoms. They originally ruled out a stroke because I had none of the risk factors. I was super healthy, didn't smoke, didn't drink. I regularly ran five kilometers. I was 41 at the time, but fitter than I had been at 21. They couldn't figure out what was going on. I had a droopy eye. And to this day, I can still see it. But it's nowhere near as bad as it was. Strangely, the rest of my face didn't droop, it was just my right eyelid.

Initially I was sent to an eye specialist to see if they knew what was going on. And then the symptoms, over the space of two weeks, got worse and worse and weirder and weirder. I had a loss of feeling on one side of my body, and then I'd have it on the other side of my body. And I would have tingling down one side and then I'd have it on my face and then I'd have it on the opposite leg. It was just such a random mix. For periods of time, I would lose the ability to walk. It wasn't that there was physically anything wrong with my legs, but I lost depth perception. I couldn't tell where the ground was. It was scary! I felt like I was an astronaut walking in space. For chunks of time I completely lost the ability to communicate. That was the scariest part! I love talking. Sometimes you can't shut me up. But not being able to communicate at all is terrifying! What I thought I was saying wasn't coming out. The words I was speaking were complete nonsense! I tried to text it out on my phone. And even that was a complete random mix of God knows what. I don't know how to explain how terrifying it is to be locked in your body and unable to communicate. Fortunately, each time that happened, it wasn't for an extended period of time, but it felt like an eternity. There were other periods of time where I was still able to communicate, but it was really slow, I felt like I was wading through mud, trying to find the words. It was just like, I know it's there, I know, I know what it is, but I had to work really hard to get it and to be able to speak it. It was exhausting. Communicating was just exhausting. And then I'd have horrendous headaches. It felt like my brain was about to explode! That's partly why I think it took so long for them to diagnose what was going on. They thought I was having migraines because migraines can be responsible for a range of unusual symptoms. They also did tests on me where they wanted to see if I could walk in a straight line. Even when I wasn't having depth perception issues, I thought I was walking in a straight line, and they said, "Uh no, you didn't."

Eventually my case came across the right desk. And the right neurologist saw it and said, "I think I know what's going on."

He sent me for an MRI. Previously I had a CT scan, and nothing was picked up on that. It turned out that I had tears in both my carotid arteries. Usually tears like that are caused by extreme whiplash in a car accident. Apparently, that's actually what often kills somebody in a car accident. The arteries are torn, and it's this massive life-ending stroke. Spontaneous tears like I had that aren't caused by trauma are incredibly rare. Incredibly rare. Usually somebody who ends up being diagnosed with that condition, it's done so postmortem because they're trying to work out why some healthy triathlete drops dead or why somebody mowing the lawn drops dead. My neurologist said they only see a couple of people each year who survive this condition. He told me that I was in such a fragile state, and we're not sure that you're going to live.

My right carotid artery was the worst. It was 95% blocked by a flap from the tear. The neurologist said, 'You're in such a precarious position that had you picked up your child, (my son was only four at the time), it probably would have been a life-ending event." As it turns out, I'd been in Tamworth, which is about four hours' drive from my home, at a gymnastics competition with my eldest daughter, so I hadn't seen my son for a few days. A lot of the symptoms were happening while I was away. One of the women who I was at the competition with was a pain management specialist at the big hospital in Newcastle, where I live. She suspected that I was in a precarious position and just arranged everything calmly. She got one of the other moms to look after Emily (my eldest daughter), to take her to the competition. She convinced me that we needed to get home so I could go to the big hospital. The hospital in Tamworth hadn't been any help. She kept me calm the whole way. And delivered me to my husband, Paul. She'd spoken to Paul in the meantime, and explained how precarious of a situation I was. He had arranged for me to go straight to the hospital. I didn't come home for several days. It amazes me how many people come out of the woodwork in a crisis who are willing to step up and help. And it's almost like the right people have been there for me and for Sophie at the right time.

So many people throughout the journey that Sophie and I have both been on have said to me, "Everything happens for a reason."

Honestly, I feel like slapping those people, every single one of them. I don't, I'm polite. I just nod and say, I'm sure you're right. Inside I'm thinking, you cow! How can you think that childhood cancer happens for a reason? The number of children whom we got to know, who died, and people would say to their parents, everything happens for a reason. It's like, that is the worst thing that well-meaning people can possibly ever say because there is no good reason for childhood cancer. There is no good reason for a child to die. There is no good reason for me to have gone through everything that I went through. There's just no good reason. But what I do believe is that it IS possible to drag something positive out of a bad situation. It is possible to find the gift in every crappy situation. And we are very good at doing that!

When they eventually worked out what was going on for my health crisis, I was told that I might not live through the night. I couldn't even reach out to Paul to support me because Sophie was having chemotherapy in the children's clinic down the hall in the hospital. I was in the Intensive Care Stroke Unit. It was me and all these 70- and 80-year-old men. I felt a little out of place, but there were no beds in the women's ward. I decided to focus on my gratitude that I'm here, I have a bed and I have people to look after me. But that was an interesting evening to go through. I felt like, okay, if I might not live through the night, I'm not going to sleep. I'm just going to write letters to all my loved ones. And that was probably the most challenging thing I've ever had to do. It wasn't for myself that I felt bad. I wrote down all of the things in my life that had been amazing, all the things I've gotten to do. But feeling like I'm not gonna be there for my children. That was hard. I felt like they weren't ready to be without me. Sophie was 7 and fighting leukemia, Andy was only 5 and Emily only 10! So I wrote them letters full of love. Other than not being there for my children, there was really only one thing I regretted not doing with my life.

I think it's pretty amazing that there's only one thing. Of course there are a few places I still wanted to go. But I decided to focus on all the amazing places that I have seen. I've been blessed with so much travel as a result of my direct sales business. I'd been on 21 five-star international trips to some of the most amazing places in the world. I felt so much gratitude for what I had been able to do and see, so I didn't feel like I missed the chance to see the world, I'd seen so much of it. I have three amazing children, I've experienced love. I've had an incredibly successful career, I felt fulfilled. The blessing from this situation is that I got an opportunity to find out what my greatest regret was. And that it was just one thing.

My greatest regret was that I gave up too soon and I never got my black belt in karate. I've always said to myself, I'll go back to it, I'll go back to it one day, I'll go back to it. And here I was, at 41, I'd given it up at 21. And I hadn't gone back to it. I thought, Uhh, I know that only one percent of people who start karate end up with a black belt. And I'd consider myself the type of person that gets through, that is that one percent. And I wasn't. I was so disappointed in myself that I'd given up and I hadn't gone back to it like I'd promised myself I would. I felt really disappointed in myself for that. So, I swore to myself, if I get through this, I am going to get a black belt in karate. A black belt means so much to me… that I've got a second chance at life, that I am the sort of person who carries through and meets this huge goal. It means that I AM a "one-percenter." The next day, the neurologist said to me, "Look, hopefully we'll be able to get you walking consistently again, in a straight line and with proper depth perception. That will be our goal. We don't expect that you'll be able to run again and certainly won't ever be able to play sports again. And hopefully, we'll be able to get you back to your regular ability of communicating."

Because they witnessed my complete lack of ability, they also witnessed times when it was like driving through mud trying to get words. So that was it, giving me hope that you might be able to get back to where you were with your ability to communicate. And yeah, we're pretty confident you'll be able to walk again. I said, "I'm sorry, but that's not good enough. I'm going to prove you wrong."

I told him, then and there, that I'm going to get a black belt in karate. He didn't say anything, but I could see the look that crossed his face. It was a look that didn't need words to say, "You are completely delusional, lady."

I had to go back to the hospital three months later for another scan to see if they needed to do surgery on the arteries to see how that was going, and if they needed to do brain surgery, for the pseudoaneurysms in the brain. I knew that I had three months to show them that I was going to be a miracle, that I was going to be different. And that's what I lived for every day for that three months. Instead of focusing on what I couldn't do, I focused on what I could do, I drew on every ounce of positivity and love and support. Everybody who offered help, I accepted. I went from not even being able to walk down the hospital corridor to being able to walk 500 meters. And the amount of healing that they saw in that first scan was unbelievable, absolutely unbelievable. There was no need for any kind of surgery. And then three months later, I set foot in the dojo.

Communicating was still a little difficult—not quite back to my normal self yet—but I set foot in my dojo. I'd been watching Andy because he started karate three months into my recovery. And I was watching for those three months, just hoping that they were going to let me do it. And by the six-month mark, they said, okay, yep, go give it a try. Just be cautious.

So I let them know at the dojo what I had been going through, that I was going to be slow progress and that I shouldn't be doing anything with extreme contact because I was still a bit fragile. Oh my God, it was so hard at the start. Anything crossing the midline or that takes multiple actions was so difficult. I'd have to break up every single move into multiple steps. They were so patient and so supportive and so encouraging at the dojo. I was there six days a week because I saw it not just as my goal, but as my recovery. It was my therapy.

Every three months I was having follow-up brain scans, and they could see incredible new neural pathways, new veins being developed in my brain because my left artery wasn't anywhere near as blocked. It was only partially blocked. So, obviously more blood flow for my brain was coming through my left carotid. It is fascinating watching the remarkable miracle that is your body when you give it the rest it needs in combination with the exercise that it needs. And as it turns out, karate does so much crossing the midline that it is probably one of the best things I could have chosen to do for my recovery. It helps that I'm so passionate about it, I just love it. I feel grateful that I can do it, and so incredibly grateful at the blessing that it's given me, because of all of that time and effort I've put into developing skill by skill. It took me weeks to learn a basic kata, which is a pattern of movement. And now I can learn it in a couple of sessions. It's just honestly, remarkable. Now that I'm on the New South Wales State Team, I'm one of three athletes in the state to have been chosen to be a Team Leader to support the Kata athletes. I've won many medals and trophies from competing. I love the challenge of it, and I'm so grateful for it. Our whole family does martial arts now. I think if I hadn't experienced that moment where I had the opportunity to find out what my regrets were I might never have gone back to it!

Karate has become a passion of mine, it has become something that has gelled our whole family even closer together. Andy and I both compete at a national level and represent our state and we are working towards representing our country in the next year or two as well. Sophie is doing incredibly well, too. It's amazing what she has achieved already for a little girl who hardly walked for two years. One of the chemotherapy drugs she was on interrupted the brain pathways to her feet. Coordination and walking were a real challenge. And on top of that, a child who's critically ill for such an extended period of time loses the neurological development that they had going through crawling and walking. All of that gets lost. So the body takes on strange patterns of movement. Karate has been such a big part of re-establishing good solid movement patterns and behaviors for her. It's such an incredible blessing. She's also won many medals and trophies. It's just amazing. Honestly, there are so many blessings that we've dragged out of incredibly challenging situations.

Another blessing is that Sophie has developed an incredible confidence to go for her dreams, probably partly from watching me going for mine, but both of us have this new lease on life. If we have a goal, we go for it now. We believe and have faith that it's going to happen and we work at it. It's amazing how many remarkable things we've both been able to achieve since those times when we weren't sure we'd still be here. It's almost like a part of that critical filter in our brains has been smashed through. It's like we assess things differently. We ask ourselves, "Is that really scary or not?"

Usually it's nowhere near the truly scary experiences we've been through. Public speaking is something that is easy for us now. It's something that we both love to do. And there have been so many other blessings in my business life as well. I don't care what people think about me anywhere near as much as I used to anymore. Every day I have on this planet is a blessing. I've been able to translate that into my business life, where I've been able to be more visible. I don't have such a loud voice in my brain saying, "You're not good enough." The other voice is so much stronger for me, where it says, "Okay, let's see what you can do with this."

My attitude is really different now compared to how it used to be. I look at how I used to be and think, huh, I held myself back from being all that I have the potential to be because I was so freaking worried about what people thought about me. I was able to build a multi-million dollar direct sales business, but there were so many aspects of my life that were still holding myself back because I was worried what people would think. And now there's so much less of that in my life. I'm not perfect at it, but it is not the deafening voice that it can be. There are so many amazing things I've achieved in these last three and a half years since my health crisis that I never even dreamed of. I'm so grateful and happy to be here. Every day is a joy, I'm focused on positivity. I go for my goals. Nothing is too big to tackle. I think globally. I'm just a different person. So, the amount of positivity that I've been able to drag out of a really scary time is something that I'm really proud of.

Q&A

Jana: I just want to acknowledge that you chose to show up for me and for the women who are going to be touched by this. So, thank you. Thank you for giving all of yourself and so much more and opening up your family to us in this way. I'm just so grateful to call you my friend. So, I have one simple question for you. What is your coconut milk?

Christine: The experiences that both Sophie and I went through have given us wings. We are able to soar over the criticisms, the voices of lack of belief. We have built a stronger belief in ourselves than is normally achieved in a whole lifetime. It's a blessing that Sophie has that at such a young age. She has such an incredible faith in herself that is remarkable to watch. I have no doubt that she will achieve some remarkable dreams because she also doesn't focus on the what ifs, the maybes or what might go wrong. She's learned how to focus on what might go right. And I think that's the coconut milk for me as well. I can focus on the dreams and the possibilities. I think about what gifts can I bring to the world? I've learned to view things with a lens that not enough people have learned how to use yet, the lens of possibility, the lens of positivity and the lens of gratitude, because every day that both of us are on this planet is an extra day. I think both of us feel that we are meant to be here and that perhaps we've already given back to the world what it was we were meant to, and perhaps we're only just starting to uncover that. But I think my coconut milk is that I'll be spending every day on this planet trying to make a difference, whether that's through my charity work, through spreading the movement of positivity, through sharing my skills in the direct sales industry. I'm not really sure what it is exactly that the universe has in mind for me, but I'm not afraid to give it my all and to live into whatever it may turn out to be. If we hadn't been through those experiences with such bitter lemons, I may not have become the kind of person that can make a true difference to the world.

Jana: Beautifully said. Is there anything that is unsaid that some beautiful soul that is holding this book might have been waiting to read in your chapter, is there anything left unsaid?

Christine: If I could speak directly from my heart and my experience into another person's soul, I'd tell them that the dream, the goal that they're worried they're not good enough for... you ARE good enough for it, you can do it. Just grab it with all of your heart and run towards it because you don't know what's around the corner and you do not want to get to your last day and have any regrets. So please just believe in yourself enough to go for it.

Jana: I love that. How much do you think a lack of connection with who we are, I mean when you think about what this world has gone through over the past two years, where we were told by our governments that it was a health crisis, yet you could drive through a fast food drive-thru, you could buy alcohol because it was considered an essential service, and we were separated as humanity, what is our opportunity, as a society, coming out of the lessons of the past two years? I just, I would love this perspective from you in this book.

Christine: I'm hoping that what the world has learned is to trust themselves and their own intuition more and to value connection above all else. Because I certainly feel that through everything that we've been through as humanity, the hardest thing to have taken away from us was human connection. The division, fear and hate that came up was painful to watch and experience. Out of that time, I also formed the strongest friendships in the fastest time with people like you, Jana, and finding like-minded souls amongst all of that was like a bright, shining light during a really tough time. So I'm really hoping that humanity has learnt about the value of connection and friendships and in finding your tribe. Whoever that may be, wherever they may be, your tribe is out there, and it's really important that you find them.

CHRISTINE TYLEE is based in Australia and has a multi-million dollar global business in the Direct Sales Industry. She has a Masters of Education and has studied extensively in the fields of Positive Psychology and Neuroscience. She is passionate about assisting others to thrive in business and life.

Christine was awarded the Australian Direct Sales Distributor of the Year award in 2019, runs a popular Direct Sales blog to share the gift of her knowledge with the wider industry and is a passionate ambassador for Childhood Cancer charities. Christine is proof that with the right positive mindset, resilience, and determination, you can go beyond what anybody thought was possible.

KAYLA

I'm a neuropsychophysiologist. This is not something that I dreamed of being as a child. I think that the vast majority of children certainly never dream of being a neuropsychophysiologist, Most people don't even know what it is. But my path to get here has been very windy. And it really has a lot to do with my upbringing and the experiences that I had in my family that were certainly not always rosy, but developed me and molded me into a scientific thinker, and into a person who's really passionate about health, especially about women's health.

Most of my family members have struggled with mental health issues, particularly the women in my family have struggled and suffered the most. I've watched most of the women in my family deteriorate mentally and physically in terms of their health because they have been misguided and misunderstood by medical professionals who were supposed to support them.

As I watched the women in my family suffer from these mental ailments, I always had in the back of my mind, "Is that going to be me? Am I going to suffer from mental health issues?"

When you have a genetic predisposition for these health issues, and people tell you you're going to follow the same path health-wise as your parents and grandparents, it's frightening! That really made me hyper vigilant about my health in particular, and it really drove me into the field of health science.

In my undergrad, I studied health ecology and planned to become a physical therapist. At the time, I worked in the physical therapy office where I saw a lot of people come through dealing with all kinds of physical ailments. And particularly, I noticed there were a lot more women who came through my clinic, especially with things like joint replacements. This and my experience with the women in my family made me wonder what is going on with women and their health. And the question of, "Will I have to suffer like the women in my family?" was always on my mind.

There was a particular event in my life that really shaped who I am, and really changed the path of my career. In my junior year of undergrad, I got a call from the hospital that my mom was there, and that she was unresponsive. My dad called me frantic, telling me that he woke up in the morning and she was lying there unresponsive and they didn't know what happened. So, I went to the hospital. All the nurses and doctors were coming up to me asking me questions and I'm trying to figure out what happened to my mom. Is she okay? What happened to her? Did she have a stroke? Did she have a heart attack? What happened? And all the doctors were saying to me is, "What did she take? What did she take?" And I was so confused by this question. I had no idea what they were talking about.

They wouldn't answer any of my questions about what was going on with her. They just kept asking what she took. It didn't even click in my mind what they were asking. I had no idea what was going on. Eventually I found out she had an opioid overdose. And I had no idea that my mom was an opioid addict. And this has been going on for years. This really shook up my world.

I actually took a pause from school and took a couple of semesters off to help my mom, and get her into rehab, which I found was a lot harder than it seems. It was a lot harder than it should have been to get her the right kind of support for her mental health and help to battle this addiction. In the end, I wouldn't say that we necessarily did get the right kind of medical help that we needed. But that year, she ended up having two more overdoses, one of which caused a stroke. And to this day, she struggles with the resulting brain damage from this event.

Thank goodness, she has, in many ways, overcome the struggles with her mental health issues and addiction. But what happened to her was completely unnecessary. And it was at the hands of the medical system, which is completely broken, in my opinion. She was prescribed medications and was taking them as prescribed, which led to a full blown addiction, all of which was fully supplied by doctors the entire time.

This event really shook up my world. I was so angry at the medical system and I wanted to figure out, what the heck is going on? Why is it that our medical system, that is supposed to support us and help us to heal is perpetuating health issues and actually contributing to the deterioration of our health? So that's what shifted me from physical therapy into public health. I went on to get my master's in public health with the end goal to work at the Centers for Disease Control and Prevention on the opioid epidemic.

When I graduated from my master's program, I did end up landing a job at CDC, but I didn't end up working on the opioid epidemic. I ended up working in global health, which was really rewarding and amazing. I loved my time there, I got to travel all around the world and work with underserved populations and different kinds of health disparities. And after a few years, I found myself at the height of my career. I had achieved all the goals that I had set for myself. I wanted to finish my master's. I wanted to get into a leadership position at CDC. I wanted to buy a house. I wanted to do all of these life goals, and I did! At the time, I was even competing as a professional athlete with Team USA and starting my PhD. So, I was doing all of the things that I had ever dreamed of doing, but my health started to deteriorate.

On the outside, it really looked like I had it all. And in a lot of ways, I thought I did. But my body started breaking down on the inside. At one point, I couldn't even make it through the day without having to take a nap. I had so much brain fog and fatigue. Every time

I ate a meal, I would crash, and I couldn't focus. But I was still just trying to push through because that's what you do. You just push through it and you figure it out.

The most frustrating part was that I had studied the health sciences my whole life, so I knew (I thought I knew) how to take care of my health. I ate perfectly clean, I exercised regularly, I did all of the things that I was taught to do to take care of my health. Yet, here I was crashing, and it was really scary. Some of those thoughts that I had growing up, like, is it inevitable that I will suffer from these mental health issues that my family suffered from started to come into my mind and it scared me. Was the inevitable finally happening?

I started to do some deep diving into my own health and started working with a functional doctor. We did so many tests I can't even tell you how many - thousands of dollars and months of tests and protocols went by before I finally got a hint of what was going on with me. It came from one particular test result, which was that of my ovarian hormones - estrogen and progesterone. I had completely flatlined. My doctor even said I had the hormones of a 90-year-old woman. At that time, I was 27 or 28, so I definitely should have had healthy hormones at that age. But I didn't, which sent me down a really deep rabbit hole into my health to figure out why my hormones crashed after I was doing everything right, exactly the way I was taught.

In that deep dive, I gained a new respect for feminine biology. But, as I dove deeper and deeper into the science of feminine biology and trying to learn and understand my own body, I started to shift the focus of my PhD research to study women's neuropsychophysiology. That is, the female brain, the female mind and the female body, and how these systems interact. My goal was to understand these systems so that I could master them for myself. It became such a big fascination and passion, as I kept digging deeper and deeper down this hole, I made some amazing discoveries about feminine biology that just propelled me into this field 100%. I put all my focus on the magic and beauty of feminine biology.

What I found was not always positive. I was shocked when I started going into the archives of women's health science research to find out that women, since the beginning of recorded history, have been left out of this scientific research because of their biological complexity. Surprisingly, the FDA formally banned all women of childbearing potential from clinical research in 1977. Then, in 1993, it was finally overturned, but even to this day, the damage has been done and women are still grossly underrepresented in clinical research. It's a huge problem that we definitely need solutions for and it's something that I'm really passionate about helping to fix.

There was actually a recent study that came out of the University of California, Berkeley that highlighted how big of a problem the gender gap in research really is for women and for their health. The researchers found that women are enduring excess negative health outcomes, including injury and even death, from being overmedicated because the clinical research and the studies that are done to determine doses are done primarily on men.

Female biology is not only misunderstood, but we're also completely misguided when it comes to our health because the research does not address us. We are lumped in with the findings of research that is done on male biology. And as a result, women are suffering. For instance, we see women burning out 200% more often than their male counterparts. We also see that women suffer from mental health issues at profoundly higher rates than our male counterparts. We see these issues going on with women's health and we even acknowledge them, and yet, we're still not doing much to fix this problem. And unfortunately, women are paying the cost.

I saw this in my family, I saw this with my own health, not understanding my biology, not understanding the cyclic nature of my feminine biology and how complex it is. Once I started to piece this together, I found the missing link - the female operating system, which I call the female biorhythm. This was the thing that the medical and scientific communities were completely ignoring. It's the main difference between men and women.

The research gap has led to a really harmful assumption about women's biology - that the biological parts that men and women share operate in the same way. This could not be further from the truth.

Over the past six years that I've spent in this field, I've been able to pull from the small amount of published research on women, alongside my own research, to figure out this female biological rhythm and how different it is from the male biological rhythm. What I found is that the male biology follows a 24-hour repeating system like clockwork. The male biological rhythm is set to the pace of the adrenal hormones - the sleep-wake hormones, cortisol and melatonin - and it repeats every day. So biologically, men are pretty much the same every day with really tiny, slow changes that occur over really long periods of time. That's why men are pretty consistent day-in and day-out, biologically speaking. This is also why the world operates on a 24-hour repeating system, because the science is conducted on male bodies. This is also where the term "consistency is the key to success" comes from. And it's true, for men.

Unfortunately for women, consistency is not the key to success. And in fact, it's the killer of our success because our biological rhythm is completely different. For us ladies, things are much more complex, and also beautiful, because we have a different biological rhythm that is set to two very different hormones - estrogen and progesterone. This was the "aha" moment that I had, where I realized that the female physiology follows a month-long biological rhythm set to the pace of the ovarian hormones that ebb and flow over the course of a month, which means that we are shifting significantly physiologically as these two key hormones ebb and flow. So, literally everything from our cardiovascular system to our nervous system, to our cognitive function, to our metabolism, to our immune system, to our neuro endocrine system, every system within our bodies is impacted and modulated by the increase and decrease of estrogen and progesterone over the course of a month.

When I started to really pick this apart, I realized that women shift hormonally four times over the course of a month through four phases. This means that we are essentially four different women over the course of a month whose basic biological needs change with each phase. And because we are four different women every month, our lifestyle, routines and health choices have to match that. They have to match the ebb and flow of our biology. Because if they don't, then we might only be taking care of ourselves properly for a few days out of the month, and the rest of the time, just be spinning our wheels, using up our resources and causing burnout.

Q&A

Jana: I'm visualizing the women holding this book, reading your chapter in multiple emotions of shock and anger and sadness and maybe some relief. Reading this chapter of yours, maybe for the first time in their lives, like with you, they feel heard or they feel like they're not. I've been told in my health journey that my pain was in my head and I was seeking attention. I believed it. For a period after that, I absolutely believed it.

Through your story, and thank you for sharing, you identified moments of lemons. I would say there were multiple lemons throughout your chapter. With all of that wisdom that you have taken from these experiences and living your purpose, what you were meant to do on this earth, what is your coconut milk?

Kayla: I would say my coconut milk is discovering the magic of feminine biology, and the magic of my own body and discovering the superpowers that not only I have, but that every woman has access to within her biology. So it makes life so fun. Now, my lifestyle ebbs and flows with my body and I'm much more efficient. But really learning these differences in my body versus what I learned in biology textbooks has really been such a blessing and such a gift to me. It's allowed me to flourish and thrive in my life and my health and in my career.

Jana: I'm sure some women are going back to the beginning and reading this again just to let it sink in. Is there a starting point? If someone's lying there in bed reading this and thinking, Kayla is my answered prayer. What does she need to know to take inspired action?

Kayla: There are a couple of first steps that we all have to take, and not only us as women, but that society really needs to take in order for us to evolve forward and properly support women. One, we need to give ourselves permission that we are different and need to do things differently. The second step is that we need to grant ourselves, and other women in this world, the flexibility in order to do things differently. We can't actually do things differently if we don't allow ourselves that flexibility or if the world doesn't allow us the flexibility. So, all of these things that we have been taught and have been ingrained in us, like work hard every single day, be consistent, that doesn't necessarily apply to us as women. And that's okay. We go through these different phases every month and we are essentially four different women every month, and we can lean into that. We can allow ourselves to do things differently through each of these phases to properly support ourselves.

Jana: For women who are thinking about their own health journey and feeling like, oh, my gosh, I've been led astray. Or, where do I start? Or, what do I do since I'm not represented in the science?

Kayla: Well, it starts by creating a relationship with your body. You don't have to be a scientist or even study biology, you can just start listening to your body. A great place to start is if you track your female hormone cycle in any way. Once we can start to track our female hormone cycle, we start to get our finger on the pulse of our biological rhythm.

If you track your hormone cycle, you want to note that there's more than just bleeding and not bleeding. There are four phases. Even women who don't have an active period still have all four phases, and those do line up with the female hormone cycle phases of menstruation, follicular, ovulatory, and luteal. So, that's a really good place to start.

Then you can start paying attention to your physiology, meaning you can start paying attention to your energy levels, your mood, your cognitive function, whether you have certain levels of focus sometimes and you don't other times, but also pay attention to social cues. Are you feeling more connected with other people? Do you have better verbal acuity? Are you able to focus more when you're learning? Are you able to communicate better with other people? Are you feeling more connected with other people in relationships? All of these things ebb and flow through the four phases. That's what I teach women about. I teach women about these physiological shifts through the phases and how it impacts our behavior, our health and our function in the world, and how we can lean into these what I call superpowers of each phase that we get that allow us to really thrive and allow us to become more proficient in the world, in our careers, in our relationships, in our health and all parts of our life.

Jana: In my 48-year-old body right now, all of my cells are feeling relieved. It is very empowering. Information and knowledge is power. I just want to acknowledge the work that you didn't fall into, I think it was very purposefully laid out for you. I just want to thank you so much.

Do you feel like there's been anything left unsaid that you would like to wrap your chapter with?

Kayla: I want all the women who are reading this book, and even the men who may be reading this book, to know that women are the greatest untapped resource in modern society that can bring new innovations, new ideas and new changes to the world to evolve us forward.

Once we can start to support women properly, once we can give them the permission and flexibility to do things differently and start to allow them to really support their biology properly, then we will see women flourish and they will be able to rise up and meet our male counterparts in thriving.

Jana: I absolutely agree. Well, that was like, drop the mic, curtain drop, end scene, all of that. Thank you. Thank you so so much.

KAYLA OSTERHOFF is a neuropsychophysiologist and women's health expert whose work has been featured on stages and media around the world. Formally trained across the health sciences with degrees in health ecology, public health, epidemiology, and neuropsychophysiology, Kayla has developed a truly holistic understanding of health and how to achieve resilience of the mind and body.

BROOKE

"I like coconuts, you can break them open and they smell like ladies lying in the sun." —*Widespread Panic*

I love the smell of being on the beach and this is one of my favorite Widespread Panic songs.

My name is Brooke Emery. I'm absolutely excited to be part of this venture and it's important that we make it fun. The title *When Life Gives You Lemons . . . Drink Coconut Milk* reminds me of vacation, fun and joy.

My first lemon to coconut milk story is about trust and guidance. I was working for a film company in 2000 to 2001, and it closed. They gave me the option to stay on a little longer or go on unemployment. I knew it was time to leave, so I chose the latter. I had just moved in with my boyfriend, now my husband. We were looking for an apartment, everywhere, to move in together. This was a big deal because I grew up in a divorced family and I had all kinds of stories about whether relationships could work or not work.

There was this one apartment that I wanted to get into. It was in Battery Park with a beautiful view of the Hudson River. My friend Sharon, who owned the apartment, was going to give me access to see the apartment. Her then subletter ran away with the keys. She was so upset that she couldn't get me in. While I was frustrated as well, I told her there seems to be a force not letting us into this apartment. So we ended up getting this other apartment, which was a sixth floor walk-up in the East Village. It's one of those places where, if you forget your umbrella, you don't go back up six flights, you just buy a new umbrella in the city for five bucks. It was a cute apartment. The sixth floor walk-up was not fun, but you got your exercise in for the day.

So, cut to my mandatory unemployment meeting.

This is a lot of lemons at once …

I didn't get the apartment I wanted, my job ended, I was going on unemployment.

It was also a beautiful day. It was one of the most beautiful days in New York. And I was like, "You know what? I'm going to dress up today." I normally wear sneakers and sweatpants. And I decided, "I'm going to wear nice shoes, and I'm going to treat myself to a taxi, not go on the subway."

My taxi dropped me off in the Financial District and I walked out of sight, headed towards the unemployment office. And, all of a sudden, I hear the loudest boom I've ever heard. In New York there are a lot of noises. There are always fire trucks, ambulances and police sirens going off, but this one was distinctively different. I turn around and walk back towards the noise … and I see this fire in one of the towers at the World Trade Center.

The first thought in my mind was that a helicopter tour had maybe crashed. I remembered the bomb scare of 1993 and then I was thinking, the tower is like a tree. Either it's going to fall this way or that way. Then I think, "I have to get out of here." So I run and I'm in these heels. Everybody's looking and staying and standing around in shock. I'm panicking and I get into this taxi and even the taxi driver is looking up, just stunned. I'm like, "Go, go, go!"

We had just moved into the sixth floor walk-up. We didn't even have cable yet. I called my husband, Lee, and told him the towers are on fire. He went up to the roof while he was waiting for me to come home, and he got his camera out. He's taking pictures and he ends up catching, on camera, the second plane coming into the tower.

I ran up the stairs and met him on the roof. I'm hysterically crying.

We sat and watched the whole thing come down from our roof. I say this from a neutral place now. But after, I went through post traumatic stress disorder. They had threat alerts that were labeled different colors with red being the highest, there were many red alerts being issued. I wouldn't go on a subway. I was a mess. It was a very traumatic experience, I had a lot of anxiety. And I'd already done a lot of personal development work, but I was like, "Oh my God, what is this?"

That ended up leading me to more deeper work and learning more about Abraham Hicks and the law of attraction. And that led me to healing post trauma disorder.

Here's what really blew my mind … (and be prepared to get your mind blown!)

Circle back to the other apartment - the one that my friend initially wanted to get me into. That apartment got destroyed on 9/11 and I can't imagine what would've happened if we'd been there.

So the message is really about when life gives you lemons, it could be your highest protection and your highest gift.

Even in the moment, it's scary, and the fear comes up and you're like, WTF? Trust that there is a higher force at play.

At least that was what happened with me. One thing led me to the first apartment. Then, with not being able to get in, it led me to a different place. I kicked and screamed through the whole process. I'm not saying it was all love and light. But on the other side of it was lots of medicine and gifts.

One of the greatest insights from that experience was from Byron Katie. I'd read her book *The Work*, where she talks about three distinctions that were very potent for me and I'll share with you.

There's your business, there's other people's business and there's God's business.

Mind *your* own business. So where that showed up for me was that I was minding *God's* business every time I heard a helicopter over the city, every time the alert went from orange to red, every time I heard about a hurricane, anything that was in God's domain. (And if God isn't your thing, you can replace that word with universe, spirit or whatever you subscribe to. I'm not putting my beliefs on you, that's just how Byron Katie says it in the book.)

That process really gave me a lot of freedom. The *other* business was trying to control what Lee was doing and his decisions. As soon as I stepped back into my business, it brought me a lot of freedom. That was an immediate insight that I got from that time that I've used in many situations and still applies today.

Q&A

Jana: There are so many moments, such as the first time you heard about 9/11, or my mom will talk about when John Lennon was shot or when Elvis died. I'm not comparing the two at all, but there are moments in your life where time will stand still, almost as a society, as an extension of a community.

Can you speak to our audience a little bit around the work that you did after the fact to ensure that you worked your way through that? Part of this book is really meant to be a catalyst, or 'the thing' that so many of the women are needing or looking for. What do we do when there's been years and years or decades and decades of idleness? How do you start? And is it ever too late to start?

Brooke: I would say it's never too late, because that's why we're here. That's why we're in a body. It's to grow. I think that's why we're here.

As you were asking the question, I kept thinking, "Why was I down there?" Because it was a very significant moment and I was meant to witness it and learn from it.

What I noticed is that one of my default mechanisms is to act almost like a newscaster. Even with the scary news stories, they always share it so neutrally. I think that I had gotten to a place where I wouldn't allow those feelings in because they scared me. I felt like Spirit had put me there to see it firsthand, because I couldn't possibly deny that it happened.

The thing that I noticed for myself is my default was to try to feel better as fast as possible. What rule and tool can I grab right now because I want to be loving life all day long, and I was spiritually bypassing my feelings because they scared me. My thoughts were, what if I stayed there? What if I don't get out of it? What will happen? And I'm still doing it. There is always a new layer of when I'm wanting to feel good, but I really need to sit with it a little longer, and feel that discomfort a little bit longer.

I would say to that person, there's always the potential to get help. It doesn't have to cost a lot of money. And at the end of the day, there's always something you can do. But it has to feel right and light to you. What's great about this book is that you're interviewing all these people and there's a plethora of resources that in the moment will be like, "Ah, that's what I need right now."

What I realized in the years of work that I've done in terms of working to release beliefs and working to release trauma is that allowing myself to feel the feelings and having that radical acceptance of those feelings so that they pass through versus being worried that I'm going to stay there.

I was at a conference a couple years ago and I saw this man by the name of Alan Cohen, who wrote the book *The Dragon Doesn't Live Here Anymore.* He speaks about the flow of life. One thing he said during his time on stage that I will never forget is, "The tide always comes back in." And that gave me peace, knowing that the emotions don't have to be the truth, but they are there and they ebb and flow through, like the tide.

Jana: Yeah, you're so right. Just the simple title of this book. First of all, it's a pattern interrupt. Because normally we'd say when life gives you lemons, drink lemonade, or make lemonade, whichever version you subscribe to. I feel like we're at this cusp of Divine Feminine Empowerment over the past couple of years.

One of the other contributors told me the symbolism of a coconut. It's the symbol of a soul, with a very hard, protected, outer layer. But once you get inside, there's the nutrition of the meat, and the milk, and the yummy juiciness. With the lemons that you were dealt, it is a gift to be able to now give back the lessons you have learnt to our readers. I'm intrigued to know about your business story, so let's segue into that.

Brooke: Right after I had my second baby, I wasn't ready to go back to work because of having two babies so close together. They were 16 months apart. But my dear beloved friend, Alan, had invited me in to do a launch for a client of his. What I do is create high-vibe and strategic partnerships for people who have courses and classes. It's a win-win to find like-minded partners to support one another in promoting offers to their lists to leverage traffic and ultimately get new sales.

The challenging part of this was it was the first time I'd ever done it. My background is public relations, marketing and film. My friend knew I was a great connector, and he thought that this would just translate perfectly. I have done partnerships before, but with strategic partnerships with luxury brands.

The opportunity came a little too early, but it felt like a yes, so I listened to it and said I'd do it. They wouldn't do any reciprocal mailings for the partners, which makes it more challenging to set up deals. I was connecting with a lot of potential partners and it was an uphill battle to convince people to mail for the offer. I spent 10 months working on the project. And though I got a little money upfront, most of my payment was tied to the back end of the performance of the launch, so I was working my tail off. I was successfully able to reach more than 1 million people with combined list sizes. I was proud of myself and I met all these incredible people along the way.

What ended up happening was, we got around 20,000 people who opted in from the mailings, but then the sales page did not convert. So I did my part, and then the sales page didn't convert. I didn't get any money from all the 10 months of work that I did, busting my butt off and taking time away from my babies. I also got walking pneumonia and adrenal fatigue to add to it all. So that sounds like a lemon, right?

But the riches of the people that I met in those 10 months is the gift that keeps on giving. I would do it all again and make no money and get adrenal fatigue because of the journey that it took me on with the wonderful, magical people I met. Sure, I was disappointed. Sure, it took me a long time to get over the walking pneumonia. Sure, I was pissed off. This was supposed to be my main cash flow. I definitely went into the victim closet. Then I took myself out of the victim's closet. Then I reflected and I said, "Okay, what was it? What's the reflection? Why did it happen this way?"

I was supposed to meet the people that I met, and then it ended up leading me to other places and bigger and better opportunities. I also realized I wasn't supposed to have a huge success on that first project because I needed to learn about being more in frequency with the people I was working with versus getting swept up by the money.

It would have been very tempting and very sexy to me had that performed in the way that we were expecting it to perform. I really believe that God was protecting me from making certain choices about my career based on the Benjamins versus what was in my highest alignment and my purpose. Sure, I would have liked both, but sometimes it doesn't go that way.

You need the lemons, and then you drink the coconut milk.

So that's my business story, and that's why I'm sitting here today, because I made that choice and I allowed myself to go through that. It changed the way I do business.

Tammy, my beautiful business partner, and I set up our days where we don't usually start our meetings until 10 o'clock and we take care of ourselves. We are very, very selective about the people we work with. They must be an energetic match and we must really believe in what they're doing. This process makes it beyond just creating joint ventures. We become an energetic force in their business. It's a frequency. That lemon is the gift that keeps giving.

Jana: Let's look at these two stories that you shared. Obviously, we had to identify the lemon in each story. And there were multiple lemons in both. When you get to the other side of the hero's journey, that's where the whole concept of the coconut milk comes in. In the lessons that you've learned in your life, as a wife and a mom and an entrepreneur and a partner, what is your coconut milk?

Brooke: I would say my coconut milk is my ability to be open to getting back to my center and my higher self because at any moment, there's an ego landmine that I can step on, and sometimes I get blown up. But I am always willing to reclaim my power back from those situations and to grow and learn from them. Sometimes it's messy and I think, "Oh my God, I've done all this work, and I'm still a mess."

And then I pick myself back up again and I go back to choosing God, Spirit, universe, angels, whatever you want to call it, but choosing that higher self, choosing the growth. Sometimes it's easier than others, but without a breakdown, there's no breakthrough. So, embracing the breakdowns, but then also realizing it's okay to not embrace the breakdown either.

It's the ebbs and flows, and I can't say that I have an answer, Jana, because I'm a human being like anyone listening, I never want to claim guru status or that I have it all together. I have the willingness and the commitment to grow. That's what lights me up and then I'm passionate about it. Sometimes I wonder, "Ugh, why can't I just be like a normal person in my everyday complaints and just be unaware?" But then I come back to my center and admit, "Okay, no, I can't do that." It's not the easier road, but it is the more rewarding road. So my coconut milk is the path of being willing to embark on the road of transformation.

Jana: I love that. I didn't plan this at all, but when I ask that question to all of our contributing authors, it's always the coconut milk coming back to within. These women use different ways of describing that, but that's what it is. You talked about the three types of business: your business, other people's business and God's business. That's where the concept of faith comes with whatever you subscribe to. There is that bit of faith and gratitude and love. We do have what's inside of us to heal, but sometimes we do need the support of external forces.

Brooke: Yeah, it's okay to ask for help. And it's okay to find a lifeline. It's just about the balance. Carolyn Myss has this great book called *Sacred Contracts*, and she has this great analogy where she talks about Dorothy in "The Wizard of Oz."

When Dorothy was on her journey to find Oz, she needed the Tin Man and she needed the Scarecrow and she needed the Lion. In those moments, they had medicine for her. But ultimately, she had the red shoes to click herself back home. To me, when I read that in the 90s, it was like a light bulb going off because that was a time when I was so lost and so desperate, and seeking all the answers. I was giving my power away to gurus, healers and coaches rather than seeing it from the place of someone being the mirror to reflect back to you what you already know. You have the power to remember versus feeling like the other person has something that I don't have or has access to knowledge that's not available to you. I love sharing that analogy because it's a little more empowering.

You mentioned the word *faith*, and even recently I've gone through moments where I have to ask myself... "Who is in my entourage, my spiritual entourage, where I can phone a friend or have a mentor?" Those are people who are sacred listeners, or committed listeners, to remind me of the truth of what I already know, to connect back to the Source and myself versus it being this person knows and is all knowing and whatever that is. That doesn't feel clean to me, but there might be a time when it may. As of right now, as we're sitting down for this interview, that's how I feel about it.

Jana: I feel like the curtain is about to draw, I feel complete. I love the messages that have come through you to our audience. But I just want to make sure, is there anything left unsaid?

Brooke: Yes. I first learned about the coconut ritual from Tosha Silver's beautiful book *Outrageous Openness*. She has this ritual where you put everything you want to let go of into this coconut on a full moon, then you smash it and allow the milk to flow through. It's a great symbol of releasing all that doesn't serve and I don't think it would be as powerful an image if you were smashing lemons. I love that this answer was consistent with the question about coming from within.

And I love that my interview is number seven, because that was my beloved stepfather's jersey number and it's his birthday on Friday. So I felt like that was like a little message from above for me.

Recognized by *Forbes* magazine as a connector, BROOKE EMERY is a creative business strategist with roots in advertising, publicity and film. She brings big vision and mixes it with intuition to connect her clients to key people and resources in her wide network to create business development strategies, partnerships and win-win-win joint ventures.

Equally passionate about elevating profits, creating social impact, and bringing consciousness to the planet she helps her clients shift their mindset from a place of fear, overwhelm, and doubt to one of positive action and possibility.

Forbes.com recognized Brooke as a natural connector who has a jelly bean jar of creatively brilliant people in her life. She is a secret weapon for many visionaries, best-selling authors, and speakers who come to her for connections and business development.

"I'm the person who talks to you on the airplane, I am a people collector," says Brooke.

Such outgoing behavior has helped her amass what she calls her "jellybean jar of people.

KELITA

Have you ever experienced a time in your life when everything was simply smooth sailing? Sure, you'd navigated your fair share of life's storms, but then found yourself floating in the most welcomed peaceful waters, no major waves crashing you up against the shore. In fact, your life had hardly a ripple. The waters were so smooth that you had to pinch yourself just to be certain this was reality. Several years ago, I found myself in that exact place. I was happily married, had a son in university, a beautiful home and a successful career as a musician and speaker. I was blessed. Yet, deep down inside there was something calling me, a voice daring me to step out of the boat.

One day, I was reading my old beat up Bible, the one with all the underlined notes and scribbles. The hard, thick cover was swollen from nearly being drowned in hot tea, and the binding was now being held together by electrical tape. But still, this book served its purpose. In one of the front pages I innocently scrawled three little words, "Break my heart." Then, I never really thought much more of it.

A couple of months later, I was at the gym on the elliptical. There was a program I was watching on the TV monitor. I started paying more attention. It was drawing me in. The voiceover was describing a dark, rat and feces infested room where children were being held captive. I leaned in closer. I saw a lineup of little girls in their nightgowns standing side by side. My heart sped up. Their eyes were blacked out to hide their identities. What I heard next shocked my very soul. Every single one of these children were forced to be raped 30-40 times in a weekend by grown men. With disbelief, I was shocked and horrified. Soon I realized I was learning the hard cold facts about child sex trafficking in Cambodia. My initial reaction was, "Oh, my gosh, does this really happen? How can this possibly be?"

I know we've been much more educated about child trafficking in recent years, but this was back in 2007. This was not something that you heard about in the news. It wasn't even in our realm of thinking... at least not mine.

As I continued to listen, I heard two Canadian gentlemen interviewed in the video who were involved in fighting this evil over in Cambodia. The program soon ended and I immediately stopped my exercise. I was too shaken to continue, so I climbed down off the elliptical and went straight home. I told my husband what I had just learned. I wept on and off for almost the whole weekend. My heart was breaking. Was this God's answer to those three little words I had written in my Bible? And if it was, what did this all mean?

This video was something that resonated in a very profound way with me. I was sexually violated as a preschool child. Then, when I was 11, my father committed suicide on our farm. That was very traumatic, obviously, for me and my family. A few months after he passed away, I wrote my first song. Thus began my journey of expressing myself through words and music. This God-given gift was a necessity for releasing all the heartache and pain I was harbouring. To this day, it still is.

As I started to process what I had seen on that program, I began to write. I had to. It's what I've always done. It was in the early fall, Christmas was coming. A new song was being born and I titled it, "Not Just This Christmas." At Christmas time, we see all the ads on TV to support those in need. We open up our pockets and the money comes out. But as I wrote, I thought, why can't we do this all year round? After seeing those little girls in that program, the question began to burn in me. Something was stirring my spirit. And my mind was busy. So, now

I've got a song called "Not Just This Christmas." What's next? Then I received a call from the TV show, *100 Huntley Street*. Around Christmas time, I've always been invited to sing a few songs on the program. Soon, I was booked for a show towards the end of November.

Before we went live to air, we had a run through rehearsal of the songs. It was at that time I told the producers that "Not Just This Christmas" was inspired by the segment they aired on child trafficking in Cambodia. Of course they knew the one. They were touched by my story and immediately called Cheryl Weber, who had produced the segment. She just happened to be in her office, so she was able to come into the studio. After performing the song live on the show, I could tell people were genuinely very moved.

After the program, Cheryl and I were able to talk about how this horrendous travesty had broken our hearts. I told her I felt so strongly that I knew I just had to do something. Of course, I still had no idea what that looked like, but the fire in my belly had definitely been ignited. She suggested I get in touch with both of the gentlemen in the video who were involved in fighting against child trafficking in Cambodia. I sent an email and explained who I was and that I'd seen the show. Only one responded, Brian McConaghy, the founder of Ratanak International. We started communicating by email and I soon learned what a beautiful caring heart this man had for the Cambodian people. I told him, "I can't let go of what I saw. I have to do something. I have no clue what that even looks like. But, I know I need to help you in some way."

Over many years Brian's foundation had served Cambodia in various capacities. But, as he began to share a new project with me, I could feel shivers down my spine. "We're beginning to work on a restoration centre for girls who've been rescued from the sex trade. We're calling it NewSong." I felt my heart soar. My sails had just been touched by a powerful down wind. THAT was it!

After some emails back and forth with Brian, the vision began to download. I would record a Christmas CD and do a big fundraising Christmas concert to raise funds for the new restoration centre. And we would educate people by raising awareness about this thing called the child sex trade. How are those words even in the same sentence? The ideas were being whipped around in my head and I knew exactly where this ship needed to sail next. Cambodia! I knew I just had to see the country and experience the culture with my own eyes. I needed to feel the darkness surrounding this evil form of slavery. I would have to if I was going to advocate for this important cause. And if at all possible, I would meet some of these young girls face to face.

Brian just so happened to have a small group heading over to Cambodia, so he put forth an invitation to me. I soon shared my story and my vision with our small home church group. People were as shocked as I was to learn about what was taking place in Cambodia and quickly became eager to join the cause. Soon, the word spread like wildfire. Before I knew it I had people filling my pockets with cash, sending me transfers and writing me cheques. In no time at all, I had enough money for my husband and me, plus our 13-year-old son, to travel to Cambodia.

Within a couple of months after receiving all our inoculations and with all the plans in place, we landed in Cambodia. As soon as we walked off the plane, I was struck by the heaviness. We saw large billboards. One was of a man with his back to us holding the hand of a small child. The child had a teddy bear in the other hand. And it said, "Sex with a child is not legal."

We were shocked to learn Cambodia ranks as the No. 1 country for child rape. The worldwide $150 million business was just so in your face in this small country. It wasn't long before we met many expats heading up organizations who were advocating against the trafficking of children. It was astounding.

Once settled, Ratanak toured our small group of seven around to visit various projects they were helping to fund. From a water ambulance to a school and even a small hospital, we could see the impact Brian's organization was having. But the one project that really warmed my heart and that I was praying and hoping I would be able to visit was the brand new restoration center, NewSong. At the end of our nearly three weeks, our leader Lisa and I were the only two invited to visit the girls at the centre.

As we walked onto the property of the very large house in the undisclosed neighbourhood, we were greeted by guards and a sophisticated security system. We saw the barbed wire on the high fences surrounding the property and on the balconies. One must remember, these girls were seen as commodities. It wasn't like cocaine or heroin. These girls could be sold over and over and over and over and over again. Once they were too old, even at 19, they were thrown out onto the street full of STDs and plagued by pelvic inflammatory disease. They were worth less than a chicken. It was unbelievable what we learned - fathers who sell their own daughters, mothers too! And it wasn't always for survival's sake, but often for an upgraded phone or a new TV. There's a lot of depravity ingrained into that society. It's been every man for himself since the Pol Pot regime that governed Cambodia murdered an estimated 1.5 million of their own people, back in the 70s.

There were 17 girls in total ranging in ages from 6-18. They were the first intakes at NewSong. The centre had only been open for three weeks. We were told many of the girls, especially the older ones, definitely didn't want to be trapped inside their new 'home.' As good as it was for them not to be abused any longer by male tourists, many coming from Canada, United States, Australia, Europe, it was still very traumatizing.

With the help of a translator, we managed to engage with these beautiful young girls seated around a long table. As I looked into their empty eyes, flashes of those first images I had seen all those months ago on the elliptical came racing back. Each girl surely had her own story. There was one in particular who spoke fairly good English. Her name was Bella. She held her head a bit higher than the rest and had a sparkle in her eye. I think she was about 13 or 14. We heard that she had been rescued from one of the worst brothels after nearly two years. I'm sure that's why her English was so good.

I was invited to sing for the girls and so I chose one of my own called "Caged Bird."

"I know why the caged bird sings, I know why she sings a sad refrain,
Even when there's no one to listen. I know why the caged bird sings."

After I sang, Bella spoke up and said, "That's so sad. It touched my heart." After the group broke up, Lisa and I were able to have a bit of time with Bella out in the spacious yard on the swings. Lisa and I asked her a few simple questions about herself like, what's her favorite color, favourite movie, to which she responded, "The Sound of Music." A girl after my own heart. That was my favourite movie when I was a young girl. By the way, these girls have all changed their names. They might change them two or three times. Once they've been rescued and start their healing journey, they might change their name again.

When we left the house, I could feel the compassion rising up. I was on fire with ambition and a sense of purpose. I was so moved by the whole experience on every level I just knew I had to support this cause. I couldn't wait to get back home. I said to myself, "I have to tell people what's going on here. I need to share what I've seen and experienced firsthand. The world needs to know!"

As soon as we arrived home, I set out on my mission! I started to share what I'd experienced with anyone who would listen. I found an arts organization out of Toronto who accepted me under their charitable umbrella in order to raise the funds needed for the project. The first thing was nailing down the funding to record the Christmas CD. It didn't take long for me to be introduced to a tender soul who caught the vision and almost immediately wrote a cheque for $25,000 as seed money. WOW! I was blown away. I had only met this man once. He believed in what I was doing and was excited to help out.

Then there were the cheques that started coming in the mail. Every day was like Christmas. I'll never forget the one from a fan named Melody. I was sitting on a bench in the mall where my post box was located. As I opened up her envelope all these cheques started falling out onto my lap. I couldn't hold back the tears. I was that moved. This young woman, also a survivor of childhood sexual and ritual abuse, performed odd jobs for family and friends to raise money for the project. People then donated money for her services and wrote cheques for the project. What a beautiful gesture. Melody had also caught the vision.

Soon I had people offering their services in accounting, marketing, publicity, design, printing, staging, you name it. Everybody started coming together and offering me their expertise and assistance for the project. At times I was a bit overwhelmed at the speed at which everything was happening. I was breathing, eating and sleeping this project and I loved every minute of my assignment.

I called the project "Heavenly Night," named after a Christmas song that I had written when my son was just a baby. That became the title track of the Christmas CD and DVD, which we later produced. By the time we had completed recording the CD, all the plans for the fundraising concert were in place. Brian from Ratanak flew out from Vancouver to the event and did a short video presentation, just enough to open people's eyes. That was the beginning of educating so many more. We kept the cost of the tickets low on purpose so that anyone was able to attend. And attend they did. Throughout the night I said, "If we can raise $10,000 to give towards the NewSong restoration center, I would be extremely happy."

You can imagine my surprise when the volunteers and I started counting all the money at the end of the night. From ticket, CD and t-shirt sales, plus all the donations, we were completely blown away when the total came to just over $50,000. I cried!

I thought this was going to be a one-time thing. I'd record the CD, do a fundraiser, and that would be it. Well, the "Heavenly Night" project continued to live on for the next seven years of my life.

Yes, I'm a businesswoman, but I will admit I'm more of an artist. And I am certainly not much of a bookkeeper. I was overwhelmed by all the money that I had started to handle. Even though I had two accountants I was working with, I was still the person in charge of the bank account. I never thought in a million years that I'd be dealing with what became thousands of dollars. That was a miracle unto itself!

Spread out over the next several years, I ended up doing many more fundraising concerts in three different Canadian provinces. There was also another CD we produced called "Heart of a Woman," which included the song "Bella." I was so inspired after meeting that beautiful young survivor that I wrote a song. There was an advocate for male survivors who heard the song and he used his creativity to produce a very touching music video.

Over the period of seven years we were able to raise over $250,000. It was certainly a voyage I never expected to take. At times it was a very harsh ride. Educating myself and others about child sex trafficking meant there were some dark places I had to go. However, it was probably one of the most profound journeys of my life. God was able to take those funds and support the place that I initially visited. Then, some years later, Ratanak opened a brand new rehabilitation home for girls who were preparing to go back out into society. We were able to donate the seed money for that new facility and program.

Ten years ago, my husband and I decided to make a crazy big move to the other side of the country. The move also coincided with me evaluating where the project was at. As difficult as it was, I realized the time had come to close down the "Heavenly Night" project. I realized that I had fulfilled what I was called to do. My heart had definitely been broken, cracked wide open in fact, to a cause of which I knew nothing.

I think as women, whether in business or not, we have a hard time letting go of things we've birthed. Just like our kids! Something that I've learned as a mature woman is that we must honour what we're sensing deep inside. Always be listening to the wisdom within and trust that voice. When it's time to let go - it's time. And it's perfectly okay. We can still be very proud of the work we've accomplished and who knows, there might be another call we're being prepared to answer once we do let go.

Q&A

Jana: Kelita, that was absolutely beautiful. The journey that you just took us on was seated with so many of those sour, lemony moments. What I received from the message in your Bible is that it almost felt like a surrender, in a beautiful way. It wasn't a coincidence that you were on that elliptical watching that program that day. Think about all of the pieces and how it all transpired. I really want to know from you, what is your coconut milk?

Kelita: I think the coconut milk that runs through me is the gift of empathy. Through losing not only my father, but also my mother, and an older brother all within six years, I had to deal with a lot of tragedy and loss as a young girl. As devastating as it was, I was forced to become resilient and the music was a big part of that. To express myself through playing piano, writing and singing my songs, I was able to feel very deeply. What deep loss gave to me was the ability to feel compassion and to understand other people's pain. I've been given a lot of lemons in my lifetime, including my husband. My married name is actually Lemon. I always tell people, "I married a lemon - but he's a good squeeze!" Life can be very hard. But would I ever change it? No. My heart is full of love and compassion and my desire to help women on their own journey has in turn enriched mine.

Jana: When those women or men have this book in their hand, and they have read your chapter, the chapter titled "Kelita," and if there's something that was kind of stirred up inside of them, what do you say to them? What could someone's first step be where they think, I can't do this, I'm just one person. What would that first inspired step be to help someone realize that no, I can take that first step.

Kelita: Well, I would say, first put the vision down on paper. Our right brain is so different from our left brain and we can jump-start the creativity when we actually write instead of compute. We also need to start verbalizing our ideas. Be willing to share your story, your concept or idea. I think some of us are afraid. We think others will think we're crazy. A little crazy is good by the way! We all have our insecurities and doubts, so choose those you know who will be supportive. Find those people who resonate with you, who get excited and who will cheer you on. Having that encouragement behind you sure helps. When they see the spark in you, the flames will grow bigger and bigger and then you'll have an incredible fire that will start to spread.

Jana: Amazing. Is there anything left unsaid before we bring this to a close?

Kelita: There is a wonderful quote I just love that I'd like to share.

"Joy is the oxygen for doing hard things." —Gary Haugen

I want to thank you for taking the chance with me because you don't even know me. You and I sat across a table from each other at a Canada Day celebration and we discovered we had one very big thing in common - moving to Mexico with our families. I understand your journey. So I already feel like I'm a kindred spirit with you. It's really special when you meet new women who share similar experiences. Plus, I love what you're doing. I checked out your websites and I was so blown away and impressed by everything that you have grown and all the great work you're doing. I'm definitely all about natural healthcare. If there's any time in our life where we need positive encouragement and direction in our health, it's now!

KELITA HAVERLAND is a 5 Time Juno award nominee and multi-award winning recording artist, songwriter, musician, TEDx Speaker, advocate, entertainer and Life Coach. Her vast performing experience has allowed her to successfully carve out her own unique keynote address, gracing the stages of conferences, concerts, gala fundraisers and retreats. Kelita wows her audiences wherever she goes. Oozing with pure talent, she creatively weaves her heart-healing original songs, hilarious character comedy and powerful messages through her personal story of overcoming. Kelita inspires, empowers and entertains!

Kelita has appeared live, on radio, TV and video in Canada, the US, Great Britain, Europe, South America and Asia. She's worked with many non-for profit organizations including Canadian Heart & Stroke Foundation, Special Olympics, YMCA, World Vision US and Canada, Power to Change, Ratanak International, Canadian

Country Music Association and Zonta International. Over the years Kelita has been interviewed countless times and graced the covers of numerous magazines.

Kelita is a respected nominee finalist for both Surrey Board of Trade Female Entrepreneur of the Year, and for WOW (Women of Worth), recognizing her as a leading female entrepreneur and philanthropist in British Columbia, Canada. Kelita is a published author and is currently writing her memoir from her home in Nuevo Nayarit, Mexico.

Website - https://www.kelita.com/
Email – kelita@kelita.com
Facebook - https://www.facebook.com/kelitalive/
Instagram - https://www.instagram.com/kelitahaverland/
LinkedIn - https://www.linkedin.com/in/kelitahaverland/
YouTube - https://www.youtube.com/user/kelitalive
Spotify - https://open.spotify.com/artist/6cDVk1BQVxvuN6i8tAgABF

AMBER

All right, here we go. I have four boys and at the time when my story begins, they were all under the age of seven. I was not working outside the home, I was what they call an unpaid, very busy, very exhausted, working mom. My husband was working full-time as a photographer in the film industry, and he decided to start a charity.

This drove me nuts for multiple reasons. First of all, I thought, "If anybody is starting a charity, I would love to start a charity!" I am an achievement junkie, I like to get stuff done, yet when you have many small children, you are doing doing doing, going going going all the time. But there is no real sense of accomplishment some days. There is this sense of what I call "running up the down escalator". Heaven forbid, you pause for a moment. It's not like the whole world pauses with you, the laundry does not pause with you, the bills do not pause with you, and the kids definitely do not just take a nap while you pause. It does not work that way. All of a sudden, the laundry gets bigger, the kids need more. You cannot get ahead of it and there is a lack of feeling like you have accomplished anything significant.

As moms, we are expected to be in a state of joy, appreciation and gratitude that we have these healthy kids, and that we can afford to feed them. I say this all with a bit of a snarky tone because yes, we have gratitude for those things, and yet, we can want more and not feel guilty about it. We can want to feel better, we can want to feel appreciated, we can want to feel happier, we can want to feel like we have our own identity.

So back to explaining more about my husband's charity and my frustration. I found it tough to be involved with a charity for sick and dying children as I could not stop thinking about the families of those children so finally I asked "can it be a charity to help anything else?" If it was something that I could get on board with, we could have just done it together. But it did not feel that way to me. It felt like he was doing something that I wanted to be a part of but couldn't because of the focus of the charity. My husband also did not seem to understand why it irked me at all. He would tell me that I can do anything I wanted to. He would cheer me on and tell me, "You can start your own charity, just go for it. Whatever you want to do, I support you." To me, those were just words, it did not match the actions, primarily because I could not see how it was possible. I could not see how I could possibly do what I was doing now and start something new without him making major changes to the way our family functioned.

Looking back, here is what I realized, my mistaken belief was exactly that. It had to be all or nothing, I had to be 100% in or 100% out. Looking back now, I sure as heck wish I had some role models, so I could see that you don't have to know the whole plan all the time before you make a decision. You do not have to know all the answers. You don't have to need verification all the time. Even if you think you know all the answers. Even if you have a plan, things rarely proceed according to that plan.

Now at this point in my story, there was a super lemony, super sour situation for me, I was resentful. My husband and I have a really smooth relationship, and this was creating a huge point of contention for us that we were not accustomed to. Both of us were not comfortable fighting. We were not practiced in it. Part of that comes from both of us being only children of single mothers who had multiple marriages. Our fathers did as well. Between the two of us, our parents had nine divorces. For us, those fights served us in some ways. It made us really value and appreciate the vulnerability of a relationship and the worth of it and not taking it for granted for anything. And really understanding that the choices that you make, and the words you say can have repercussions. It helped us in that way. Then it hurt us in a way that made us fearful of conflict. So sometimes things weren't said because we were afraid of what that outcome might be. We did not have the skills yet to communicate compassionately, honestly, effectively.

I remember a key moment for us where we were standing just outside our kitchen and we were having our eighty-seventh argument about his charity. The conflict did not resolve in the argument. I remember saying, "Okay, I can't talk about this right now, I'm gonna leave the house for a moment." So I went to this little office we were renting and something just clicked for me. I keep this little notebook where I keep making plans for myself. I keep dreaming up ideas. I keep dreaming up businesses. And I write all these lists. I write all these ideas, and I plan it all out and I strategize it, and then I analyze it to its death. I come up with all the reasons why it won't survive, why it's not viable, why it will die, why it will cost too much money, why it costs too much time, why it won't succeed, why people won't want it. I would do this over and over again. And you know where it was getting me? Nowhere! And I thought, huh, Jamie had an idea for a charity, and I don't think he wrote one damn thing down. I don't think he analyzed any of it. He just started moving. He just started taking action. He just started talking about his ideas. He started doing the things that felt aligned with helping sick children. For him, that started with taking our kids to Toys "R" Us, buying the types of toys that people in hospitals can receive. Then he would load up the grocery cart. And he would take our kids and they would decorate little bags, and he would take them to the hospitals. It was not simple. The hospitals would say, "It's not Christmas, what are you doing? Okay, let me get a manager, I don't understand what you're doing here." It wasn't simple, but he just kept doing it, he kept showing up and he kept talking to people.

My moment there in this little office, I thought to myself, hmm, so what I'm doing is not really working for me, personally. Not even the impact I wanted to make, it just was not making me happy. And Jamie is not only happy because he is doing something that he feels passionate about, but it is actually working. He is actually helping people. As aggravated as I wanted to be at his approach, because he did not research it, and he didn't do all the things and plan incessantly, his approach was working much better than my approach was working. So what if I approach this like he would? What would I do if I thought with his brain? What would I do? What would Jamie do? That's what I thought. The first thing that came into my head was, I would start a school. That was what I was passionate about at that moment. I got really excited, I just felt this flood of endorphins and adrenaline and joy. It was the answer and it came full force right away to me. I immediately took action. I texted a friend of mine who was another parent at the school where my kids were at that point. I said, I am starting a school, do you want to partner with me on this? And she wrote back, 'YES', with five exclamation points.

So I acted on this good feeling, this good intuitive feeling. Which was a struggle for me my entire life. I was a planner, I was do-er. I do not do anything unless it makes logical sense to my brain. If my heart wants something, then that means it is wishy-washy. That means it is not to be trusted. That means it is weak. I had all of these wild assumptions. That means it's not logical, it is silly. All of the negative things you can think about, plus I had somebody point that out to me like, ouch, wow! Not only had I not been tuned into my intuition or my heart, I had actively smashed it down. I would say to myself, you don't know what you're talking about, you are a mess, this is stupid, that would be so embarrassing to trust you. I was like really not listening to it. For me to take action from an intuitive, heart-based feeling was super new to me. It felt really good, and that was the beginning.

My friend Eve and I spent the next nine months visiting schools, researching, planning, doing all this stuff that I really like to do, and taking action. At the end of that nine months, I realized that I did not want to run a school. Because by the time I built the school and found funding for it, and developed it, and found the land, and hired the teachers, my kids wouldn't even be able to use the school, they wouldn't even be able to be there. I would have spent four or five years building this program for other people's children, which is fine. But I realized at that time, I did not want to do that. Instead, I wanted to take all those things that I had learned about education in that previous nine months and take my kids out of traditional school, and travel, and homeschool them in a unique way.

Never ever, ever, ever in my life would I have gotten there if I hadn't first spent those nine months giving myself permission to go down the path of "I want to start a school." I think of it like a highway. So I got on the Build-a-School Highway. It journeyed and went up and down, and I learned things. Then I saw this exit that was called Travel and Homeschool your Kids. I knew it existed, I thought it was only for crazy people or people very much not like me. But once I traveled down this first road for quite a while, that road made all the sense in the world to me, and it all clicked. Jamie was on board before I could even get the sentence out of my mouth. As soon as we did that, a second road appeared. My kids are all musicians. One of them was quite proficient at drumming. I had a friend who was involved in the theater world. She said, "Oh, there's a Broadway production that is looking for kids who are musicians first, and who they can teach to sing and dance and do all the other things. You should send a recording of Cameron playing drums."

So I sent it, thinking that would be funny. He was called for an audition in New York!! Six months later, he was offered a role in the touring company. We would be in a different city every couple of weeks. I'd have to homeschool from the road, so thank goodness I had six months of practice homeschooling and really understanding what that meant to me. It meant reading lots of books, having a math tutor weekly. And then the rest was open.

Every new week, we would explore the city, we would say what's here? We would go to all the children's museums, all the science centers, and then we would just explore. If I had never gotten on that path to build my own school, I would never have seen the exit. And if I had never gotten on that road, there is no way in heck I would ever have agreed to go on a Broadway tour with 150 other people, and travel for what ended up being 16 months across 60 different cities throughout the US and Canada. That never would have happened. Not only would it never have happened, but it would not have seemed fun. It wouldn't have been enjoyable, and it really was.

It took me having faith in myself, and having that alignment with what was important to me and what was not. I left behind the thoughts of 'what are other people going to think when I take my kids out of school? What are the people going to think when we put our house on the market and join this tour? What is my mom going to think about homeschooling?' My mother and my stepmother are both lifelong educators in the public school system. So explaining to them what homeschooling really was and how I was going to approach it, and why, and what I saw as the benefits for my kids. Doing that with confidence and clarity instead of waiting for permission felt exhilarating. Having that clarity so that I could have that faith in myself was crucial. That is the first step in having that faith in yourself.

Somebody asked me the other day, what do you do about those women who give you the side eyes, that give you that judgy, I can't believe you're doing it that way look? So here's the thing about those people, they are just reflecting something that's already doubtful inside you. If you have zero doubt, and all the confidence and clarity about what your choice is and what you are doing, I don't care if somebody looks at you and screams at you that you are the craziest person on the planet. You will not care. Because it is so clear to you, it is so aligned. Having faith in yourself is about becoming really clear and this means you can change your mind like I did. I didn't say, well, I told myself I would start a school, so I am going to start a school whether I like it or not. No. I learned a lot during that process, and then I made better choices. I saw options that were not options previously. Those nine months were not a waste of time. They were a gift. Often it is not about making the right choice forever, it's about making the right choice for you now. Then you continue to grow and learn and make the right choice for you in six months, and in ten months, and in two years, and in 10 years. I just encourage everybody to give yourself permission to get that clear. Once you have that clarity, then you can have faith in yourself to make those decisions. Circling back to the gratitude piece, holy mackerel, you can find gratitude so much more easily when you are really in alignment with what is most important to you.

Q&A

Jana: There was so much in your chapter, Amber, but I'm going to ask this. What was your coconut milk? Was it Jamie's support? Was it the faith in yourself?

Amber: I think it was trusting myself. Because support from other people is great. But if you do not trust yourself, then it doesn't have any place to land.

Jana: For the amazing beating hearts reading this book who are just getting back their confidence and their girl power, if someone doesn't know how to do that, where do you even start? Where do they start to get that faith in themselves?

Amber: The very first step is figuring out what is most important to you, right now in your life, given your values, given your lifestyle, given your personality, given your family dynamics, just right now, what is most important to you? What are the three to five things that are most important to you? Then, the second step is to ask yourself and try to answer honestly, how much of your time, attention, resources, energy, are you spending on those three to five things?

I talk a lot about being overwhelmed with my clients and with my community. People will ask, How do you get less overwhelmed and what creates overwhelm? I love being busy. I love doing doing doing, going going going. I believe that overwhelm is spending a lot of your time, or a lot of your energy, or a lot of your resources, or a lot of your attention in ways that you do not care about. That is what leads to being overwhelmed.

The flip side of that is trust in yourself, and have faith in yourself. This comes from first identifying what is really important to you. Then every day, more and more, moving your time, energy, attention, money, resources to those things that are most important to you. The more you can shift your time and energy to what is important to you, the more confident you'll become, the happier you'll become, and people around you will see those changes as well. When you are in alignment, it affects not just you, but everybody. I also call that self-care. It is really how you spend your time, money and energy. When I say this about self-care, I want to reiterate and really leave you with the understanding that self-care is not a luxury. Self-care is a responsibility. It is a responsibility not only to yourself, but to your children, to your families, to your community, to your career and to your future. I really believe in that.

AMBER TRUEBLOOD is a licensed therapist, best-selling author, speaker, and mother to four sons. An avid reader and learner, Amber curates courses, hosts seminars, and works with private clients to reduce stress and anxiety in their lives. She's gone from a divorce, infertility diagnosis, bankruptcy, and traditional therapy practice to a two-decade relationship, four children, complete financial freedom, and now serves thousands of women worldwide. Amber believes the most effective route to raising the consciousness of our planet is to help women thrive.

SUSAN

Unlike most women, I'm defined in great part by my sexuality. As an author of passionate lovemaking techniques, I lead people toward the intimacy and connection they crave.

It's said that your greatest wound becomes your greatest gift. This was true for me. I remember the pivotal moment of my sexual awakening. I was standing at the door of my beautiful Silicon Valley mansion watching my husband drive away for perhaps the last time… I'd asked him to move out.

My six-year-old little girl was standing beside me in the vestibule. As a child, when Taylor was nervous about something, she would rub the satin edge ribbon of her baby blanket on her lip to soothe herself. She was doing that as she looked at my husband, suitcases loaded in his car and said, "But, will you still be my daddy?"

At that moment I thought, "What am I doing? What are we doing? My beautiful husband is about to drive away and leave me in this giant house all alone. Why are we breaking up our daughter's family life? We are ruining her childhood all because I can't have an orgasm from intercourse."

I had gotten tired of sex. I never came and it just felt like my husband was constantly needy for sex and never satisfied. Sex felt like work. I avoided it at all costs. But I was wiiling to try to figure out why sex was never as good as I expected.

I rushed to the car as it slowly backed away and said to my husband, "Don't go. Let's try and figure it out."

First we tried a marriage therapist who said, "Oh, hey — you know — sex just doesn't stay the same as when you're first married.

64

You can't expect it to be good forever." When we left, my husband said, "We are not coming back to this therapist. I believe a couple can have a sex life that gets better over time, instead of worse."

This possible divorce all began when we were 11 years into our marriage. On our anniversary, I had one too many gin martinis and I said, "It's not working. I love you, but I'm not in love with you anymore."

He took a deep breath and replied, "You're avoiding me. And we've lost our intimacy. And we never have sex. And I'm sick of begging for it."

And I fired back, "It's just not good for me. For 11 years I've dutifully had sex with you without ever having an orgasm from it. I just can't do it anymore but I don't want to lose my marriage." (I could have an orgasm with a toy, but not with my husband during intercourse.)

That was 20 years ago, mind you, when there were barely any decent toys. And I felt like a failure. And I no longer wanted to have sex if it meant not reaching an orgasm. And I was trying to get out of it all the time, avoiding him. I had a million excuses, but I felt guilty and I felt bad.

Pretty soon he came clean with me. He said, "I'm actually having an affair with a married woman whose husband doesn't have sex with her."

I was devastated. I felt, more than anything—shame—like I was a failure because I couldn't keep my husband satisfied. This is what our patriarchal society does to us. We're supposed to satisfy them whether it feels good to us or not. And I felt that burning shame.

I talked to someone who does "The Work" by Byron Katie and she said, "Oh, honey. He didn't have an affair to hurt you. He had an affair because he loves you. And he's trying to stay in the relationship with you and keep your family together while getting his needs met."

Our problem was sex. And back then, therapists were not trained well in sexuality. We couldn't find one that seemed right. So we decided to try attending sex workshops. The very first one we went to was called the Human Awareness Institute. We did "Sex, Love, and Intimacy" levels one through four. Later on, we started going to Tony Robbins'

"Date With Destiny" and "Unleash the Power Within." We went to an ecstatic love-making workshop, a Tantra workshop, we went to classes on orgasmic meditation.

After all that, we realized that we don't REALLY have any problem with sex itself as an act. We just didn't know what the heck we were doing in bed!

The minute we started learning sex skills, we totally transformed ourselves. I remember in the tantra workshop, we were supposed to create this sacred space. And we were supposed to put things in and take things out of the sacred space we were creating together. And my husband put something in that practically broke my heart.

He put in a mirror for me, which worked magically, to see how beautiful my body was to him. And how beautiful my genitals were to him. I've never really looked at my genitals, and I was 40-something years old. I really didn't celebrate them, love them, and know them intimately. And that was really touching for me.

And over time, we just kept practicing. And we got better and better and better in bed together. And in time, I learned how to have orgasms from intercourse. I did what I now call crossing the "gasm-chasm".

We had a realization that there was absolutely nothing wrong with us. And there was nothing wrong with all our friends who were getting divorced. It wasn't money problems for them either. They were all Silicon Valley executives.

It was sex. And the guys were going to go on to get new, younger wives who hadn't realized that they didn't want bad sex. It was still new to them. So my husband and I came together. Brainstorming. Thinking...

"How do we nip this in the bud? How do we help people realize how easy it is to have great sex? We wanted to help others discover how to undo the shame, religious programming, trauma, abuse and the anorgasmia that women take on as something that's wrong with us rather than the system. "

And to this day, I talk about how the system is a patriarchal system. Sex is a patriarchal system. The way we think about sex. And when I say having sex, I mean people think it's just that a penis goes in a vagina. That's what sex is in the patriarchal view. And it's really not. It's so much more than that.

If we just understood how women's pleasure works — if our male-bodied partners understood that better — everyone would be more satisfied, more deeply connected, more surrendered to their pleasure, more intimate with each other their whole lives long.

So, that's when we decided to start a company together in this renaissance of our relationship where we were having the most incredible sex together.

Where I began learning how to have orgasms from intercourse...

Where I experienced G-Spot pleasuring for the first time...

Where we learned how to have female, ejaculatory orgasms...

I could squirt my heart out and completely release my feminine waters, my divine nectar that all women have inside — if we were not shamed out of it and holding back.

And it was at that time that I realized that I wanted to change my career and become a sexpert, and to help women and their partners understand how to have these orgasms.

Even a year ago, 17 years into this business of teaching people about sex, I sat here in my summer home and I wrote how to have all 20 of kinds of male and female orgasms every human body can have.

Most women know there are a few kinds. They know, "Oh, okay, I could have a G-Spot Orgasm. I could have an orgasm from my nipples being played with. I could have an orgasm from kissing my partner. I could have an orgasm from my clitoris being stroked. I could have an orgasm during intercourse, a cervical orgasm, and an A-Spot orgasm. I could have a female ejaculatory orgasm. I could have analgasms. There are also throatgasms. There are orgasms with toys. There's erotic hypnosis, where I can have an orgasm on command without you even touching me. There are so many kinds of orgasms. There are regular orgasms, multiple orgasms, extended orgasms and expanded orgasms. There's also orgasmic meditation. Number 20 is a "wildcard orgasm" because there are ways that people are orgasming that I don't even know about.

I have devoted the last nearly 20 years to bringing out sexual education, sex techniques, orgasms skills, bedroom communication skills and sexual health to people who know in their hearts that sex can be a source of super powers and incredible pleasure and connection.

I also talk about how to conceive, how NOT to conceive, how to protect yourself from sexually transmitted infections and how to date and sleep around safely. Everything from how to fix the loss of lubrication, incontinence, painful sex, vaginal thinning, loss of orgasmic intensity, how to fix our partners' erectile dysfunction and their premature ejaculation, their delayed ejaculation and even the loss of libido for all people across the gender spectrum.

And it's been the most incredible, love-filled experience. People appreciate me so much. I am so loved by the people whom I help. And it is my joy and pleasure to help everyone who comes to me — because I don't do one-on-ones. I don't do therapy. I just give away free advice to anyone and everyone who asks.

What I do is publish passionate lovemaking techniques, techniques that transform having sex into making love, heart-connected, conscious, love-making techniques. My online programs are available to everyone around the world. They are self-study content. Most include audio, video and ebooks.

And the single most important thing that I teach is how to ask for what you want in bed. Because so many people are afraid to speak up. Sex is quiet, it's silent. And it doesn't need to be. Because when we speak up, when we use sexy talk, when we moan and when we find our sexual voice, we become more deeply connected.

I have a technique called the Sexual Soulmate Pact. It's an agreement between lovers, wherein we acknowledge that our bodies want something different every day, every second. And when we honor that changing desire, we become more satisfied. When we can speak up we get what truly pleases us.

For example, "Today, I want to be held, stroked, petted, loved and to be nurtured. And then when I've gotten that, maybe now I want to pounce on you like a tiger and ride you like crazy, like you are a wild stallion."

When our partners understand that in our female bodies, we go through these moon cycles that really change what we want — not from not day to day but minute to minute — then we are deeply satisfied. The pact is about understanding and honoring that within us.

So many women say, "I don't know what I want. I just know that what I'm getting is not it."

To reframe that mindset, I say to women, "Oh, you DO know what you want. You just have to listen to her. She's talking to you all the time. Who? Your Yoni, which is a beautiful tantric lovemaking word for your vulva. Your genitals know what they want all the time. And when you speak words for her to your partner, when you're on the same team, (My husband and I call each other 'Team Sweetie'. That's us, and we have been that way for 31 years now.)

And when your partner realizes that it's nothing they did wrong—that they're doing everything right by listening to you—by giving voice to your desires—it's like being on fire and turned on every moment—adjusting and flowing with it.

Then, suddenly they're empowered. They're winning. You respect them more for being that lover who listens and you feel heard. And then your sex life gets on what I call "The Upward Pleasure Spiral" where sex just keeps getting better and better and better.

Last night in bed, here's what my husband and I did. It was what I wanted. My neck was hurting because I did these crazy lunges up the hill yesterday. My trainer came over and he made me do lunges up a steep hill. And I did all these shoulder presses and they torqued out my neck and I was super achy last night. So I said, "I would like you to rub my neck with my THC pain cream," —which works like a charm and it doesn't get you high," ... and I would like to hold your penis in my mouth and just enjoy and take my pleasure with it."

And I laid my head on his belly and I put his penis in my mouth as he rubbed the pain cream on while I suckled his penis like a baby. And it was really fun. He didn't need to ejaculate. My pain cream felt good. I was like, "That's good babe, I'm gonna go to bed now, will you tuck me in?"

I like it when he pulls the cover up over my shoulder when I go to bed and pats it for me. It makes me feel so good and safe.

Then, when he got up this morning, he was like, "That was really fun last night."

And I said, "What did we do?" I couldn't even remember because we are always doing something different.

And he said, "Oh yeah, you know, I rubbed your neck and you gave me a blowjob."

And I said, "Oh, that's so good. Yeah, that was really fun! I'm glad you liked it."

He goes, "Yeah, it was great. It seemed effortless for you."

And I was like, "Well, it wasn't effortless. I was working, but not in a bad way, in a good way. I love the peaceful acts and connection we show each other."

He said "Yeah, it was really intimate."

And I said, "Yeah, I know. I love that about us."

And when I think about the level of variety and the novelty and just the whims of whatever comes up — and my willingness to ask — and his willingness to ask — and he feeds me fantasies that sound fun. I mean, I literally cooked him pork chops the other night in a Bavarian barmaid outfit because that's what he likes.

It's just such a wonderful thing when you have a partner, and the sky's the limit. Sex keeps getting better. It never ends. There's always something new to try, do and experience.

When you trust each other, you listen to yourself and you feel good about whatever you need to ask for and have.

This is the Sexual Soulmate Pact at play, that ability to know what you want because you're listening to your woman's intuition—or your man's intuition—or your body's intuition.

And your partner's like, "Yeah, that sounds good, I'll do that. Let's do it." And you can just listen to what your body wants in the moment over and over and over again.

The ability to make course corrections in real time with no worry that you're hurting anyone's ego allows you to feel free and open and flowing in your sex and connection. And that's what I want for all lovers.

But there's one last thing that I want to leave you with. And that is my number two most important thing for sex. And that goes back to this idea of the patriarchal versus the matriarchal view of sexuality.

In the patriarchal view, the man wants to put his penis in your vagina because it feels good to him and it's his favorite thing. And for many of us, we haven't achieved the learned skill that all women are capable of doing, which is having orgasms from intercourse without even touching the tip of our clitoris.

We can become fully orgasmic from penetration even without manually touching the tip of our clitoris if we get enough foreplay and blood flow to our entire vulva. We rush penetration and then we don't have enough sensation to achieve orgasm. When we slow down and allow ourselves to get completely turned on, orgasms from intercourse become easy.

All orgasms are learned. If you haven't done it yet, it's just because you haven't learned the path to it. On my website at personallifemedia. com, I have a series called "Come With Me: The 20 Kinds Of Male And Female Orgasms."

But here's what I want to tell you about the patriarchal view of sex. I want to show you two pictures. So, this is our vulva.

This is the mons pubis up here, the labia, the outer labia, the inner labia. The opening inside the labia is called the vestibule. The clitoral hood actually becomes the labia and comes down to this little area at the bottom that meets called the fourchette, which the French named, means fork.

Inside the vestibule, underneath the clitoral shaft, there's the clitoral tip under the hood that goes in and down to a shaft that's our penis essentially. Then there's your urethral exit, which is where your pee comes out. And that's the first area of your G-spot and around that little area is spongy tissue. I call it G-spot number two.

And then, here's the opening to your vagina which is called your introital sphincter. It's a round muscle. And then, when you go inside, you have the vaginal canal. And on the upper top portion of the roof of your vagina, you have the G-spot number one.

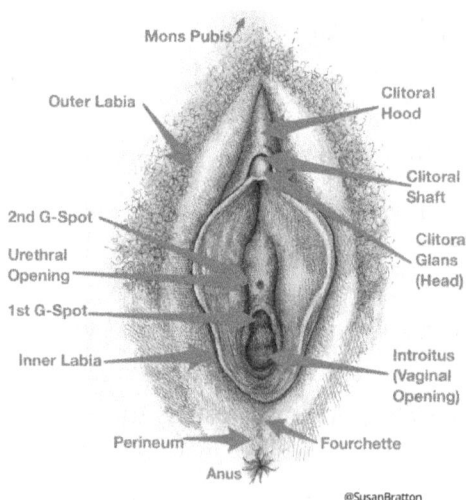

Mons Pubis
Outer Labia
Clitoral Hood
Clitoral Shaft
2nd G-Spot
Urethral Opening
Clitoral Glans (Head)
1st G-Spot
Inner Labia
Introitus (Vaginal Opening)
Perineum
Fourchette
Anus
@SusanBratton

Now, I'm going to show you what a G-spot actually looks like. I often say, "The G-spot isn't a spot. It's a G-area." That's because it is actually a long tube. Next, this is your perineum down here. And this is your anus here. And then if I take away the skin and show you what's underneath, these are your erectile tissue systems. This is the head of your clitoris. The shaft of your clitoris, the arms of your clitoris, and the legs of your clitoris. This is that tube of sponge, the G-spot, which is a tube of sponge. Layer buds pop out; this is the introital sphincter, or opening to the vagina. And then this is the perineal sponge.

So, you have three erectile tissue systems in your vulva. You have the clitoral, the urethra, and the perineal. Just like inside your male body partner, he has three spongy chambers. Those three spongy chambers are the two corpus cavernosum and a corpus spongiosum.

Half of it is outside of his body, and half of it is inside his body. And this is all erectile tissue. And the thing is that those straight shots of tissue get hard. He gets hard much faster. He gets swollen, erect and full of blood in a minute or two. Whereas for women with those three very complex systems, it takes us about 20 minutes to get a full erection.

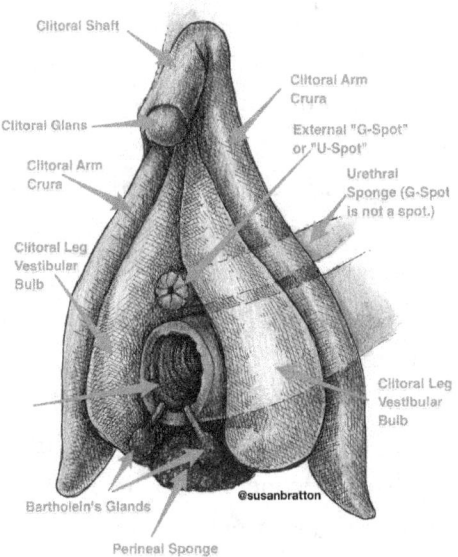

For most of us women, we've been rushing ourselves to intercourse forever—and we never really get a full erection. And if you ask any man if he wants sex with or without an erection he'd be like, "With please, that's the only way I really like it." And not just because it's hard and straight and penetrable—but because if you take small amounts of tissue, it has X amount of surface area. If it's expanded, and it's large and plump and fluffy—it has double, triple, and quadruple the amount of surface area. And when it's touched and there is sensation, it sends double, triple, and quadruple the number of pleasure signals to your brain.

And so, the number one thing that I want women to know is that what you want is always right. And the more you listen to your body and get in touch with her, the better your sex will become.

All sex techniques are learned skills. So, spend a lifetime learning them. And don't rush sex. I literally don't even believe in a quickie.

My husband wouldn't even give me a quickie. I'm like, "Let's do a quickie!", and he says "No, you'll just be cranky afterward." Because women have to become fully engorged to fully enjoy sex. You need a lot of gentle massage and stimulation.

So, to bring this all home, I have faith that you can put yourself on a journey that will take you a lifetime of joy and pleasure to achieve that sex never stops being great. And that you can enjoy sex for the rest of your life. And your sexual maturation will continue to grow and expand.

I have a desire for you to love your body exactly how it is now. It's an amazing, beautiful thing. There's nothing wrong with you, you are perfect. And estrogen makes you so critical of yourself. So, you need to push self-criticism out of your little monkey mind and love yourself fully. Embrace all of your beauty—especially your remarkable, marvelous genitals. And I have gratitude for Jana for having me here —so I can give you the opportunity to learn more about the things that someone should have told you, and that I have just done. Thank you so much.

Q&A

Jana: Susan, that was really great. I need to ask, you shared so beautifully about your lemons when you talk. You had us there, in the moment. We could see and feel the silky part of Taylor's blanket and you took that lemon on so many different levels—not just personally but professionally. Tell our readers, what is your coconut milk?

Susan: My incredible orgasmic experiences. Feeling deeply connected to myself rooted to Gaia, which is the word I like to use for Earth and my connection to all living things. My comfort and groundedness in my own human skin, my love of my beautiful vulva, my breath, my body. Even at 60 years old, loving myself for exactly who I am. My connection to my husband and my lovers, my partners. The joy that I have that I think so many people are missing. I mean, people have their family, they have their faith, they have their food and they have the things that bring them joy, but if they only had a little idea of the amount of pleasure that is created through sexuality—I wish more people could tap into that particular coconut milk. And I would say just knowing how many people are helped by all the "thank yous" I get all the time from so many people for the work that I do to make sexuality something that fuels and expands people. So I think that's probably one of the things too is that I get to give my gifts and they are received with joy.

Jana: So if there's a reader, right now, and she's reading this book, maybe there are tears streaming down her face. Sometimes we are so concerned with who others think we need to be that sometimes we actually forget who we are. Where does that woman with this book in her hand start?

Susan: Self-pleasure. Start with masturbation. Start by finding your own orgasm. One of the things that I like to do is I like to explain to women that you can cross-train orgasmically. You can try different types of sex toys that give you different types of orgasms. Whether you're using an air stimulator or you're using a buzzy vibe, or rumbly vibe or you're using a G-spot wand, or using a G-spot vibrator, or any number of different types of thrusters or pulsators. There are all kinds of toys that can help you expand your orgasmic potential— even without a partner. And if you're with a partner, solo pleasuring masturbation can work really, really well. One of my favorite things to do, even after I have sex with my partner, is to give myself some orgasms at the end with a vibrator because I've got more in me than they do. They are in this paradigm where they will have full-body orgasms, and then they ejaculate, and then they are done, and they need to rest. And sometimes I'm just getting started. And so they love that too. They're like, do you need to use your vibrator? Do you need more? Do you need to have some more orgasms? Sometimes I'm like, "Yes, I do. Can you please play with my nipples?" Enjoy what you have, knowing that no one's there to judge you. That is absolutely so healthy and good for you.

Jana: Is there anything that you feel has been left unsaid that you want to make sure lands with our audience?

Susan: I've already given you enough to get started. There are 1 million more things I could tell you. I mean, I've written 5,000 articles, I've produced 200 videos, I've published 20 programs. I've authored 35 books. So yes, there are so many things you need to learn, whether that's how to have better orgasms or how to do a dirty talk or tantric lovemaking techniques or whatever it might be, seduction skills or how to do a floor show or a pole dance or, like, it's an endless amount of things that I need to tell you. So you need to get started.

Jana: Amazing and I love that advice. Just get started. Right. Today is the day.

SUSAN BRATTON, "Intimacy Expert to Millions" is a champion and advocate for all those who desire intimacy and passion their whole life long. She is co-founder and CEO of two corporations: Personal Life Media, Inc., a publisher of heart-connected lovemaking techniques and bedroom communication skills and The20, LLC., a manufacturer of organic and botanical supplements that enhance sexual vitality.

A best-selling author and publisher of 34 books and programs including Sexual Soulmates, Relationship Magic, Revive Her Drive, Ravish Him, Steamy Sex Ed™, The Passion Patch, Hormone Balancing, and Hot To Trot. Susan has been featured in the *New York Times* and on CNBC and the *TODAY* show as well as frequent appearances on ABC, CBS, The CW, Fox and NBC.

You can find The Susan Bratton Show® at BetterLover.com, her personal shares on Instagram @susanbratton, and her lust-for-life supplements, FLOW and DESIRE at The20store.com.

DR. SHARON

Hi Ladies, I'm Dr. Sharon Stills and I learned pretty early on in my life - I'm now 54, but at the age of, I think I was about 25 - that when life gives you lemons . . . drink coconut milk. And so, I'll share how I learned that and how it affected me personally and how it's affected my thousands of patients who I've been working with throughout the years now, and how it can affect you as well.

I was 25, with two little boys. I was a single mom, and we had just moved to Tucson. I was doing my undergraduate work so I could become a naturopathic physician. I was at the University of Arizona, and I was a massage therapist. I was working really hard. I had a clinic I would go to see my massage patients. I was also doing iridology and colon hydrotherapy and nutrition and all sorts of stuff. I was going to class to do my undergraduate degree, I was having to run a household, I was doing my best to be the best mother I could be because my kids were the most important thing to me and still are, (obviously, along with my now grandchildren), but I wasn't really getting to see my kids. One day I picked them up from the Montessori school that they were attending and I was told that there was an outbreak of chickenpox. And I thought, holy crap, I had never had chickenpox, and I wasn't a physician yet, but I had heard that rumor that chickenpox was really sucky when you have it as an adult. So, I called back home and asked my mom. "I don't remember having chickenpox ever. Did I?" And my mom confirmed I had never had chickenpox. And so, my eldest son got a few pox. My younger son got a few pox. They were ill for a couple of days and then they were fine and had natural immunity. And then I got chickenpox.

I got chickenpox from head to toe and in every nook and cranny that you can imagine, including down there. It was not an enjoyable experience, and I got super sick.

At the time, I was a single mom working my way through school. We lived in a one-bedroom apartment. I gave my kids the bedroom, I slept in the living room on a futon, and all of a sudden, the futon and I were inseparable. It wasn't like I had chickenpox for a day or two and got better. I had chickenpox for a week, and then two weeks, and then three weeks, and four weeks. So, I was sick, lying horizontally on this futon for a month, just literally miserable. And you know the saying that doctors don't make the best patients? Well, that's definitely true. My family was back East. We were in Tucson, Arizona. I had to rely on friends who became family, and neighbors who pitched in and would take my kids to school. I remember my chiropractor would come to the house and adjust me because my neck would go out and I had chickenpox all over my neck. It was just miserable, and I am itching just thinking about it now.

From the chickenpox, I went into pneumonia first followed by chronic fatigue. So finally, the pox crusted over, and they stopped itching. However, let me remind you pneumonia is no joke. I wasn't a naturopathic physician yet, but I knew I was going to be a naturopathic physician, so I sought out a great naturopath locally in Tucson. I told him I wanted to treat this naturally and so he prescribed many things including a very powerful herb called lomatium which was extremely healing for my lungs. So, he was giving me all the correct herbal treatments, and I was eating organic broccoli, and I was taking vitamin C, and I was doing all the 'right things', but I really wasn't improving. And there I lay on my futon, watching the neighbor come to get the boys, barely being able to put together a gluten-free sandwich for them to take to lunch, waving goodbye and just lying there, just feeling like death, and feeling hopeless, and feeling helpless, and feeling disconnected from myself, and disconnected from my life, and disconnected from my children. It didn't matter what I took. I took more vitamin C, I took an extra dose of lomatium, or I had an acupuncture house call, but nothing seemed to be helping until about a month later when my lungs started to finally heal but now in my third month, I was experiencing complete and utter exhaustion. My adrenals were just shot. I did have mono as an 18-year-old. My Epstein Barr was reactivated. And I was just lifeless and desperate and crying. And here I was, I had just moved with my kids. I was on my journey. I was supposed to be completing my undergraduate work, I had this great job, in this new office, doing massage. I had a great boyfriend. Life was supposed to be happening, and I was just lying on my futon. I was just lying on my futon, and life was not happening.

So, there I was lying on my futon three months into this ordeal when I had an aha moment. I started thinking about my life and what was not working in it. I was so insanely busy. I was always at the office or always at school, and my kids were getting older. I was feeling disconnected from them, I wasn't feeling like I was being the involved parent that I wanted to be. I didn't want to just be a ship passing in the night with my children. And as I was lying there in month three of extreme illness, I had this aha, this idea that, what if I took my kids out of Montessori school and I started to homeschool them? And what if I went to night school instead of day classes? And what if I stopped working at the massage clinic, which was a 30-minute drive one way from my home, and I started doing massage out of the apartment? What if I did that? What if I could spend all day with my kids, so when it came time for the neighbor to watch them at night, I wouldn't feel guilty leaving them, I'd actually probably feel relieved because I've been with them for nine hours –kidding not kidding ;) When I had that idea, I literally went from horizontal to vertical. And I started to feel better. I got my life back; I got my energy back. It was such a powerful experience for me because we all talk about the mind-body connection. Sometimes I think we just give it lip service. We don't really lean into it. We really don't embrace it. We don't experience it. We don't even create the space for it to occur and show us how it materializes in our lives.

In this moment, I had this powerful understanding of how the mind truly does affect the body and how our happiness and our connection affects our physical body. I took that knowledge with me, and I did it! I acted on my thoughts. That was a very busy bedroom we had. It was a classroom, and it was a massage room, and it was a bedroom. But I turned things around and instead of sending my kids off to school, we would go to the natural foods co-op and math class would be counting the change or figuring out how much a pound of bananas would cost. We went on homeschool field trips and played in the park with other homeschool kids. I started massaging at home, so I didn't have to leave and do the commute. Both of my sons I had attuned to become Reiki Masters when they were young. And my younger son, who actually now is the naturopathic physician, would come while I was doing massage and he would start to hold his hands out and do Reiki on the clients lying on my massage table!

It just gave me so much joy and so much connection that my children were involved in my life, and I was involved in their life. And it was a very powerful thing to learn for someone who was becoming a physician because when I went through naturopathic medical school, I had this powerful experience with me. Although I've been in practice for more than 20 years, I've seen thousands and thousands of patients, and although I do rely on giving vitamin C or giving the proper herbal prescription. I also know and often prescribe leaving your job, or taking a vacation, moving cross country, reconnecting to your husband, getting in touch with your guilt and really creating the life of your dreams. These emotional events can really weigh heavily on our physical being. If you have chronic fatigue, sometimes the answer is a vitamin C infusion. But sometimes the answer is writing that book, or taking that dance class, or finding a new partner, or reconnecting with your partner, or having that baby, or not having that baby, or getting that dog, or whatever it is. Our lives are intimately connected with what we think, what we drink, what we eat, but also with what we do and how we find our place in the world.

Q&A

Jana: I love that. Okay, That was fantastic. Thank you. As a naturopathic physician, you offered some advice just towards the end of your chapter that maybe people who haven't had any experience in the world of naturopathic medicine would like to hear. I think for many people, we're used to going to our MD and getting a prescription, not maybe for an herb or a supplement, but for a manufactured drug, which maybe that is necessary in your world of naturopathy as well. But for those women who have this book in their hands right now, can you give them a little bit of insight because not everyone knows what the world of being a patient of a naturopathic physician is like. Can you explain that for us?

Dr. Sharon: We have been taught in society that when we are sick, there is a pill, and that is how mainstream medicine has been cultivated. You go to med school, you learn how to name or diagnose a disease process, and then you learn which pill is going to suppress those symptoms. And that is the kind of standard of care that we have been taught to believe is acceptable. The reason why I went to naturopathic medical school and now have a totally different paradigm when working with patients is because that system didn't work for me when I was a child. I was extremely ill as a child. I couldn't walk outside if they were cutting the grass without being sent into a huge asthma attack which then had me being carted off to the hospital to go under the oxygen tent (and now I'm dating myself).

I don't think they have oxygen tents anymore in the hospital, but that was the treatment, it was like the girl in the plastic half bubble.

When you go to see a naturopathic doctor, we have a philosophy that we practice by, and one of the philosophies is to treat the root cause and that everyone is an individual, and that the answers to healing us often lie in nature. When you come to see a naturopathic physician, you typically spend an hour just sharing your story. Because your story often contains the answers, whether it be you are only sleeping four hours a night, or you drink one glass of water daily and you're dehydrated, or you're super stressed out and unhappy, or you have unresolved trauma or whatever it is. We do not just treat and name a disease. Honestly, the disease process is really not that important to me when I'm working with a patient. I'll tell you a quick story because it really illustrates this idea. I went to medical school to become a pediatrician because my son had a lot of issues when he was born. And I didn't find answers through antibiotics at the pediatrician's office, and back then there was no internet, so it wasn't that easy to research. But I researched and I figured out how to help my son heal his chronic ear issues.

So fast forward four years of medical school. I'm out in practice. I just opened my clinic. I'm on my own, a brand-new doctor. The seventh patient who walks in my door is an elderly gentleman in his late 60s. I guess it's not elderly really, now that I'm in my 50s. A spry young gentleman in his late 60s walked in, and he was diagnosed with stage four pancreatic cancer, and he was told to get his affairs in order. He saw my sign on the street that said, "Naturopathic Solutions, A Center for Balanced Healing," and he said, "They've told me I have no hope and I want to walk my daughter down the aisle."

And I thought, oh my goodness, because you hear that pancreatic cancer is the worst one that's not curable at all. And I just took a deep breath. I remembered that my belief is that the universe only sends us what we can handle and only provides us with what we need to learn and grow. And I thought, okay, here we go. This is not a kid with a tummy ache. I said to him, "Look, I'm going to be honest with you, I've never treated cancer before, certainly never stage four pancreatic cancer, but I have a set of philosophy and principles of how the body works and how the body heals. I'm happy to apply those to you and see what happens."

And fast forward, he's cured, his cancer reversed, and he went on to live another 10 years. He got to walk his daughter down the aisle. He later died from a cardiac issue which was totally unrelated to his cancer diagnosis. This experience taught me a huge lesson. Here's another lemon to coconut milk scenario, which was to trust in how the body heals and to trust in my medicine, which is naturopathic medicine.

We Naturopathic Physicians are all different because medicine is a science and an art, and it's the practice. My experience with the cancer survivor taught me that the body innately knows how to heal itself. When you come to work with someone like me, if you come with migraines, I know that herbs like butterbur, magnesium and B vitamins are really helpful for migraines. Now, my pills are natural, and my pills don't have side effects like pharmaceuticals, and they don't deplete nutrients like pharmaceuticals, and they don't create other problems like pharmaceuticals, but is that really looking at the whole being of you?

When you work with someone like me, I may give you those herbs and those nutrients, but I'm also going to look at your lifestyle, I'm going to look at how you're hydrating, how you're sleeping, your community, your connections, your relationships, your stress levels, because I had such an extreme experience of going from horizontal to vertical, just because I changed my lifestyle and how I was living my day-to-day. I've never forgotten that lesson. I know that is true for other human beings as well. So, yes, you may have a migraine because you're low in magnesium, but why are you low in magnesium? Stress will deplete magnesium. Why are you stressed? I am always looking to get to the root cause. That is why I take a longer amount of time with patients. I cannot possibly get to know you and the whole gestalt of you in a five-minute visit. All you have enough for in a five-minute visit is, What are your symptoms? What is your disease? Here is a pill. Have a nice day. It is a very different paradigm of working with patients.

Jana: Thank you for that, and for that story. Very inspirational. You have shared with us lots of your lemons and you have also shared lots of the coconut milk that's come out of the shift in the direction that your life has gone because of those lemons. If you had to look back over your short 54 years, if you had to attribute your coconut milk to one thing, what would you attribute it to?

Dr. Sharon: I attribute it to the way I see life. I see life as I am a spiritual being having a human experience. So, everything is not happening to me, it's happening for me. There is always a lesson or a growth edge I can take from every experience. It is just a matter of me being mindful. Mindfulness is another one of my huge tools. I discovered mindfulness meditation when I was still a naturopathic medical student. That is the other big piece of medicine that I provide to patients. I believe that when we are mindful, and we are introspective, and we are seeing and experiencing what's happening, that there is always a lesson in it for us. I believe we are here to evolve, and as a soul we choose to incarnate because maybe we have to learn how to forgive. Or maybe we have to learn how to slow down. Or maybe we need to learn how to speak out. Everything that happens is just part of my spiritual journey that I can take with me.

Jana: That's beautiful. I pull a Super Attractor card every day and the one I pulled today reads, "I slow down and listen to the guidance that's available to me." You just mentioned that and it's in those moments of slowing down and being mindful that we can actually hear the messages. I feel like sometimes women have been told that we have to be these super moms, the super partners, these super entrepreneurs. And that was me, I would wear that like a badge of honor. It impacted my health in a negative way. People would say, "How do you do it? How do you do it all, Jana?"

And I would just feel my ego double in size. Like, how am I going to walk out of this door? My head is totally blown up here. And yet, it sometimes takes the physicality or the emotionality, or the spirituality of our being to have its dark night of the soul or its contraction phase. Maybe that is what your chickenpox to pneumonia to adrenal fatigue was, because when you told us that story, almost every aspect of your life changed because of it. And maybe it would have evolved and maybe would have ended up getting there. But to think that there was this 90-day period, where for some people that would be enough to surrender. And yet the 'what if' questions opened you up to the endless possibilities, and that delicious coconut milk.

Dr. Sharon: It really did change who I was personally, but also who I was as a physician. I give thanks for all my experiences and trust me, I have had tons of hardships and lots of stories I can tell, but I give thanks to all of them because they all have made me wiser, more empathetic, more able to understand the human condition. I think it's really important for the readers to understand that I'm not saying I don't get upset or I don't get angry, or I don't get any of the "negative emotions." Because I do experience those and I allow my body to experience them because all emotions matter. All emotions are equal. When we experience a negative emotion there's a reason for that experience and there is no need to shame ourselves over it. It's just a matter of, do we get stuck in them, or do we dance with them? Do we move through them? Do we learn from them? And do we let them leave? I love the poem, "The Guesthouse," by Rumi. It is really a beautiful poem, inviting in all the emotions to the home. But you know, come for a cup of tea, you don't have to move in. I think there is this toxic positivity where sometimes we think, oh, I have to be spiritual and I have to be positive, and that is not what I'm saying. I'm saying, through feeling the depression, the anger, the anxiety, whatever it is, I've been able to come to this place because I do not ignore it. I feel it. I experience it. I learn from it. I dialogue with it. And then I'm able to see it from a higher perspective.

Jana: Yeah, that's beautiful. I just want to ask; do you feel complete? Is there anything that you feel has been left unsaid? Do you have any last bits of advice or wisdom?

Dr. Sharon: One last story that I believe can be of benefit for the readers. When I was in naturopathic medical school, I had a boyfriend. We were together for a couple of months. And I was about to break up with him because I did not think he was a very nice person. And I ended up pregnant. I already had my two children (remember the ones who gave me the chickenpox ;), I was in school, I never wanted more children, I was done. But all of a sudden, the hormones took over. And I was like, I'm going to have this baby. And he was pressuring me to be with him. I was 32 years old, and I got pressured by him and my father to marry him even though I knew inside this is not what I wanted. But I did it because I wasn't 54. I didn't have the wisdom back then that I have now. We went to the courthouse and got married. It is never a good thing when you get married with a discussion ending with the words "Fine, I'll marry you."

Off we went to the courthouse with my two boys and his three children, and you could certainly tell it was a last-minute decision because in the wedding pictures, all the kids were in T-shirts and shorts. We got married and not very long after there was an incident where he was physical and dragged my younger son across the room. Obviously, this was unacceptable to mama bear. I quickly divorced him and had to make a decision about my pregnancy.

I was a struggling single mom in med school. I already had my two boys. They were eight and 10 at the time. I had to make a decision about what I was going to do because I did not want to share a child with someone who was physically abusive. I then saw him be physically abusive to his own children. And I was trying to become a doctor and I was trying to take care of the two children I had, and I had already struggled as a single mom, and I just could not see it. I made the very hard decision to terminate the pregnancy at about 10.5 weeks. I cried and I processed, and I thought that was it. And then fast forward eight years in practice, and I am always talking with the patients who come in about their issues, whether it be sexual abuse or having to terminate a pregnancy or, you know, the hard things in life, the challenging things. Patients would say, no, no, I'm fine, I'm not upset about it anymore. You can't really argue with someone if they say they're fine. I thought I was fine too. And then one day this meditation rolled into town.

I was in New York at the time, and it was called the AUM meditation - awareness understanding meditation - by Veeresh, a student of Osho, an Indian spiritual teacher. My friend said, come on, we're going into the city, and we are going to do this meditation. Me, being up for anything, was like okay, cool. So, we went. I had no idea what we were going to do. This was not like an ohm sitting there quietly meditating. This was a social, dynamic, interactive meditation where you go through 12 emotions, from anger and love to Kundalini and laughing and crying. And during the crying part of the meditation, I started screaming about the baby that I had terminated, I was pretty hysterical and was processing it and went through it and was blown away thinking, holy wow, that was eye opening. I didn't even think this was an issue for me.

The meditation came back to New York again, so I went again. The same thing happened. I lost it again during the crying part with a little bit less intensity. Then the meditation came back a third time, through town, and I did it and I was complete in the crying part. It was a very powerful lemon to coconut milk moment where I really, again, learned that the body stores our experiences. Even if we consciously do not think it is affecting us, it could still be affecting us. It could be just buried. It is important for us to explore, not just mentally, not just with words, but to explore somatically what is going on and what is holding us back and what is keeping us ill. So, there was that big awareness, which was like a gallon of coconut milk. On top of that, I decided that if this was this powerful for me, this needed to be shared with others. I traveled to Holland and spent three weeks at the Humaniversity Center where they teach this meditation, and I became one of the only US certified teachers to lead the AUM meditation to share with others so they too can process through their emotions and live happier, healthier lives.

Jana: Wow, wow. I'm assuming, and correct me if I'm wrong, this process of this meditation can only be done in person. Is that right?

Dr. Sharon: Yeah, it's an in-person experience with actual people in the room because it starts off by pairing up with another person and you are screaming, like, "F*ck you!" You are getting your anger out. Then you go into hugging, and it is a cool thing to let the emotions flow from anger to love. Retreats are coming soon where I will be able to share this for everyone to experience and heal. I mean, it had and still has such a powerful effect on me, especially for me as a physician, using all my lemons to make coconut milk to not only help heal myself, but to heal all my patients and fellow humans, such as the readers of the book, to make an impact so that they can think differently.

Jana: Oh, Dr. Sharon, thank you, thank you, thank you. This is like going to be a lighthouse book for many women who end up having it in their possession. Thank you for opening up your heart and your soul to us, and for inspiring. As feminine beings, we are much stronger together.

As a gender, I think we went through a period where maybe that was not the case. This feels really good. Thank you for inspiring and impacting our audience with your story.

DR. SHARON STILLS is a Naturopathic Medical Doctor who helps perimenopausal and menopausal women to pause and evaluate life so they can live the second act of their story stronger, healthier, and sexier while aging backwards. Using her 20+ years of experience and extensive training and background in European Biological Medicine, pro-aging therapies, and Bio-identical Hormone Replacement, she has successfully helped thousands of women transition gently through the different stages of their lives with all natural methods. Dr. Stills is passionate about spreading the word about her signature RED Hot Sexy Meno(pause) Program – the philosophy she developed for you to Reinvent your Health, Explore your Spirit and Discover YOUR Sexy so that you, too, can create and live the life you desire and deserve! She founded and ran one of the largest and most successful naturopathic clinics in the country for a decade and is the host of The Science Of Self Healing podcast. She is an expert physician for Women's Health Network and she educates other physicians as the Co-Lead North American lecturer for the Paracelsus Academy in Switzerland. Patients work with Dr. Stills in a variety of ways: through telemedicine consults and her life-changing retreats for individuals or small groups in healing and rejuvenating locations around the world.

MARUXA

So, this is really a story about the power of resilience and determination, and the marrying of the two. Of course, faith and gratitude are part of that too. But the truth of the matter is, life gives us the opportunity to really lean into life at its fullest form, if we so choose to play with that. So, I'm going to share these two stories from that perspective of really looking at resilience and determination as my guiding lights, as part of the faith journey and as part of the experience of continuing to say yes even when it feels weird, and uncomfortable, or different, or unlike anything else you've ever experienced. The third piece of this would be that it's also out of the box. Life is an out of the box experience if we allow it to be. It doesn't have to fit all the same things that anyone else has given us in the past, or told us we could be or not be.

For me, it started in 2008. I was in the middle of my first ever big crisis of my life. And that crisis was when I found out I was pregnant with my oldest daughter and my husband was out of work for 18 months. I'm in the career that I absolutely love in higher education, I'm also working 100-hour weeks. I was excited to be a mom, I was so thrilled to become a mom, and I found out here, hey, you're actually going to finally be a mom after trying for six months. And also your husband's out of work, and also these 100-hour weeks, they're not going to slow down. So, what is your next step? Oh, and separately, in addition to that, I was also getting my master's in counseling. I was finishing up my final semester in the spring of 2008. Realizing all of those things had to happen: taking care of my husband as he's in a depression because he's out of work for 18 months, being pregnant, running an internship plus running a division of the college, the Multicultural Affairs Division. And all the while, I'm pregnant and about to have a baby. So, I did what any sane mom would want to do to take care of her baby, and that was to quit my job, in the midst of my husband not having a job and everything else. So, I decided in May of 2008, hey, I'm going to have my last day in June. Maya wouldn't be born until September 2008, so it gives me three months to figure our stuff out, have Murph (my husband) get a job and move on with our life and everything will be perfect. I didn't think anything of it. I just knew that I could not work 100 hours a week anymore and be the kind of mom I want to be. With faith, I made the decision to leave.

Well, as you could probably imagine, nothing ever goes the same exact way that we think it's going to go. So, at that point, September is now getting closer and closer and closer, and I'm getting bigger and bigger and bigger and Maya is ready to be born. Murph is now a bank teller making $9 an hour at the time, basically just practically minimum wage to make ends meet and then he would take some temporary jobs whenever he could fit it in with his bank schedule. At this point our savings are just about done. And we're now going into our 401k and cashing out there. So I am thinking ahead. If need be, I'll start taking jobs as a therapist, because I just graduated with my master's at that point, and start seeing what's out there. So, I ended up waiting until the baby was born before I started applying for jobs, I ended up needing to apply for jobs. I became a therapist where I would work with children who were in the system and meeting those kids in their private homes or in their schools. And seeing very quickly that this work didn't light me up. It was hard to see these children, many times in abusive homes or situations where not much was available to the children to care for their wellbeing.

Add to that having your own first child! I struggled to make sense of it all. So it was a very, very, very, very stressful time. And what the worst part at that point for me was having to take on work when Maya was only four weeks old. I started going back to the office or to get clients while Murph was being a bank teller. We were still not able to make our bills. And I had to finally get to a point where I looked myself in the mirror and I said, goodness, here I am with a master's degree, having just won all these awards for the way I was teaching in higher education and these innovative projects that I was working on. I was being published about it. And I'm about to apply for government freaking aid, government aid, a WIC check, WIC check coming to me. I had to sit in that office as a number being called and wait until my turn was called to verify that that was my identity, and to pick up a check for myself and for Dennis and for our daughter. It covered items like beans, rice, milk, formula, cheese. And every day I had to go do this exact thing for a season of my life.

It was a humongous hit to the ego. And I'll never forget, Maya was about four weeks old around November of 2008. I would go to the local Walmart because that's where I would cash my WIC checks. And I would go to the cashier and give her that check, with the beans and the rice and the milk and all the things that I was allowed to get that week. Maya was brand new. I mean, she was four weeks old and I still was at the place in my life where I didn't know how to read the baby's signs really well. What does it look like when she's starting to get hungry or when she is tired? So, I walked into Walmart with a hungry baby - without knowing she was hungry. Well, if you looked at me, and depending on the day, depending on what I'm wearing, depending on the area or place I'm in, people will make assumptions on my racial identity. And that day, the cashier at Walmart decided that she thought that I didn't speak a word of English. And that I must be, you know, quite poor because I'm there with a WIC check and at this point a baby who's starting to get kind of irritated because she's getting hungrier and hungrier.

So, she starts talking to me as if I am a person who doesn't speak English. And she says, "Do you have two forms of ID?" And I'm like, "Yeah, totally, I should." I pulled up my driver's license. And I am looking for the rest of my IDs but I cannot find any other form of ID in my wallet. "I'm so sorry, here is my debit card, here is my credit card, I cannot find the other ID. I'm so sorry. But here's the WIC check and all of it matches." And her response was, "You need two forms of ID." All at the same time, Maya is starting to scream, and I feel like I have the spotlight right on my head, just saying to me, "You are not meant for this world. This is not the world that you're meant for. But here you are, enjoy the pain." And just the feeling of embarrassment and shame and anger, and complete surrender to the fact that I have no idea what the heck I was supposed to do in this situation, except I have a screaming baby and woman who's not going to give me my food, the little bit that that I need to feed the rest of us. And there's a woman behind me who I call, lovingly, *The Angel*, and she came to me and said, "Sweetheart, is there any way I can pay for this for you? I'd love to take care of this." And I was in such ego at that point, such shame around the situation, I looked at her with just complete and utter disbelief that this is my life, and ran out of Walmart with my screaming baby and left all that food sitting right there on the conveyor belt. I couldn't do it, I couldn't have someone pay for me. And I couldn't imagine what that would feel like to be that loved by somebody else.

I walked out, got into my car, and started nursing my baby while also crying uncontrollably. And calling my husband, who thinks by this point, like, something is super wrong because I'm bawling my eyes out at him. And I'm basically just saying, never again. Never again will this happen, I will never allow this moment in my life to happen again. He was kind of in shock. He had no idea what was happening other than hearing me bawl my eyes out. So, I finally got myself okay enough to head home.

I decided then and there that I would never allow that to happen again. And if I can help it, this is what I'm here to change in this world, this feeling that people have that they are beholden to the system, and that the system is better than them. That is not what we're put on this planet to do or to be. And so, with that said, he and I made that commitment to each other that we're changing this. This is not us. And there's nothing wrong with being a bank teller or taking the jobs that we did. We knew that we were made for something more, but we had no idea how the heck to get there, to get out of the situation. So, we did what every sane person does, and that's get on your knees, put your hands in the air and just surrender to the higher power because there has to be something more than this. And so we did that that day. And I'll never forget just the amount of tears that came out of my face, and the feeling of anger and sadness and pain that just left my body that day.

Within a few hours, Dennis had this idea, hey, you know, I'm going to reach out to this guy, David, in Texas. David is somebody who had been a mentor to Dennis for a long time in the marketing world while Dennis was in mortgages prior, and then a bank teller. Dennis also had been studying online marketing since 2000. It was more of a hobby for him and he loved it, but he didn't see how he could make a life out of it.

He met this guy David at an event. Well, he and David became friends and in 2006, just a couple years before, David thought Dennis was a bright guy. He wanted Dennis to work for him and he wanted to train him on how to really do online marketing the right way. David was already making millions in the early 2000s. Dennis wasn't ready for that. I wasn't ready in 2006 with my career and everything. So we kind of didn't think anything of it at the time. But now, Dennis just felt like, you know what, I'm just gonna give it a shot. I'm going to call David and see if he has an opportunity for me, or at least referrals for people here in Florida who want to have

David's systems implemented in their business. So Dennis called David and David said, there's no way I'm going to refer business to you. And Dennis is like, uhh, what? David told him, no, I've wanted you to work for me forever. Get your butt over to Texas and let's see what we can create together. So, literally, I'll never forget, Dennis came out of his office and he goes, hey, Maruxa, and I'm here nursing Maya, what do you think about Texas? And I was like, what's in Texas? And he goes, well, David said that he might have an opportunity for me to run a division of his company. And I was like, Texas sounds great. Let's do it. That was January 19, 2009, a couple months after the *surrender*. And it was at a point where we really started to recognize we are not going to make it if we are a bank teller and someone who is just taking on clients here and there as a therapist. We are going to lose the house, and by this point, we also lost all of our 401k. We had nothing left because we used it to just take care of life expenses.

Within one month of saying yes, we're going to Texas without any knowledge of where we're going to live, what we were going to do. But I set out an intention for myself, and it was this: I loved my career, I loved the work I actually did to help people be *in community*. And as leaders of these communities, in higher education, really see those communities thrive and come alive while making people feel at home and make people feel they are a part of something bigger than themselves, and create meaningfulness and belonging, become these communities. I knew I wanted to do that, but I wanted to figure out how to do it virtually because I knew the world was going virtual. And in 2009, and this is in the middle of the recession in Florida, I started to see that people were really being impacted by that. So, I set the intention and I want to figure out how to really do this leadership training that I was doing.

We moved to Texas. And while we're in Texas, I was literally given an opportunity to have a conversation with David. It was just going to be Dennis and David building this company. The company was called TELUS summit events. It was the first of its kind. There were no TELUS summits back in 2009. The idea was to bring bestselling authors, speakers and trainers, and bring conferences to people in the comfort of their own living rooms. Because, with the recession, as we've just seen with the pandemic, no one was traveling. So, we wanted to continue to build business while no one was traveling. So Dennis was going to run operations and marketing while David was going to be the face. So, we decided, okay, let's go and make this happen and start to make this a reality.

Now, these summits were a side business for David. This was everything for Murph and me. We literally moved our family across the country for this opportunity. Being that it was a side company for David, he was busy with his other company. So, while he had this beautiful intention of being the host of all these summits and talking to all these bestselling author friends of his and all these big names in their respective industries, he actually didn't have the time to do it. In fact, he barely did one. And we knew we'd either be out of work if we didn't find another host, or we'd have to spend every single month just begging and pleading with David to put some time on his calendar to interview these bestselling authors and trainers.

For the first two months of being in Houston, I really felt lost. I lost my identity as a career person and suddenly became this new identity of a stay-at-home mom, and I really struggled with it. So, this conversation over dinner with Dennis and David happened after two months of being in Texas. And I wish I could say it was so intentional, but it really wasn't. It was me being in my full heart space of pain, and of true desperation to figure out who the heck I am as a woman and as a mom. And how do I do it all with joy in the way that people told me I should be happy as a mom, I should be happy with my career?

We are at dinner, and David asks how I am enjoying Houston? And I look at him and I say, "the better question is, David, why are we here?" Dennis is kicking me under the table. He's pissed. He was like, you do not talk to my boss that way. The energy of like, what are you saying? And I kept leaning in. "Why are we here? Why am I here? What are we doing with this business anyway? You don't seem to have time for this project that you brought us all the way across the country for." Again, Dennis is literally making a bruise on my leg at this point, he is so upset that I'm disturbing a good thing, what he thought was a good thing. And David actually played with me on it. "Well, it's a good question. And I'll be honest, I thought I'd have way more time to do this than I'm giving myself time to do. And that's not fair to you." And I asked, "Well, how would you imagine we change that, David?"

So I'm literally in this conversation with David, and Dennis is beyond himself, like, disgusted with me, just shocked. Like, I did not know this part about his wife. Holy crap. And I didn't know that part about me either, honestly. But I was in such pain that I needed answers to be able to know that I could be here and do this. And his responses were so powerful, we ended up having a two-and-a half-hour conversation. And I helped him really get clarity on this division that he's created in this company. He now has Dennis, who is super invested in the company, and a wife who's super invested in making sure it works and that we have purpose in being here. And at the end of this two-and-a-half hours he says to me, "Maruxa, you are so good at asking great questions." I'm sure it's my counseling background coming out. And next he says, "I really want you to be the question asker of these bestselling authors, speakers and trainers." And I'll never forget that moment, being like, huh? What? I thought it was the perfect way to not be a stay-at-home mom. That was my motivation to say yes. At that moment I thought to myself, it would get me out of the house at least for a few hours a day. Done. I'm doing it. Pay me $5 now, I don't even care. I didn't really care.

What happened was that all of this intention, the intention I brought in to figure out how to do this beautiful career that I had in person working 100 hours a week was starting to be put into action. I didn't know what that box was going to look like. I thought it was going to look like something I did before. But really, what I was creating was this beautiful new space of opportunity. Next thing I know, I'm the interviewee of these bestselling authors, speakers and trainers and all of these different practices in marketing, different ways to do marketing online and in person. And they would, over and over and over again, tell me, Maruxa, that was one of the best interviews I've ever done. Maruxa, how did you get that out of me? No one ever gets this out of me. Maruxa, you saw something in me that I didn't even know was there. Wow. The next thing you know, not only did we end up building 22 summits, we grew our audience to 250,000 people. We turned that side business into $2.5 million. And these gorgeous humans whom I got to interview became friends. These bestselling authors in their industry became my friends and my colleagues. And they started to ask if I could create, with them, their own Summit, and their next summit and their next summit. And next thing I know, I actually had a business. Who knew I could do such things? And so, that was for me the beginning of this career, then this journey of totally being able to just surrender and have faith in the process of not knowing. And yet, at the same time, trusting that what I really wanted to create was possible, that I could and I'm allowed to create something that's really possible.

That actually led to me selling that business in 2015, a few years later, and then helping grow a business incubator into a $6.5 million business from a vision into this beautiful, powerful and incredibly uplifting community of entrepreneurs, investors and influencers called The Tribe. I left that company after two-and-a-half years, to run a coffee company that's all about inviting women to step into their power, called Perky, Perky, which to this day is still in existence. To this day is still empowering incredible women to rise every single moment of their day, all the while continuing to use my artistry to help friends, to help colleagues, to help all these other humans build communities that are also about raising up others. That's a through line through everything I do. But I was just doing it as if I was breathing. It was just like that for me. It was so in flow. And the whole while never fully owning my power in these conversations other than recognizing I've had cool successes, great, but never fully owning it until I found myself in my life, in my career, where my husband's career was on the mantle. His career was the thing that seemed to be what mattered more than anything else. And it took us to a lot of places. It took us from Houston to Austin. And then it moved us down to Delray Beach, Florida. It felt like he was really at the height of his career in Delray. He had these incredible $1 million-plus budgets that he would work with. One day, he ended up finding $81 million in cost savings which led to a full time opportunity with that company. And so, again, I felt like at that point in my life it was time for me to slow my career down again. Now, instead of one kid, just being present with my three kids and be that stay-at-home mom who forgot that she had a coffee company, and who also just created a $6.5 million business, and also just sold a company, and also, and also, and also, and all these beautiful wins that I've had to be home with the kids. And that was fine. It was beautiful until I realized I was resenting the process again. I was missing me, and the fullest version of me. Was there a world where I could be both mom and I could be an incredible entrepreneur. Is there such a thing? Was that a possibility?

I knew the answer was yes. I knew that was a possibility, but I never allowed myself to fully embrace that until this moment. That moment was in March 2020. Dennis came to me one day, and he says, "I'm done. I'm done with our marriage. I am done with the kids. I am done with my career. I'm out. I don't want to do anything anymore. Just letting you know, if you don't see me tomorrow, that's why." It was literally the worst message that anyone could have given a wife who feels already so disconnected to her own life, and the life that she really wanted for herself. And so that was me. I found myself in this place, at this time, feeling like instead of doing this together, like that first story, doing this on my own and having to figure out what to do with now three children, a house, living away from any real friends and family whom I knew at that time. I had some really sweet friends but we just moved there a year and a half before that. So, they weren't like deep friends yet. And so I went and found a therapist. As I started to do that, I realized, oh, my gosh, we're in a different place. It's not the same as 2009. This 2020 experience allows me to give him a break. He was burnt out and he needed a sabbatical. So after realizing I could figure it out, I invited him to sabbatical. It also invited me to stand not from a place of resentment, feeling like I have to be a victim to my life circumstance again, but from a place of love. The Creator who has created the most beautiful sunsets and the most beautiful flowers and oceans is also the Creator who lives inside me and inside all of us. So, if that Creator could create that gorgeousness out there, why wouldn't he create that gorgeousness within me? And from that, I leaned in and I said, well, if I was using my mind like I know I can, what would that bring? And what would those thoughts want to bring to the world? I sat with that for a week, and I journaled like crazy. And from that, I started to see the patterns of this beautiful Creator, having created this divine divinity, through my hands into the world, through the relationships and through the people and through the opportunities I've had, up to this point, to create such massive and beautiful magic in the world.

That really led me to telling Dennis, with clarity and with confidence, I believe in you. I believe that what you probably need is a sabbatical. And I believe in myself. Even though I totally didn't, by the way, I was also in, like, full-on, just like, I think I can do this, I hope I can do this, let's see if I can do this, maybe I can do this, and this is my one shot. I went from just taking on consulting clients when I could fit them in between my kids' lives and schedules to turning the business from primarily Dennis's baby to tripling the business that year.

Building the business around my superpower, my magic, which is community and designing communities in a way that feels focused on the heartbeats in the room, generated a lot of money for the companies that we work with. I was able to do that in one year and then take that business and systemize it, create programs from it, and really start to serve more people and multiply my impact in the way in which I have been able to serve. But again, it goes back to that same idea of surrender and determination. What I see on the outside is not the actual story. The actual story is the surrender. The actual story is the faith that we need to have to be able to loosen the grip of trying to figure out how to make it happen. You just have to be present with what is and let those beautiful things bloom to get us to that next place. And this is the story of my life. And if there was one thing I know about both those particular life examples and stories is really that the more I tried to control any situation and put more tension around it, the more tired I became in the process. But really, this is a life of adventure. This is a life of bravery. This is a life of constantly saying yes and seeing what that next door has in store for us. And if we can't ask the universe for guidance in this process and then surrender to the arms of the universe, we will never fully understand what else is possible for ourselves and our lives.

Q&A

Jana: There were so many lemons. You also touched on multiple points where there was coconut milk or there was that lesson. If you had to pick one, what is Maruxa's coconut milk?

Maruxa: I would say my coconut milk is just eyes wide open into the adventure. Yeah, that's it. I don't know what tomorrow brings. I literally don't know what tomorrow is going to bring. None of us do. And yet what I do know is that there is sweetness there. Even if tomorrow doesn't go your way, for example, like the other day every one of my meetings no-showed. And then the one had tech issues. Even if it's stupid stuff like that, right? It's so sweet. Because at the end of the day, there were lessons to be learned. There were opportunities to gain value from those moments. And when I see myself as an adventurer, as a brave wild one, saying yes to the journey, my gosh, everything gets fun. Overall, there are hard days, but it gets fun. And I get to come to conversations from that place of, oh, guess what I got to learn today? Oh, guess what? I find that those of us weird ones that like to think this way find each other and we get to all be that together. But I had to be brave enough to find that as well and say, ah, wow, I wonder if all the technology issues today were really about the fact that I had to deal with this thing in my life. Ah, look at that, that's a gem. Did you see that gem? I saw that gem, you know, and be in that space together where all these beautiful coconut milky gems get to play?

Jana: And so, tell me as the mom of girls, and I ask this because I'm the mom of boys, and I mean a mom is a mom, but I do think there are very big differences between raising girls and raising boys, as the mom of girls, how do you start to instill this love of adventure and play into them?

Maruxa: Part of this is gonna be theoretical because I'm just moving into that phase with my daughters. My oldest is 14. And my younger two are nine and seven. So the younger two are still in the play space. But my 14-year-old is literally in this right now. And what I'm seeing has been the power of the consistency of being that example for her. I'm open about my struggles. Just a couple days ago, she saw me making coffee, and I was sitting there with my coffee pot, and she could see I was in my head. She says, "what's going on, Mom?" I responded, "You know, I'm actually dealing with something right now, and it feels really hard, and it feels really scary. I know that I'm going to be okay, I know that this too shall pass. And I also know that this is what I'm learning through it." So having that transparency with her has been so powerful because she's able to hold space for me in a way that I didn't know a teenager could for their mother. Not that I'm telling her all the details. I'm not trying to put her in that weird place of being *my mom* at all. I'm very aware of that because I had that happen to me when I was a kid. So I'm very aware of that. But moreso, just to help her see how we can process through difficult times. And without having to know all the details and just be like, you know what mom really needs right now is just a hug.

So, as she's been seeing me in that, I'm noticing that she's holding herself to that also. And she's coming to me, or she's that person in her friend circle who is talking the way mama talks. And her friends think she's the weird one. And you know, they love her for it. But they're kinda like, okay, here's Maya going at it again, you know, but hey, she's going to love this part of her when she gets older as well.

I also recognize that every kid is so different. So, she's my discerning one, she pays attention. My second one is much more about, are all the systems in the right order? If it is not in the right order, it cannot move forward. So I'm going to see how that's gonna turn out one day. And then my youngest is like, I do not give two F's about anything but me. Okay, I matter the most. And so we're just going to deal with that. Do you see me? So, we'll see, we'll see. I think it's a work in progress for me to hold space for them. But I am willing to be fully authentic with them in that process, and I think that's probably the most important thing.

Jana: Has anything been left unsaid that you feel the beating hearts that are reading this book need to read? Or do you feel like you've given all of you to this amazing chapter and it is a beautiful closure?

Maruxa: I'm here as a stand to bring humanity back to the human species. And part of that has to start with us as leaders, making a choice to live as humans, to be fully human in the work. And to embrace that there is nothing wrong with feeling anger, shame, pain, or hurt. Own it, embrace it, walk through it, move through it, so that we can see the fullest version of us, as you, as me, as leaders in this world that we are meant to serve and the way in which we're meant to grow and love others.

MARUXA MURPHY is an award-winning community experience designer, strategist, entrepreneur, author and catalyst for change who has been transforming communities in person and online since 2000. She leads national and international initiatives with a deep understanding of the dynamics of how people connect and share information. Maruxa is further changing the game in community experience design while working in the travel, business, personal development, parenting, and coaching industries shifting how communities can be designed from "the inside out" to transform their industries from the core.

Her clients include Netflix's "spiciest" show Sex, Love and Goop's stars Jaiya Ma and Ian Ferguson with the Erotic Blueprints (grew this community to 1M people on Mighty Networks), Kajabi, the Uplift Millions brand, Spryte Loriano with Awakening Giants (an community owned conscious media network), multiple metaverses (alternate reality worlds) as well as creating and designing communities for brands revolutionizing their industries, like the Maui Resort community, the Women's Prosperity Network, The Vision School, The Traveling Diary and the conscious dancer mentorship experience with former Rockette dancer Gina Pero.

Maruxa specializes in bringing people together to create profitable enterprises that do good in the world—while empowering all individuals to live their fullest. Her work has been featured on Forbes, Reader's Digest, Fox News, The Huffington Post, NBC, and The Austin-American Statesman as well as featured as one of 10 women-owned brands to be on the lookout for at the United Nations on Women's Entrepreneur Day 2019.

TAMMY

"The two basic items necessary to sustain life are
sunshine and coconut milk."
—Dustin Hoffman

Tammy: Why am I here? What am I doing here? I ask myself that question every day. What am I doing here? What am I going to do today? What is the best impact that I can have? Where can I best make a difference?

Or, if I'm having a rough day, I'm thinking about how I get through the day with the least resistance and the most grace and allow myself those moments when I need to just take care of myself.

When I'm feeling up for it, I go forward with intention. I ask for guidance in baby steps. I ask, "What's the next right action to take?" Then I listen to my guidance and intuition and proceed forward.

I do this knowing that I'm doing the best I can in every moment.

Even so, I aspire to leave every situation and interaction better than when I entered into it.

And I try to apply this knowingness to anyone I interact with, so I don't take things personally.

Because everyone else is doing the best they can in every moment.

Jana: You run a successful business, you travel, you have a loving relationship. There are all of these aspects of your life that I think people see at the moment. You almost gave us your coconut milk right at the beginning, where you shared your perspective of how you see the world, so there must be a reason why you see the world that way. Or, there must have been a time when those eloquent thoughts and words didn't just spill out of your mouth like they just did. Could you take us on a journey on what brought you to being able to be in that energy day in and day out?

Tammy: I started out in this world seeing everything through a lens of black and white, right and wrong. As I've gotten older, and through the constant transformation that we all experience, I've gained more wisdom and a much more expansive perspective. Now, I see all shades of gray and all shades of the rainbow. It's not black or white. What is black or white, or gray or purple, for me, is yellow or blue or red for somebody else.

I've learned that every experience that I'm viewing is through my lens, and that somebody else is viewing that experience through their own lens. There's no right or wrong, it's just a different experience for every person.

I started out being very regimented with the mindset of things must work this way, and I have to do things perfectly. I used to get upset if I didn't get the best deal on something because I thought I only got one chance to get this life right.

I would think of everything in my life as debits and credits. And I used to think my bank account had something to do with my worth. And if I wasn't constantly doing and contributing, I felt less than. And I didn't want to look back on my life and think I could have done this so much better. That mental process was exhausting for me. It was exhausting.

Gradually over time, it was a letting go of control and attachment. I realized I don't have control over everything. That's a fantasy and it's a huge self-imposed burden that's not necessary.

We can set intentions and control our thoughts and beliefs so we can be in the higher vibe frequency to attract the things we want. We can make plans and we can take inspired action. We can surround ourselves with the right people to help us reach our goals.

We can take little steps every day to get to what we want. And, ultimately, we just need to put all of our ideas and passion out there and let the Universe know what we want. And then, we can sit back and allow the Universe to surprise and delight us and bring us something better than what we could have imagined.

Sounds easy, right?

Letting go of the control and releasing attachment to the outcome is still a challenge sometimes, even with all the knowledge and tools.

I forget and need to be reminded.

I also have to be very aware of the stage of creation for the projects I'm working on or the dreams that are in transition. And I have to practice patience when I'm waiting for something to show up.

I allow for a lot of self-love and self-care into every day and I highly recommend everyone does this for themselves.

We're in a constant state of moving between doing and being. You are a human being, and you can't always be the giver. You have to be the receiver too.

The words haven't always come so eloquently or easily, and they still don't some days now. Every time I write something, I scrutinize every word.

I get nervous about an interview like this because I don't want to say the wrong thing or have something I say be taken in a way that I didn't mean. I just set an intention before that the right words will come, and that my true intention will be felt.

And I forgive myself daily because I don't know everything and I'm constantly learning and growing.

All you can do is step into being who you are and being honest about how you're feeling in the moment and not apologizing for it. You're going to learn and grow from that experience no matter what. I think we have to learn to laugh at ourselves and relax more.

My parents were very young – 15 and 16 - when I was born, and they divorced when I was 10 years old. My sister and I lived with my mom, and being the oldest, I felt like the adult of the family. If I didn't wake everyone up in the morning, we wouldn't get to school or work on time. It was a huge amount of responsibility on a young kid. So, that's where the pressure and the people-pleasing tendencies started.

I've had to unlearn some of that. I'm experiencing my life backwards. Right now. I'm learning to be a kid again, to play and do things for the fun of it, and without the heavy responsibility. My goal each day is to experience joy, do good and have fun. It's that simple!

What if we could all wake up each day and just do what's fun and in our highest excitement?

You don't have to prove anything to anyone. You don't have to act a certain way or work at a job you hate or even at a job you enjoy for 10 hours a day to be successful.

If something isn't working, you can change it or let it go. There's always a different route you can take; there's always a chance to course correct.

In those moments, I can take a look at the situation and decide if I still want to continue down this path. Do I want to make changes? Do I want to let this person go from my life? Do I want to keep this person? Do I want to let that project go or this client?

You get a chance with every experience to turn lemons into coconut milk to make it sweeter, to make life sweeter.

I am blessed to have so much support. I have a few close friends, a wonderful husband and family that I can lean on in times when I feel lost and need clarity.

My journey has been learning to let go and not just stay on the given path. I was climbing the corporate ladder 20 years ago, and I got up to a management level. At that point in my career, I could hardly get out of bed in the morning. I was so disenamored with my life that I didn't even want to wake up and face the day.

I went to therapy because I thought there had to be a problem with me because I'd spent seven years building this career and I couldn't understand why I didn't want to do that job that I worked so hard for anymore.

I didn't realize it was sucking the life out of me. I was climbing the corporate ladder because that's what I thought I had to do to be successful. I was miserable because I didn't enjoy it, but I didn't want to have wasted the last seven years... I didn't want it to be for nothing. I felt shame and guilt.

I wasn't listening to that part of me that was trying to tell me, "This is not for you anymore. You need to go on a different route." And I held on to it for months and months. Finally, I got to the point where I was ill, and I decided I had to quit. I had to let it go.

My husband, Reede, is a teacher and has summers off, so we decided to travel. We were gone for two months and went all across the U.S. It was a literal journey and a spiritual journey for me.

I felt so much guilt and shame and it took me a while to recover from being burned out and uninspired. We spent a lot of time in nature, camping in the woods, going on hikes and bike rides, just enjoying each day without an agenda and living in the moment.

I was able to look back on my time at the former company with gratitude. I learned so much there, and I'm still using some of those skills today. And I'm so grateful for it, but it was no longer the right environment for me to thrive in.

When we returned, I decided to try out different jobs to see what I wanted to do going forward. I felt like I had the whole world opened up to me. I didn't have to go back into a high-pressure sales position or a corporate track.

And I always really wanted a career where I had more flexibility so we could travel in the summers.

I did substitute teaching for a few months and decided that wasn't for me. I also tried a couple of other jobs that I couldn't see myself doing long-term.

Then I got an offer to go work with a company where they taught people how to start their own business as a copywriter. I got to see so many different sides to that industry and expanded my skill levels and knowledge. I knew the sales and the relationship marketing part of it, but I didn't know the online side of the world, and I didn't know anything about copywriting at that point.

I spent three years there and really enjoyed the job and the people I worked with. I got to travel and interact with people at live events, and it was really fun.

Then, out of nowhere, I got laid off. I got laid off on a Friday morning and decided I didn't want to go back and work for anyone else. I had been telling other people for three years how easy it was to go freelance and start your own business, so I took my own advice.

I started reaching out to potential clients on Friday afternoon to let them know I was available. By Monday, I had my first client. That was in 2009. I started out doing project management and building websites, but it morphed into something else. I carved out a successful business as a joint venture and affiliate manager and have been fortunate to work with some amazing people in the personal development and health and wellness spaces.

I've also worked on other projects and co-founded other companies along the way. I have the flexibility that I wanted, to travel in the summers, and I only work with people I admire and projects I want to be part of. I also make a lot more money than I ever did before.

That was a huge transition point in my journey of working for someone else for all those years and putting my effort into their companies. I was good at the jobs I did, but I wasn't fulfilled by them. And I started over in a whole new capacity where I had no clue what I was doing. I found out how to set up a corporation and opened a business banking account.

The Universe was giving me signs along the way and I didn't pay attention as soon as I could have. That's another lesson ... you don't have to wait until you get hit over the head with a metaphorical brick. You don't have to wait until you're so sick you can't get out of bed. Listen to your intuition and make adjustments early on.

I could have never imagined how great things would have turned out. Sometimes you just have to trust and have faith that if you take the risk and step off the edge, you'll learn to fly!

My whole business and the cornerstone of my career goes back to relationships.

It's all about taking care of people and treating people the way you'd like to be treated.

Always under promise and over deliver.

Do what you say you're going to do.

Follow up and follow through.

I can't stress that more importantly than anything else to people who are starting a business, or who are working in business, or even just in their relationships.

Having that care and consideration for the other person and making sure that everyone feels heard is important.

I've had the privilege of working with some of the biggest names in the personal development industry. Through high-vibe and aligned partnerships, I've contributed to millions of dollars in revenues and added billions of subscribers to my clients' communities. I've been able to connect them to methods and programs that transform people's lives for the better. I feel really blessed to be able to work with amazing people who can provide that solution for them.

Jana: At the beginning, you explained the feeling of being frozen and not wanting to get out of bed in the morning. I'm going to go out on a limb and say that you're probably not the only person who's ever felt that. And I think you did the natural thing that many people would do. I'm going to go to therapy, and I'm going to work out this problem. I'm going to get a solution and then I'll be able to get up in the morning and feel like

I'm contributing. What would you say to those women who are feeling stuck? Their ego is maybe saying you're making this salary, you've got this title, you've got all this responsibility, this is what you've been working for. What do you say to them when they come to the realization where either it's not enough or I deserve more versus was this whole last seven years, nine years, five years, a waste of time? Because I think as women we can very easily fall into that mindset of, I've just got to push through. I hear that all the time, I've got to just push through till next year, and then I'll be good. What do you say to that woman?

Tammy: I would tell that woman that you are enough just as you are and you don't have to push through anything. You have to get in receiving mode. Let go of the attachment and let it go early. You can always change your mind and course correct. Don't be afraid to take chances and say this is no longer working for me. Sometimes you have to let something die or let go of something, give it a metaphorical death, in order to make room for something amazing to take its place.

You can't keep stuffing things down, biting your tongue, or filling yourself up with stuff that doesn't give you joy. If you're not getting some joy out of it, some fulfillment out of it, then it's not working.

Don't get discouraged because you get to benefit from all that experience. You will learn some new skills along the way. You might even meet some people who are going to be detrimental to your success in the future. None of it's a waste of time, and we can always take away a lesson or a teaching from each experience we go through.

I think we get caught up in the fact that we're supposed to be farther along or that there's something wrong with me, or there's something broken in me that has to be fixed.

Even today, with all the experiences, triumphs and defeats I have been through, I am still evolving, so I'm constantly discovering who I am in each moment.

Just recently, I realized I have been looking at myself through a lens of being broken instead of the whole person that I know I am. I invite you to look at yourself as a whole person.

Sit in a quiet space with your eyes closed and pen and paper ready, then ask yourself … If I am whole and in the perfect place in time for me, what would be my next right step?

Listen, then jot down the guidance you received, whether it's a word or words or an image or a feeling.

Jana: You touched on the essence of your coconut milk right at the beginning. Now that you've shared more of you with us, I'm going to ask you the question, what is your coconut milk?

Tammy: I spent a lot of my life downplaying my abilities and advocating for my invisibility. I was afraid to stand out and I didn't want to bring attention to myself and shine. I didn't want to be seen. Even with the trauma I experienced, I would downplay that as well.

I would say the essence of turning lemons to coconut milk is being able to acknowledge in every single moment whatever you're feeling with honesty. Whatever you're experiencing, whether it's joy or pain, love, hate, frustration, pride, shame, guilt, whatever it is… just allow yourself to really feel it.

Be in the moment with it, express gratitude for it, then release it with a cleansing breath.

Don't stuff your emotions down, especially anything that feels heavy. Allow your emotions to have a voice and be heard. Then, let it go.

I spent a lot of time tamping down anger because my mom had a lot of anger, and I was scared of it. I wouldn't allow myself to feel anger or sadness or even happiness. I was always the even keel, never too high and never too low.

Suppressed emotions create trauma in our bodies, so don't give them a chance to take root there. Talk to someone you trust about what you're feeling or put what you're feeling in a journal.

Let yourself feel those emotions and just be who you are.

One other thing that I was guided to share with everyone today is the Oracle card I pulled this morning. I use Oracle cards to connect to my intuition and higher self on a daily basis. It's a great tool for me.

The card is called Treasure Island and it talks about how you already have the treasure inside of you. It might have been buried, but it's uncovered now.

Now you just have to hone your ability and find your sweet spot. Take a look at each opportunity that comes your way and ask... is this the right opportunity for me? Is this not the right opportunity? And then trust your intuition to help guide you.

Jana: Okay, that is really amazing. And I want to share something that really resonated for me. I love that you framed it that way to me because there are moments in all of our lives where we either want something so badly or we think we want it for whatever reason. Maybe someone told us what you're doing is amazing, and you're thinking I don't really know if it is that amazing, right?

My 21-year-old son has been watching me go through a process in a professional sense. What you just said made me really think about this conversation we had. And I asked him yesterday, "Tyler, as an observer of what your mom does, you've been observing this for the past six months, what have you learned? What have you taken out of this experience?" And he said, I've learned three things, Mom.

1. *Not everything is going to work out the way you think it will, but trust that it worked out as it was supposed to.*
2. *Know how to value your time, your worth and your energy.*
3. *Know when it's time to walk away.*

And I think that's exactly what you're saying. As women we are innately nurturers, we are the divine feminine. There can be a lot of beliefs and values that we don't even know where they came from, or we try and trace them like, when did I start believing that or when did I start saying that, right? And I just want to thank you for the way you dropped these gems of information. There are beating hearts on this planet who are going to have this book in their hand, and you will be an answer to their prayer. So, I just want to thank you for that.

Last question. Do you feel there's been anything left unsaid before our readers flip this last page of your chapter?

Tammy: I just want to comment on what your son said. They don't teach you any of that in business school. As a mom, you just hit it out of the park. He already knows those valuable lessons before he's really gotten started, which is amazing. And that's what I want other people to feel. I want them to feel like they're getting these gems, and this wisdom, and that you can bypass the last 14 years that it took me to learn any of this. If you apply those three things in your life today, you've totally shortened your learning curve.

Take everything with a grain of salt. Take what feels good and use it, even if only for a little while. If it doesn't work, let go of it. Try something else. There are so many ways to do things and there's a plethora of tools out there to help you get what you want.

And you really have everything you need inside of you already. You are whole where you are in this current moment. You have your own intuition, your own guidance inside of you, and that's really all you need.

I've tried a lot of different tools, and sometimes it takes those tools to really learn to trust in those things for yourself. Don't be afraid to reach out for support. There are always women out there who are willing to share their time, to be supportive or to connect you to a resource.

You're a rock star goddess warrior and own it!

Jana: Own it. I love that. Tammy, thank you so much for your time, your wisdom and your message.

TAMMY LAWMAN has been making a difference in the personal development and wellness industries since 2009. As the CEO of Lawman Communications Inc. and Co-Founder of Link Lab, LLC, she is a master connector and Rock Star Joint Venture and Affiliate Manager who has collaborated with dozens of the top transformational leaders to up-level their visibility, multiply opportunities to grow their email list, sell more programs, and create conscious impact and awareness for their work that benefits all of humanity.

She excels at creating strategic and impactful business partnerships that bring in a loyal audience and 6- to 7-figures in revenues. Her creative solutions have generated $20+ million dollars in revenues for clients through thousands of successful win-win-win partnerships and collaborations.

Tammy is also a Conscious Business and Marketing Strategist skilled in creating engaging funnels, free gifts, e-book, webinars, marketing copy, and graphic images to attract new leads and convert them to buyers.

JANE

I couldn't believe this was happening.

My life was falling apart. I was truly afraid for my future. How did things change so quickly? I was at the lowest point in my life, my body wracked with pain. At that rock bottom moment, my soul spoke to me.

Just a few months earlier, on my 50th birthday, I was strong, vibrant and healthy. The freedom years were coming up, and the nest was empty. I was looking forward to retirement with my husband. We planned to travel, and do everything we couldn't do in our working lives.

But a month later, I woke up one day with pain in my shoulder so bad my arm had to go into a sling. Then the next day, it was the other shoulder. The pain moved down to my knees, my feet, my hands, my jaw, my elbows. Within three months, I was nearly disabled from the pain and inflammation.

I had just come through a really stressful year. My mother had died suddenly, and she was my best friend. I felt like I had lost my champion. I also had to deal with the house my parents lived in for almost 50 years. They were collectors, so there was a ton of stuff. And I have three siblings, so there were the normal stressors that you would expect after someone dies. I had a lot on my plate.

After the pain began, I thought, okay, I just need to get the house sold and have all this taken care of, and then I'll be fine. But I wasn't fine. I got worse. The pain got more intense and spread throughout my body.

At my rock bottom moment, I was curled up in pain and just feeling like my life was falling apart, my body was letting me down. And then I heard a voice... a voice I believe came from my very soul. The voice told me I would figure this out and then I would tell other people how to do it. I was still in a lot of pain, but I knew in my heart that I would do this.

I'm an engineer, and we are problem solvers. We figure things out. So I got to work.

Although nothing out of the ordinary was showing up in my tests, my doctor scheduled an appointment with a rheumatologist. My amazingly progressive doctor told me that food can sometimes be related to joint pain. I was kind of blown away by that idea. I thought, what? Joint pain and food? How can they be related? But I was desperate to get out of pain so I completely cut out gluten and dairy. Incredibly, within five days, I had a significant reduction in pain.

I still had a lot of pain, but now I was in a position of power. I didn't feel like a powerless victim anymore.

I started researching. I started tracking things. I was making graphs on how different things would affect my sleep, and my weight, and my pain. I kept on trying more things and I started figuring out that I probably had an autoimmune condition. When I finally saw the rheumatologist a few months later, I was diagnosed with rheumatoid arthritis.

There are no concrete remedies for getting rid of rheumatoid arthritis completely. The medications for it have horrible side effects. I knew that I wanted to avoid the medications if I could. I started researching stories of other people who had healed from rheumatoid arthritis. I learned about the autoimmune paleo protocol (AIP) diet so I tried that. Then I discovered functional medicine. I started researching more about it. I read a book by Dr. Amy Myers called "The Autoimmune Solution." In that book, she said, if you reach a plateau in your healing, which I had, then it could be some other thing. So I found a functional medicine doctor and found out that it was small intestine bacterial overgrowth, which is quite common.

I worked with the practitioner for about eight months to get that cleared up. I got a little bit better, but then I plateaued again. I just knew there was something else that had to be addressed. I wanted to learn more about functional medicine, so I signed up to do the health coaching program with the Functional Medicine Coaching Academy.

Every month in that program we had a module on mind-body medicine and the mind-body connection, which I found fascinating. I finished my program and really started diving in more to the mind-body medicine.

I realized that I had been coming at all this illness like a warrior: "I'm going to fight this, I'm going to beat this." I came to realize that actually, all of this was happening FOR me, not TO me. Illness was actually a gift. I didn't really understand what the whole gift was, but I knew that there was a reason.

In the past I had played around a little bit with numerology. My Life Purpose number is 33. It is a master number, the compassion number. People with this number have a special task. I had known this for years but didn't know what my special task was. Perhaps my task had found me.

Although I was an engineer, I also had a spiritual side. I had trained in Reiki years ago, so I knew about energy. I practiced yoga regularly. I was always really interested in energy and spirituality, but I didn't really see that initially as part of my health journey.

When I started to learn a little bit more about energy and health I could see that everything I had been studying was all coming together: the spirituality and the science. Quantum physics tells us we are all energy, everything is energy. Ancient spiritual practices and world wisdom traditions told us that we have a spirit that is timeless.

Even though I loved being an engineer, what I really wanted to do was help people. I knew I was meant to help people. I also knew that the stress of my job was keeping me sick. So, I decided to leave my engineering career and become a health coach, the wellness engineer. I started speaking on health topics, coaching clients and creating programs. And I love what I do.

Now I KNOW that everything is energy. The pain that I was experiencing was energy not flowing. This pain that I was experiencing was a gift, letting me know that I needed to examine my life. The pain wasn't something that needed to be beaten or covered up, and I was not meant to live with it forever. The pain was my body was speaking to me to tell me that it needed some loving attention. So it really was a gift. It's a gift in strange packaging, but it is a gift.

I see now that when someone has dis-ease - I had pain, but it could be anything, it could be anxiety, it could be an illness, any of these things - these are really here to awaken us to become a better version of ourselves. The version of ourselves that got sick or created pain was not the best version of us, obviously, because we manifested this problem in our life. So really, it's there to awaken us to become that best version of ourselves and learn to love ourselves.

I realized that it was actually a lifetime of people-pleasing and perfectionism that started from, "lowercase t" trauma when I was a child. I always had this feeling that I wasn't as good as others, and I think a lot of women feel that. Many of us are perfectionists and people pleasers because that's how we try to feel worthy. But really, that doesn't work. People-pleasing and perfectionism are simply behavioral adaptations we make to cope with the fear that comes with feeling unworthy. We carry this little stress around inside of us all the time, and when we carry that stress around we are creating a state in our body that's not conducive to health. This is what stops the energy from flowing.

This is how I see it now, that it was all a big gift to awaken me to become a better version of myself. I wasn't living up to that 33 number, but I feel like now I'm getting closer to it. So I do see it totally as a gift now, and I wouldn't have changed anything. It was all happening FOR me. It brought me right to where I am now, and I wouldn't want to be anywhere else.

Q&A

Jana: The theme of this book is, when life gives you lemons, drink coconut milk. Your lemons were the joint pain that really took over your body despite feeling healthy. I feel like I've been in the health and wellness world long enough to know that most people who have experienced what you did may have just surrendered to the diagnosis, and lived decade's worth of life in a very different way than you did. Help the women who are reading your chapter right now understand, what happened with your mindset that shifted you? Was it the voice that brought a different set of lenses? Or was there something more going on there?

Jane: Part of it for me was my parents. My father had a lot of health problems. He had his gallbladder out when he was a teenager. Now they say that probably was gluten intolerance. He had a triple bypass when he turned 50, he had diabetes, he ended up with cancer. But even when he was on beta blockers, and on insulin, he used to go to a place in Utah for a month every year. While he was there, they would put them on a paleo type of diet. He would exercise every day, and he would go off his medications. So I knew that you could do something. My mother was not on any medications, and she was very proud of that. So we kind of had this thing in our family about thinking maybe there's another way to approach treatment other than medications.

We all go to Dr. Google, but what we type in that search bar matters. Because if you type certain things in, you'll get those pictures of the grotesque joints and, for rheumatoid arthritis, you'll see the treatment and you'll read about the medications and that's all you'll know. Whereas I was typing in things like natural treatments for, and how to heal from rheumatoid arthritis naturally. So I found some people who have natural remedies for all sorts of illnesses. It's even more so now with the work of people like Joe Dispenza, the HEAL documentary, there are podcasts that are just based on stories of people who have healed naturally. I just started having a belief that there was something I could do.

I was so fortunate to have a family doctor, a conventional doctor, who said food could help, because not many doctors will say that. That initial result of cutting out the gluten and dairy and then five days later, having a big reduction in pain, that empowered me. We're not really taught to be empowered in our health. We're taught to give all of our power over to the doctor. Seeing yourself as being the person who's at the center and then getting support from the different members of your health team, that's a different point of view than saying, "Well, the doc says I got to do this and that's all I can do." We are told things like, oh, it's genetic. What I've learned is that less than one percent of illnesses are genetic. You may have a propensity for something, but the genes can express. They're like dimmer switches. They can turn up or turn down, based on the environment.

The environment is our thoughts. It's the food that we're eating, it's the air we're breathing, it's what we put on our skin. All these other things become the environment, and that changes us. That's the environment that our cells are living in. Our cells are reproducing all the time and changing over. It's kind of interesting to think that we're not even physically the same person that we were seven years ago. We're changing all the time. So create an environment where those cells are bathed in vitality and health and in an environment that's going to allow them to be strong and healthy. There's a lot we can do with our thoughts and that changes our feelings, which are vibrations in the body, which is the energy.

Jana: You very beautifully identified some of the lemons in your life that not only shifted your wellness, but your career. I also am a Numerology junkie so I love how you are stepping into your 33. But I have one more question for you. What is your coconut milk?

Jane: My whole life, I always felt like I was in a shadow. I felt like there was more for me to do, but I always felt like I couldn't get there. I was stuck. I couldn't get out of the job that I was in because it was a good job and I felt like I should be satisfied. So my coconut milk is just that feeling of being empowered. First of all, empowered in my health, but also empowered in my life, being the creator of my life. Being an entrepreneur now, I am creating my life. There's no one else but me. All of that has been such a huge gift, Jana, to really feel that I am the creator. That is what quantum physics tells us we are. We are creating our future by who we are now, what our thoughts are, what our feelings are. If I continued being the way I was before, the timid, playing-small kind of person, well then I'm going to keep getting that. But if I want to change, I have to feel and embody that person that I want to be. It's fun doing this.

Jana: Looking at each of the authors in this project, it would be very easy to have people say, oh, she's so lucky. Look what she does for her job. She gets to work with people, she gets to speak, she gets to do what she loves, she gets to manage her own schedule. I don't know about you, Jane, but as a Canadian, if I had a toonie for every time someone said to me, you're so lucky, I would be living on some fantastic Island. But it is not luck.

If you had to leave one last piece of advice that maybe has been left unsaid at this point, for the women holding this book in their hands, or reading it on their laptop, what is one thing they can do now that would begin to create that environment where their cells are being bathed in vitality? Because sometimes we get frozen with the overwhelm of, well I could never do what she did. But what you did was start with one thing, and then you did that one thing, and then it was rinse and repeat. So what is the one thing that you would leave our audience with as an inspired action?

Jane: We think we're limited, but we're not limited. Sit down with your journal, and say, if I was not limited by time or money, if I could do anything that I want, and have anything that I want, what would it be? What would my life look like? And just write it all out. Write out what you would want. And then feel that. Feel what that life feels like. Create a vision in your mind of what that is and give it lots and lots of detail and feel it. Then start building on it. Come back to that vision every single day. Maybe you keep adding to it, Oh, I never thought about that, well put that in there too.

Just create. Think about what you would want because really, if we're the creators of our lives, why would we limit ourselves? We're the only one limiting that vision, so put whatever you want in there. But keep focusing on it. The law of attraction, I know a lot of people might feel like, ah, that's woowoo. But it's physics. We can't attract what we're not a vibrational match for. The vibrations come from our feelings. So keep feeling the feelings of what you want to have. This is one thing I did early on. I was picturing what I would be doing if I was totally well again, and I would imagine climbing up the mountain and arms raised in victory, and on a sailboat and pulling up the sails and being strong, playing with my grandchildren. These are the kinds of things I thought about. It would just fill me up. Every day I would think about this vision and then I would build on it. Well, what else do I want? What if I left my job? If I could leave my job, would I leave my job? What would that look and feel like? And I've made it happen!

Jana: Oh, Jane, thank you so much for opening up your heart to the audience, and to this project, and beyond what we do. We don't know the extent of our impact, and that unknown is pretty spectacular. So thank you for being with us.

Jane: It's such an honor for me to be here. This is my mission. This is what I'm here to do and I'm so honored to be part of your project, Jana.

JANE HOGAN, "The Wellness Engineer," blends science and spirituality to help people release chronic pain using the mind, body and breath so they can become empowered creators of their own health.

Her personal experience of reversing crippling rheumatoid arthritis using natural solutions inspired her to leave a 30-year engineering career and become a Functional Medicine Certified Health Coach, Certified Yoga Teacher and wellness educator.

Combining ancient wisdom with leading edge science, Jane's Wellness by Design Blueprint has helped hundreds of people release chronic pain naturally. She is the host of the Wellness by Design podcast and her empowering message has been featured on numerous podcasts and summits. She has been published in Thrive Global and Elephant Journal magazines.

LAJJA

Okay, here we are. I'm Lajja Reser.

It was summer of 2000, in the middle of the night, I woke up to an inner voice. I was told, you can take my hand and come with me now (meaning leave, die) or hold on tight and I'll be with you. I had been in an unhealthy relationship for many years at that point.

I didn't go back to sleep, rather I lay there for a few hours in a total state of panic holding tight to His hand. When the sun came up, I got up, put on my running shoes and left; my beautiful home, good job and husband of 10 years. I was training for a marathon then and like Forrest Gump, I went for a 20 mile run and never went back. That was the first time I heard the voice that gave me an immediate sense of awareness and clarity. As painful and dramatic as that day was, I knew deep inside it was right. I couldn't stay, I had to listen. And from that day on, I also knew I needed to learn from where that voice was coming.

Shortly after, I went to Puerto Vallarta, Mexico for a couple of weeks. A friend introduced me to some people who invited me on a surf adventure two hours north of town. Having just left a married life, living and working in a city a month before, I found myself for the first time on a surfboard in Mexico; with people I just met the day before; in a precious little coastal village in the middle of the jungle; the scene felt surreal.

In the ocean looking back at the jungle, there it was again; this time it said, you're going to move here. I got out of the ocean with the same crystal clarity and told my new friends I'm going to move here! Three months later, the truck packed up, my dog and I began the drive from Portland, Oregon to San Francisco, Nayarit, Mexico.

No fear, no doubt, simply a knowingness I had to follow the voice again. When messages are clear, you can't ignore them. Call it blind faith, but is there blind faith? Faith is based on experience, based on belief. Once again, I put myself into the hands of something greater, in the unknown.

I had some tremendous journeys that first year in Mexico. One day after surfing, my friend and I stopped at her friend's house to say goodbye, as he was moving the next day. I had never met this person and have not seen him since. As I didn't speak much Spanish, he gave me his only book in English, a book on Ayurveda Self Healing. I began reading it immediately. It felt so familiar, as though I was remembering something I've learned before. Ayurveda made perfect sense to me. A few months later while traveling in the jungle of Chiapas, I again got a clear message, it's time to study Ayurveda.

Five months later, I drove from San Francisco, Mexico to Sarasota, Florida where I lived with my Ayurveda teachers, studied and apprenticed for three years at their Ayurveda Pancha Karma Center. In addition to teaching Ayurveda's cleansing and balancing of the body, my teachers' great emphasis on healing the emotional body and mind. Living with them, I found myself on a deep dive of healing inner child and childhood trauma.

Near the end of three years, one day flipping through a magazine, I saw a full-page ad of a Yoga Teacher Training course in the Himalayan Mountains in India. Immediately captivated, I knew I would be there. I signed up and was off a few months later.

Before getting on the plane to India, I set an intention. I asked God, I'm ready for my next teacher, for what's next on my journey. Two weeks into the four-week training course, I extended my stay for another five weeks to attend the Advanced Teacher Training Intensive. We were in a small ashram with 35 people, high up in the Himalayas on the Ganga River. So high up in the mountains, you saw only a few people a day, in a country of over a billion; it's unheard of. It was so quiet. In that quiet setting, one can see the movement of the mind even more, which pushes you into watching it, observing it. One random day during a quiet Savasana relaxation pose, the boldest of all voices came straight in my heart saying exactly, *It's time to go to Mexico and get started!*

I had no plan to go back to Mexico. My plane ticket, my life, my plans were all in Florida. However, "We plan, God laughs." Again, I had to listen, I had faith. The last month of the Intensive course, my mind created so many ideas for an Ayurveda Center in Mexico. Endless were the details I would dream about.

My roommate in India was from Germany and she inviting me to visit her on a spiritual pilgrimage in California the next month. Perfect, I would stop to see her on my way to Mexico. After the Training course and a bit of travel, I left India and made my way to Los Angeles. Claudia was there with 25 other Europeans and her Guru, Swami Vishwananda. On day three of the pilgrimage, Swami agreed to see me for a private interview. Growing up with a Christian faith, I knew very little about Guru's. Claudia prepared me to have a question or two ready before the interview as she said your mind often goes blank in His presence and it will last about 5-10 minutes. When my time came, I waited calmly in the meeting room and when Swami walked in, my mind remained calm and clear. However, my heart ..... it exploded out of control sending an expansive endless wave of love over me. Words simply cannot describe the experience. Little did I know at that time, Swami Vishwananda is the embodiment of Divine Love and He is here to guide us in connecting with this love within us all. After 45 minutes of talking, I told him about the message to go to Mexico and get started, that I was on my way in a few days. He smiled, tapped my hand and said, I'll come visit, I'll come visit. Before we finished, He gave me a mantra and said to chant it continuously and I took his instruction literally. As I left with my heart full of love, it was clear Swami Vishwananda was my "next teacher."

After the pilgrimage, I flew to Puerto Vallarta, Mexico arriving on a Thursday. On Friday, I met a realtor Katherine and told her I was looking for a 4-6 bedroom beachfront Villa in the Bay. Saturday we saw two Villas that were clearly not it. On our way home, she remembered a new listing nearby and we decided to have a look. Driving down the windy jungle road to the gate entrance, a knowingness came over me that this was it. When we pulled into the driveway, I told Katherine, for the record, this is it. We had a tour and when we saw the little room adjacent to the kitchen for the Herb Apothecary and small room off the master for my meditation room, Katherine too was convinced it was it; a 5 bedroom double wide beachfront Villa with property to build the Ayurveda Spa. We spent a whole three hours together that day. Six weeks later, I had purchased the property and was driving from Florida to Punta Mita, Mexico with my truck of belongings.

From the moment I heard the voice in India, to meeting my Guru, finding the property, coming up with funds, family and friends questioning the move, never was there once a bit of doubt or fear. There was only faith. When God speaks, you listen. I had clarity and now, I had a mantra and a spiritual teacher.

It took two and a half years to remodel the Villa and construct an Ayurveda Spa on the property. What a wild ride that time was! Living alone in a foreign country, barely speaking the language, family a country away, friends an hour away. Then, I knew nothing about construction, had no cell service, little internet and yet never once was there any doubt. I became the general contractor; daily meetings all in Spanish with a team of architects, engineers, electricians, plumber, painters, artists and the 25+ workers six days a week. I meditated every morning and repeated the mantra constantly. It kept my mind focused, taught me to let go of the stress and gave me the energy to keep going. Guruji was my saving grace, His grace saved me!

I later learned why constant repetition of the mantra called Japa is so powerful. Man - means mind and tra- means protect; the mantra protects you from your mind. There is no difference between the name of God and God Himself. So mantra repetition strengthens your inner connection, intuition, strength and relationship with the Divine. The mantra became my best friend, it saved me from myself. A year into the challenging construction project when I traveled to see my Guru, all I could say to Him was thank you thank you thank you; I have endless gratitude for your gift of the mantra, my saving grace.

For 16 years, Villa Ananda Ayurveda Spa & Suites has been serving humanity through detox and rejuvenating programs, Yoga Retreats and events with my Guru Paramahansa Vishwananda, other Spiritual Masters and Monks. It provides a safe environment for people to cleanse, heal and experience something greater within. I still repeat the mantra constantly.

We know we can accomplish our goals with a clear mind. With Japa practice, you learn to distinguish if the mind is controlling You? Or are you controlling the mind? Who is winning, the monkey mind or the mantra? You begin to observe the mind, it's tricks and chatter; positive thoughts and limited beliefs. You decide who is in control and what you want to give energy to, discernment. It's a tool to keep you connected with your inner voice and intuition. It brings us back when we lose our center. And my favorite part, it's so easy to do!

Q&A

Jana: Okay, that was amazing. So, a few follow up questions. Can you give us an Ayurveda 101, for someone who is reading this chapter and says, what is this?

Lajja: Yes. Ayurveda is ancient natural medicine of India, dating back 5,000 years. It teaches one how to live a conscious life. It is an integrative approach at educating people how to live life in balance based on their unique body mind constitution. We all want to wake up and feel good every day. Ayurveda teaches you how; and teaches you what to do to realign when we get out of balance.

The basis of Ayurveda is in the five elements, Earth being the only planet that has all five elements present in the Universe; space, air, fire, water and earth. These five elements are all present within us. We're like little microcosms of the macrocosm.

We all have the elements in differing proportions; one might have more water, less fire, another more earth and less air, etc. And each element has different physical, mental and psychological characteristics and emotional tendencies. When you learn your unique constitution, you learn what you need to do to stay in balance. In Ayurveda, like attracts like, yet it's the opposite that balances. We look at each individual and teach them what they need to reach and maintain balance. It's an intuitive art and science, I love it. The number one answer you'll get to any question you ask an Ayurveda practitioner is, "It depends." What is one man's medicine, could be another's poison. We look at your constitutional makeup and where you are at today, then help educate you to make choices to reach that optimum balance, in your power, in your strength. From here, you keep reaching up for higher conscious living.

Jana: So, through your story, you gifted us with moments of "The Lemon" And not to oversimplify things, but if you had to identify one aspect of your story that was your coconut milk, is it the voice that led you to your experiences and your Guru and how that supported you? Or is your coconut milk something different than the voice?

Lajja: The coconut milk would definitely be my Guru, His voice. And the gifts that come from listening to Him.

Majority of the time we do not listen, more so, we do not hear because there is too much chatter in the mind. Or if we do hear, there is doubt. It's really quite simple, if we can control the mind, we can hear the voice. For me, I am eternally grateful to my Guru Paramahansa Vishwananda and his voice guiding me on my way.

From Portland, Oregon to Puerto Vallarta, Mexico! After working in radio sales and marketing for 6 years, in 2000 LAJJA MINDY RESER came to Mexico for "three months" and never went back. In Mexico she discovered Ayurveda and went to study in Florida obtaining Associates Degree in Ayurveda then Massage Therapy. Next stop, India to Himalayan Mountains Sivananda Ashram for Yoga Philosophy and Advanced Teacher Training programs. Whilst in India, the call came, "it's time to go to Mexico and get started."

Lajja took this message to heart and without a moment of doubt. En route to Mexico she met her spiritual teacher, satguru Paramahansa Sri Swami Vishwananda who became the guiding light in her life. Upon arriving in Mexico in 2005, after three hours searching, Villa Ananda revealed itself. For 15 years now, Villa Ananda Ayurveda Spa & Suites has received clients for detox programs, yoga retreats and spiritual events. The intention of Villa Ananda is to give clients an experience of something greater – through the art and science of Ayurveda, Functional Medicine, healers and educators; new levels of balanced health, mental clarity, internal peace arise.

Lajja's life's purpose expanded to include raising two beautiful babies born in Villa Ananda, Al Vicente in 2010 and Viviana Patricia in 2012. She is blessed and full of gratitude to share her passion of balanced health and connection to Self with every person that graces Villa Ananda.

TASHA

I was about two years old when my journey to being a strong human started. That was when my dad first was diagnosed with cancer. Following my dad's initial diagnosis, he subsequently developed cancer four more times, which included two liver transplants, spleen removal, two-thirds of his liver dissected, part of his aorta cut out, adrenal glands removed, and radiofrequency ablation. Many things that made my life unstable, yet, with his unconditional support, I somehow thrived and survived to the present day. We're gonna fast forward quite some time and go to about two and a half years ago, so winter 2019/2020. In February of 2020, things started to progress to where I am today.

My dad hadn't been feeling well for about four months prior to that. The doctors kept saying, "Oh, it's a pulled muscle, oh, it's a pulled muscle". And he said, "No, I've had a pulled muscle. This is not a pulled muscle." But nothing was showing up on scans.

In February 2020 my parents went down to Palm Springs for their winter vacation to golf. While he was down there, he called me and said, "I just miss you, I need you to come down here. Book a flight." So, I went down there for a week and had an absolutely unbelievable time with my mom and my dad. But he was in pain. He couldn't stand for any length of time. He could golf, but we were carting. I was thinking that something was up. So, we came home and things started to progress to normal life.

Then a few weeks later we got a call from the doctor's office. It was not good. We got the diagnosis that he had cancer for the fifth time. This time it had spread throughout more of his body, so there wasn't much we could do. With him having a rare form of cancer, epithelioid hemangioendothelioma, there's not much literature on what to do, what works, what doesn't. So, he progressed to go through some chemotherapy treatments. Ultimately, those worked to progress his life for about a year, but they were no longer working entering the summer of 2021.

Summer of 2021, he got very sick and went into the hospital. Now, at this time you could only have two people as visitors in the hospital and only one at a time in the room. I have a younger sister. She has two children and a husband. So, my mom was the only one visiting and then we decided as a family that I would be the second one visiting as she needed support to support my dad. I had an unbelievably strong relationship with my father. He was my best friend. I worked for him for about eight years in my adulthood, and probably another eight years part-time back when I was a child and a teenager. He was my person. I talked to him every day, I told him everything. I saw him every day. He was the one person who knew me inside and out and never judged me. He always supported me no matter what. So, this was a hard time for me seeing him really sick.

As an entrepreneur, I owned two businesses, so I still had to keep my businesses flowing. I had to pretend like this wasn't affecting me. I had to work all day and go to the hospital when I was needed. Through those hard times, you thrive and you survive. You just do it. You don't think anything of it. You wake up at five in the morning, you go to the hospital, you come home, you work all day, you go to the hospital again at night, come home, sleep and repeat it all the next day. And it was fine, it was great. That's what I was meant to do. Then my Dad got put into palliative care and luckily, I was able to work from palliative care. I basically moved into his hospital room. That was great, but part of me felt like you're just supposed to pretend like nothing matters, and that you're not grieving, and that you're not allowed to fear that you're gonna lose the one person who's been there unconditionally your whole life.

Now, my mom's amazing. She's supportive, but my dad and I are the same person. We share the same passion for life. He was the reason that I always chased my dreams and inspired me to do everything that I did. I have lost many people in my life. I was in the hospital when my grandpa died. I was in the hospital when both my grandmas died, I have been there. I always survived it. It was fine. I knew my purpose and kept going. As an entrepreneur and a business owner, you don't get days off. Emails still come in. You're supposed to act like everything's okay, however in the corporate world, if you're losing somebody, you get bereavement leave, you get leave, and your emails go to somebody else. I didn't have that. And I don't wish for that life because corporate life is not for me. But you're just supposed to continue day after day doing what you've always done, taking care of your body, taking care of your mental health, taking care of your team, taking care of your responsibilities, taking care of your family. And you don't even realize what's going on and then suddenly everything hits you all at once. Slam! It's like, holy crap, here comes the grief.

August 22, 2021 was when my dad passed away. From that day on, things shifted for me. I was so extremely thankful for my almost 33 years with him. I knew that I needed to be resilient and chase my dreams to prove to him that I could still thrive. I know he's with me every day, so I've been thankful for that. But when you've just been in survival mode, being the person there for your mother, being the person there for your sister, being the person there for your dad. And at that time, I was single, so I didn't have that person to be my backup. I had some phenomenal friends and colleagues in my life, but it's just different, right? So that took a lot out of me, but I just continued. I took a couple of days, planned the funeral, and all of that as well as a full-time freaking job while you're still doing your regular job because you still need to do everything.

Fast forward to September, it was my dad's birthday on the 10th. We had a nice memorial golf day for him. September 12th is my birthday; we are both Virgos. After that busy week, that's when things started to shift. I was in a relationship, I kind of kept it hush hush because you don't want to bring somebody new into this situation. So, there's no right time to have this person come into your life. And then all these thoughts run through your mind: What are people gonna think? "Oh, my God, she got into a relationship. She just lost her person, her best friend, her dad. Shouldn't she be focusing on that? Shouldn't she be focusing on her business?" And you have this level of pain and I'm gonna say judgment that is happening that you don't know about. And you're supposed to still put yourself first again, physically, mentally, metaphysically, all those things, and that's really, really hard.

So, I got into this relationship. Things are going really well, and the relationship is moving fast. We bought a new home together, and I moved in with him. That's all great. I even moved my two businesses into that home. Everything is amazing. It's picture perfect. My mom's feeling strong, I'm feeling strong. Of course, I have my rough days, but I'm getting through. Then February 2022, bam! Everything is flipped upside down. I'm locked out of my home where I have my two businesses located. I have no idea what's going on and I just have this flood of emotions that I just need to keep going on. So, I continued to work, pretending like nothing's happened. I tried to go through life for about two weeks as if nothing had happened. I kept telling myself, "Just keep going. Take it one day at a time."

But that mindset I created and the situation I was in was not fair. As women, yes, we're meant to be motherly and strong, but it's okay to not be f*cking strong. It's okay to cry all day and be weak. When I got locked out of that house by my partner at the time, I had to regroup. I hit ground zero, it was the first time I'd never had a backup plan. I still owned a house, but I had renters in it. I had a fitness studio. Where was I going to move this? Did I have to close it? Where was I moving my business consulting and bookkeeping business? I was put in a completely unexpected situation, and I had to come up with a plan in days.

Being the strong woman that I am, I was not interested in taking this lying down. My ex was a well-known member of the community, so I felt a strong instinct to protect myself, my reputation, and my businesses. I posted online about my experiences and received an overwhelming amount of support and information from other women. It turned out that this was not the first instance where a woman was taken advantage of or lied to. I felt betrayed, of course, but I also felt a sense of pride that I may have saved another girl from having the same experience. It is never okay to destroy others' lives. I am very particular about who I allow into my life, I like to make my own decisions about people and am very rarely swayed by the opinions of others. I can understand that my ex may have had a past or a chapter that he wasn't willing to share with everyone else. However, just like me, we are all responsible for our own communication and healing. Bad behavior doesn't always make you a bad person, but it's our individual responsibility to heal so that we don't repeat toxic actions with no regard for others. No one deserved to go through this, but I am incredibly proud of the way that I handled that situation and that I spoke out when I did.

This is where my lemons turned into my coconut milk. Through this experience I had the greatest realization to the types of people who were in my life. It was like, holy shit, at one of my lowest points of my life, I had the most support I've ever had. My family's massive, I had aunts and uncles from Alberta who were willing to drive to Saskatchewan to pack up my stuff to get me moved. I had best friends staying with me every day to make sure I was okay. My mom was helping me get everything into storage so I could move on with my life. I had clients who called and were like, can we send you money? What can we do? Do you need to work in my space? That's when I realized, I do not need to be as tough on myself as society's norms have made me believe in the past. I can be broken, I can have bad days, I can miss deadlines. I'm human, I can be imperfect. This level of perfection that I've put myself up to be is unrealistic. If people in my life can't see that I need a breather, they're not in alignment with me and my journey.

It took me a while to regroup. I've always worked out throughout my life, and now I wasn't working out. My fitness studio had been closed, not by my choice. By somebody else's. And that was always my outlet. At the time of all this, it was winter and now I'm living in a basement, and I don't want to work out in a basement. Just all these things that kept piling on top of each other. I began to overthink every little detail. Am I doing this right? Am I doing this wrong?

Once I took a step back and detached from the situation, I just grounded myself and told myself to live in the present. I don't need to be perfect. My dad was never perfect, but I know he never gave up. And that's what I knew I had to do was to never give up. To be passionate about what I love, to find my safe place again. Where did I feel safe? Was it in nature with my feet on the ground? Was it with the people who unconditionally supported me whether it was a phone call or just being in their space. And trusting myself again, knowing that it's going to be okay. Putting one foot in front of the other, refocusing. And does grief still show up in my day-to-day life now? Absolutely, all the time. And I bawl my eyes out. But I know that I'm not going to live there. That's for a moment in time and I'm going to keep moving forward.

For anybody who's struggling with a huge, major life occurrence, just know that the universe throws us what we can handle. So, if you're getting thrown something, you can definitely handle it. And it's okay to think you can't for a moment, but you need to pick yourself up and get yourself out of that. Because at the end of the day, you are strong enough, and you can do it. So, my advice is, be real. Be real to yourself and be real for others. It's your responsibility to heal. It doesn't matter how long it takes you to heal, but it is your responsibility because life is beautiful. Even in the muck and grossness and all these lemons that are thrown at us, there is a bright light at the end of the tunnel, and hopefully you can see that even just a little bit. Because it'll get brighter and brighter. So, be supportive to yourself and love yourself. Give yourself a little extra love on those tough days. Trust me. It will be worth it. You will look back and you will be amazed at what you can persevere through.

Q&A

Jana: Tasha, that was so beautifully said, I have a few questions. You obviously identified a few lemons and I mean, that's been the whole theme of this book. These lemons are there for you, they're not doing something to you. They are there to show you something or shift you on onto a different trajectory. You also talked about a few key coconut milk moments, including loving yourself and how it's your responsibility to shift out of those dark spaces. But if there was one main piece for you to share with others, what is the one main coconut milk in your life that you keep coming back to?

Tasha: It is my dad, but it's going to be his journey. Not him specifically, but his journey. I honestly have no idea what physical pain is compared to him and what he experienced through his cancer. I can't even fathom what that feels like. But the fact that he pursued every day to live a life for his wife and his daughters is going to be my coconut milk probably for the rest of my life. Because I don't know what it's like to be that strong. And to be 90 pounds and still fighting for your life. To be told, we don't know if you can live, and still telling doctors, you're gonna make me live, we're gonna find a way, I'm going to do this. That's going to be my number one coconut milk, his journey.

Jana: For that woman who is feeling frozen, maybe they have gone through similar situations of grief or breakup, or questioning their ability to ask what's next because it's really easy for our sympathetic nervous system to take over and just freeze us, the question of what's next can feel extremely overwhelming. Sometimes staying frozen is the option that so many women choose. To that woman, what is the one thing that she could do today or tomorrow that would start to shift a little bit of momentum in her favor?

Tasha: I would say it's okay to exist. That is a healthy place. But we aren't meant to just exist. We have a voice. Use it. Whether it's to one person or if it's through an online medium, trying to find somebody who's been through something similar. A lot of us have a story. There are people out there to support you. A huge part of me sharing not just my journey as a child and an adult with a sick father, but my journey with a horrible breakup, was having a voice for a lot of women who experienced the exact same situation but weren't strong enough to say anything. Find those people in your corner who, if you don't have the voice or the strength, that they have your back and your strength until you're strong enough to do it yourself.

Jana: Amazing. Anything left unsaid before we wrap this chapter?

Tasha: Know you are amazing. Tell yourself you love yourself. You are worthy. You are enough. People are going to see your beauty, but also make sure you see the beauty in yourself. Because you have one life and this is yours.

TASHA BAIER, B.Comm., is a business owner and entrepreneur located in Saskatoon Saskatchewan. Along with Tasha's passion for business, she is a certified personal trainer with accreditations in Active Aging, Eat Clean Foundations, and Stress Resiliency, along with a multitude of other educational courses. Outside of work, Tasha is a daughter, sister, aunty, friend, and Virgo. Tasha believes in living a balanced life and has a passion for healthy living which includes helping others reach their true potential.

HELENA

When I returned from India in 1991, in a few weeks my son was just going to turn four. I had been living in the ashram Ganeshpuri India at the Gurudev Siddha Peeth Ashram with Gurumayi Chidvilasananda for two complete years in India.

While in India, I was appointed to be one of two psychotherapists "on duty" in the ashram, and it was just myself and a psychiatrist from the UK, Dr. Richard Gillette. The referrals were coming in directly from Gurumayi Chidvilasananda. They handed me a typewriter (yes a typewriter) and asked me to write a report for each client. Was it a mother or father issue? This lifetime or a past lifetime issue? Once she received my evaluation she would select the therapist (Richard or me).

This went on for a couple of years. It was quite intense. We had people flying in and out, people including international celebrities. It was very busy with famous people flying in for darshan and having issues. They got referred to us. I started to realize these clients had trapped in their emotional body such deep issues that we were challenged dealing with the issues in such a brief time as they were often flying out rather soon.

During those years it was when we were confronted with the rather intense limitations of "talk" or "emotional expressive" therapy as they could not free them. We tried everything from emotional release therapies in teepees to talk therapy.

They were doing meditation, chanting, eating this pure vegetarian diet, having Darshan, living in an ashram in India, and yet we found there was abuse in the family or emotional issues going on in the family. It was not nurturing. Beyond the surface of the garb that spiritual seekers usually wear, you know, the image that they project. There were issues in the families and in the relationships. And so we were kind of, we didn't know how to get this emotional work done in a short time. It was challenging for both of us. Sometimes they were literally in, we'd see them, and fly out. They would arrive in the morning and fly out at night.

At the end of these two years in India, I had an intense desire to remain in India. It was peaceful, and my son was growing up nicely. We loved it there. It was so beautiful and serene. So, I didn't want to leave. Gurumayi had another plan for us and had the travel office issue a return flight for myself and my son, whose Indian name was Sacci. We left Mumbai (then Bombay) the day after Gurumayi's departure. Back to the "real world" of the USA. We flew back to Honolulu!

Gurumayi gave me one message before she left for the USA... "Your dharma, your purpose, your gift is to be in healing."

I made a deal with the universe because I had been very concerned about our results of the therapy we were delivering. I said, I'll go back into the healing work if I can find something really efficient that actually addresses the deep patterns that sabotage our progress emotionally, physically, financially, just our overall experience on Earth.

I know that's a complex question. So I met up with the psychic, and a deep trance channel, Darlene. She was able to go into a deep trance state and deliver messages from the quantum field. She said your mission is in sound and tone. So we went in search. It was pre-internet, about 1991. The internet was being created, but nobody was using it yet. What happened was, we finally found Don Campbell, and I went to his event. Then a couple days after he asked me to be his manager, meaning I would be running the 'mysterious girl,' which my husband was not thrilled about at the time, but we moved to Boulder, Colorado in pursuit of this knowledge and it immediately resonated.

I had been studying classical piano and modern dance at the Boston Conservatory throughout my entire childhood. Most of my weekends were with the Director of the Conservatory and his wife (head of classical piano) as they were my best friend's parents.

I knew I was very resonant with sound and music. And my mother was an opera singer. So I dove in and started doing this work in toning and sound. Then one day, the late Don Campbell, who is now a New York Times best-selling author, called me and we would talk quite frequently. Don was quite a well known classical pianist who decided mid life to teach the world about sound healing and toning.

He said, I'd like you to go over to the University of Honolulu, tonight. A very famous ethnomusicologist is doing an event at the university. So I went, and this machine showed up with Rytwin Lee, and he put the frequencies on. It was a computer with a million wires.

Rytwin played these "Awaken To Christ Consciousness" frequencies and I immediately went into samadhi, a state of meditative consciousness, in seconds.

My joke at the time was that I had spent two years meditating and training in that state. It was amazing to me how quickly those frequencies flipped the switch. He said it was Christ consciousness. As we were leaving, I said to him, "Give me your card; I'll call you."

I called Rytwin the next day and invited him to my home, which was in Hawaii Loa Ridge, to bring that machine, which I didn't know what it was called, or anything.

I'll call these events: "The Sound Laboratory." And added, "I'll have every alternative practitioner on the island at my home to see your machine, everybody who's available, if you accept my invitation." Forty people showed up the first night.

He showed up with the big machine. The place was packed because everyone actually really wanted to see this house, it was a gated community overlooking the Pacific Ocean. So I got them all there. I don't know how I knew them all. I have no idea. But somehow,

I invited them all. We had this extraordinary first experience. We chose someone in the audience who was not working in the healing industry, whom no one knew. And we did her frequencies. And we had a pleasant experience. It was very smooth, and then everyone went home.

The next day, the woman called me, and she thanked me. And she shared something interesting. She said, "I'm so grateful. I was going to have kidney stones removed. I had a surgery scheduled, but I passed them in your bathroom after you did my frequencies." I just about fell on the floor. I was like, oh, no, no, here is my first lawsuit already. But she was not upset, she was thrilled. She went to the doctor and the doctor said they're gone. I don't know what you did, but they are gone. That was the beginning of the journey. I decided I had to invest in this technology. So I did. I had to borrow money, because we'd been in India for years, and spent pretty much everything we had. I had to borrow money from my father, actually, and get through my brother as the gatekeeper. It took a lot of persistence.

I immediately opened my practice, which was interesting, and started traveling with the machine, but mostly people were coming to my home. We decided that we had to move back to New York. The islands were not quite right for the businesses we were running. So we went to New York, and what transpired there was actually really interesting. I had the machine at this point. I had it shipped over to New York. I opened two offices in New York, one in upstate and one in the city. The minute we got to New York, things just kind of blew open. Someone brought a healer who was really sick. He was dying, he had pneumonia. He was not recovering. He'd been in bed for three or four weeks. So they brought him and I did his frequencies based on his voice analysis, and he became well. At that moment, we actually removed the source code, which was a lung. He was having pneumonia, so it was lung and loss. He went back to the city. He was a Reiki Master and started referring clients to me and word spread. My private practice exploded naturally. We started seeing a lot of phenomenal changes: changes in people's lives, changes in their emotional status, changes in how they communicated. So I started speaking and delivering talks.

The thing about this was that it was built on the Amiga platform and Amiga was going to go out of business. Some people say Amiga was a derivative of Apple. But anyway, they went out of business, and of course, Apple soared. I had this place I used to go to get all my equipment. We had all this stuff in his basement. When that stuff stopped being produced, I had to make a cosmic life decision, which was, do I join Robert Lloy to help him bring this project back online.

I received another level of spiritual awakening at this point. After a lot of "spiritual nudging" I decided not to talk to a human because I knew that they could be misguiding. I created this contract with Source again. Now I had to get the signs from the universe in my subconscious that this was a good decision because I had to move to California and give up my practice in New York. The answer came in "yes," and I was given several dreams and messages. In one of the messages I traveled to the Council of Sages and I was sitting there, and my partner, Robert Lloy, was there with Shirdi Sai Baba, and Shirdi Sai Baba said, "You will take care of him in the final days." I didn't know what that meant. But I knew that I was supposed to be with Robert.

So I accepted the invitation and on April 21, 2002 I got on a plane, and shipped my jeep to move to California.

We invested the next 20 years creating, evolving and developing what we have now, available at: https://www.quantumsoundtherapy.com.

- Quantum Sound Miracle iQube
- Quantum Sound Tesla iQube
- OmPocket
- Voice Code Software Version 6.0
- Scalarwave Structured Water

What I didn't know at that time was the precariousness of Robert's health. He had great technology, which kept him going, and a steel will. I knew that we were definitely twin flames here to do a mission together. But his health was not strong. And until you are really with someone, you do not know that. Within the next 20 years, not only did we create, but we innovated as well. As Tony Robbins once said, when you don't have a billion dollars to build something, or at least a million, you learn how to create and innovate.

And Robert was very, very innovative and received his visions as picture images and inspirations from dreams, from spirit, and soul. We went through this journey of 20 years, walking side by side and creating these technologies and using whatever funds we could muster, to create this work. We were living simply knowing that healing people was really important. We developed the technology together piece by piece, following his dreams and instructions. That is not my thing. I do not receive visions of what component is needed next. This journey went on for almost exactly 20 years. As the mission grew, we were not quite able to clear all of his health issues. But what happened was we built the technologies and the spaces and the places for the manufacturing facilities to be created.

Over time, we continued to see the purpose of the technologies were to help us to align with these new frequencies and the new energy. At this point, we developed a library of millions of frequencies with a number of different formulas and ways to build the technology so it would last an entire lifetime. During this time of development and expansion, I was observing that there had been damage to Robert's health from his journey. So we continued our journey to Hot Springs, Arkansas and built a facility and continued to evolve the concept around the technology. The technology did not become a shield, but did become a technology that could be used without any negative side effects. Scalar is not that easy to contain the heat because it is a huge energy field. We continued that process until it started to become really clear to me that Robert's health needed to be addressed. Hot Springs is extremely hot. So we took a little sabbatical from the heat. At this point, it was really about his health. We developed a residence in Florida solely to help him heal. What happened next was quite surprising. He actually developed a brain condition. So here we are, we have the technologies that are developed to help us use our brain better. He was making the technology stronger and stronger to heal himself. That was what he was being guided to do. He added frequencies like organs, glands, including the Pineal, just everything to nurture everyone's consciousness and his as well.

The big surprise and the caveat was that we were not able to completely heal his brain, and he started to progressively experience memory loss. Now, keep in mind he had all this toxicity from 20 years of working in uranium mines that we could not remove from his body and brain. He continued to contribute and be active and do everything he could do to keep his brain moving to maintain neuroplasticity. In the end, he was not able to, and he started to experience loss of memory. It was very difficult for him because he was brilliant, which is not uncommon with some of these diseases, they impact people very quickly. He did continue to decline, although there were ups and downs and ups and downs, and I kept believing the entire time that something would start to work to heal him.

It was conscious and subconscious. I had been fighting this battle since I understood his health condition. It was 20 years. We had gone on raw diets, we were walking miles and miles. We were juicing and doing everything. Including making the technology stronger and stronger, to help others and himself. But what happened over time was that he lost his abilities, not his spiritual abilities, but his mental abilities.

Eventually, it became advanced. It was a very terrifying experience. But I had been given the assignment to take care of him in the final days. I was still determined that there was a solution, and maybe I would figure it out, or someone else. The last few years were very, very challenging. But, his health was pretty stable even though his brain had a little less capacity.

We went through this experience of losing him physically. It was very dramatic towards the end. A lot of things can happen with this type of disease, and he was completely relying on me. We had a long process where we were up at night a lot just trying to keep him steady and stable. But nothing was really working. Towards the end, I started to realize that it was not going to be reversible. The other aspect of this is that I had always thought we were going to ascend together, that we would be leaving together. I had this one vision of holding hands and walking out over this lake. So I thought, oh, we are going to finish our work and then walk out into the sunset. So I had this very romantic vision about how we were going to be creating our future. And sadly, though there was tremendous love from the beginning to the end, I feel so fortunate that I had over 7,000 days with him. Because he is a great master, as his body deteriorated, and I understood his soul, I realized I had to let him go. I had to let him go. Not that I wanted to let him go, I had to let him go. When the brain stops functioning, there is really no memory. It is quite a challenging situation, because there is no memory, and there is really no frontal lobe, which is the personality and what drives you forward. He was hospitalized a couple of times, and on May 26, 2022, he was put on hospice and he passed away. I'm still processing that because it was so very recent. It was where I realized, of course, I wanted to go with him, but I also realized I had to complete the work.

Here is the big takeaway of this lesson. We have a lot of psychics in our community that informed me that Bob and I were still ascending together. I, in the body, finishing up the work, and him on the other side. I actually went through the experience when his magnetic field was disassembled. I actually could feel it. I was standing in the kitchen, and I said, "Oh, this is a weird kind of feeling." I didn't really understand it, I just knew what had happened.

The magnetics were kind of disassembled, and then you go into a light body. So at that point, I actually started to realize what a gift he was going to be. As he became this light-being I started getting phone calls and text messages and things from people saying, Bob came in and he said, I need to continue to do this work. He said, you need to do this to make your work better. And then they started telling me that he's still overseeing the project.

So he took it on as a guide. Although he was given several options, it appears he chose to oversee the project in his own light body self. The takeaway has been that nothing really matters. It is a matter of freeing yourself and feeling joy. I started to realize the whole thing is for us to be in this flow, and to accept the flow, but also to be light and joyful. I also realized a strange thing about me, which even cracks me up now, and it is that I've never been alone. I had children and a husband that I've always been taking care of. It seems I have always been second on the list. You know, when you have an infant or somebody who is really sick and needing you. I have also seen that it was orchestrated as part of my own evolution, that I would have this experience. I definitely consider him the love of my life and my twin flame.

One of the biggest messages right now is that we are in this continuum of time. We are at the end of the Atlantean cycle. Some people say 12,000, some people say 16,000 years, it doesn't matter. Nothing really matters, but that particularly does not matter. The truth of the matter is that we are drawing from and assimilating and completing many of the lessons, the relationships, the emotions of the past, so we can clear it and move into being sovereign, powerful, female light leaders.

All of the acts, experiences, are feeding into this vast energy field that we carry, so that we can become that. When we were in the emergency room, at one point he looked up and he said, "You didn't fix this." He looked right at me, with two nurses, me at his feet and a doctor to the right. And the doctor said she couldn't. I realized right then that I believed I could, that I could fix that. And obviously, he must have thought that too. I feel as though this expansion is at this crossroads in time where so many of our experiences are coming in, to be completed, to be acknowledged, to be loved into the next octave. So, in some ways, our relationship continues, but it is now in another octave where he is invisible. Sometimes he is a little visible. And I'm in a physical structure. This is for the highest good, for some reason that I don't fully understand yet completely. But it is very important to pay attention to the very subtle energy that's coming in. That's one of the messages that he has been delivering, because there are signs in the universe.

Many of us are going to go through grief. We are going to lose and gain. It is part of our immersion, and it is part of our expansion. To accept the holy flow of secret synchronicity, to accept whatever experience life is sharing with us at the moment, it is for our highest good if we can live it and just accept it. For example, grief comes in waves. It's very unpredictable. Where all of a sudden it is all-encompassing, and then it's gone. So grief is part of our game because human life is short. We need to understand that. We need to understand that death will eventually come to all of us, but what has been gained is this tremendous love and compassion.

In his parting, I realized this very interesting paradox. He was capable of not having the frontal lobe, but experiencing and sharing profound love with me. So that was another aspect. When the mind and the brain go, you can still be loving, you can still love. You can still beam and share your light, you can still be human. I really have not digested that fully, that we operate so much from our mind in the west. But this is so important because he was going through frustration and confusion. But he still had this capability. The soul, the heart, the spirit remains and the body goes. As we ascend and as we work with all of these energies that are convening right now on

Earth, it is for our growth. Even when we are going through these times of loss, we have to accept now and surrender and do the work inside ourselves. I was not only grieving his loss in this lifetime, but we had also been separated in Atlantis when Atlantis was going to sink. He had gone off to Egypt and I had stayed behind and that was the real pain of separation. That was probably what brought us together so strongly.

My message is to really go deeply within yourself and pay attention. Do not just go on the surface. Pay attention to the signs that are being gifted and given to the experiences for the fulfillment of your soul and your purpose. Once you understand that, even if there is sadness, or grief, or loss, you can carry on and continue your purpose and fulfill it and have an amazing life. But also gain spiritually, gain in the soul. Gain from the perspective of love.

What I learned was that nothing is really that important. The things that we attached to, oh, I have a spot on the wall that needs to be painted. Well, how important is that? Oh, somebody left their clothes on the floor. Well, how important is that? Towards the very end, it was as if nothing was really important but love and learning to love yourself. Harmonizing and loving those that we have been gifted with. It is a gift, and it will not last forever. It is precious, life is so precious. Sometimes we miss that. We think, I have to do this, I've got to write that, you know, we have a long to-do list. In the west, especially. As female entrepreneurs, as female healers, as female light leaders, as female whatever, we need to remember what is really important, and it is the humans, and walking in their spiritual journey and supporting it so they are safe enough to be in their hearts. I realized when Bob passed that I had given him that experience. I had given him the experience of being unconditionally loved. It is really an important time to prioritize what is in our life and appreciate it with great, great gratitude and love. The other aspect is what we are working through now is separation. But we are really never separate.

In the quantum field, we are always connected and we are always one. Separation is a huge illusion. And you may miss the body, but the separation is a huge illusion. Surrendering to our experience and appreciating the divinity of each one of us is the key that opens the door to the quantum field, and to your enhanced experience of your lifetime. There is no greater teacher than death or grief. There is really no greater teacher because it shows you your ultimate destiny, but also that time is limited here. So, respect it. Time is a great gift. And that is my story.

Q&A

Jana: That was beautiful; it was wise. You led us on a journey. I really only have one question. There were so many moments where you had these lemons, where you were like, what do I do? Or you could have taken that, like, why is this happening to me? And so my one question to you simply is, what is your coconut milk at this moment?

Helena: My coconut milk is knowing that I fulfilled my purpose and that I have reconnected to my soul. And that all I invested has come back to me. Different psychics can pass on their various gifts and talents to you when they pass because they cannot use them. Certain gifts you do not use on the other side, you do not need to heal a person because they are not in physical bodies. The coconut milk has been the gift. It was kind of like pulling off a Band-Aid, but it has resulted in a much fuller, more embodied expression of Helena. Everyone from my own son, people arrive and they say, now it is time for you to do Helena. And that's the gift. If you have ever been a caregiver, any caregivers will know what I am saying. I did not have a second. I cannot even figure out how I did that. But at the moment, we had so much support. As you transition into the next stage, it is the evolution of your own soul. Bob gave me this huge gift of evolving my own soul. The other coconut milk is that in many ways we do not always fully understand what's going on. But it is for our full soul expression. It is being orchestrated and created by us because of our intention. Mine was always enlightenment and liberation. But it is the surrender. That was where even when I was weak, I did not want to surrender to the fact that he was going to die. I don't believe in death; I guess I should say that he was going to transition.

The other gem is to turn our wounds into wisdom. If you have lost someone, or someone in your life is really sick, and you are working to reverse that, just understand that there are divine powers, there are higher powers. We cannot control the trajectory of time in someone's life. The date or the time in which someone passes is not really up to us. Even with the best supplements in the world, the best sound frequencies, the best scalar technology, we are still going to die. In doing that, we are also going to expand our consciousness. So, in many ways the gift is that he freed me, and also freed me from that pattern of always taking care. Well, we will see in a few years. I am always taking care of others before myself. That is a second gift. We do need to pay close attention to what is going on in our lives. That is the huge, huge coconut milk. Pay very close attention, do not miss the signs of what is happening. Love is all around us, it is so rich. It is really the love that makes us rich.

Once Bob's physical body was gone, it was so clear to me that, yes, we do need flow, we do need to create, but it is the love that is sustaining us. It is not the money, it is not the success. It is not about prosperity. It is not where we live. It is the love that is sustaining us. That is the ultimate coconut milk.

Renowned Quantum-Scalar-Sound Therapist, HELENA REILLY, MA, is the co-founder of www.quantumsoundtherapy.com. She is a pioneer in the use of sound frequencies and immersive quantum scalar energy vortex technology to effect lasting transformation and decrease the impact of stress and burnout. Her mission is to harmonize humanity. The Voice Code Software that she developed with her partner Robert Lloy automatically depicts the nuances of the subconscious and delivers a harmonizing soundtrack that releases the hidden stress that sabotages well-being and human potential.

Helena did her graduate work in Psychological Treatment at the University of Chicago. In 2015, she received the award for Best Therapist and Therapy From Who's Who Of Distinguished Alumni.

Realizing the limitations of her academic training, she sought to create a modality that was more effective than talk therapy. She applied Sound Therapy and Quantum Sound Technology in her upper west side Manhattan-based private practice.

The Quantum Miracle iQube synergistically combines the science of scalar energy with sound therapy to effect permanent subconscious transformation. Helena is an expert in applying Voice Code Sound Therapy and Quantum Technology as cutting-edge methods for Stress Management and Anti-Aging of the Burned Out Professional. Connect with Helena at https://www.helena360.com.

KIM

Whether you are a business owner, a mother, sister, friend or all of the above, some days you are in your stride, knocking it out of the ballpark and high-fiving on the way to home plate. Other days, you might get on to first base with a line drive, and sometimes you strike out. The important part is taking what you've learned and getting back up to bat.

This story will never go down in history as a top play by business owners. But what happened did prepare me for what was around the corner waiting for me, whether I was ready or not, a comeback of epic proportions. I was growing my marketing agency and things were picking up. We were getting a lot of clients in our local community that we were doing marketing for. I discovered direct response marketing and was starting to apply the principles to social media, meaning if we posted on social media, it wasn't just about getting likes or comments, it was about getting customers. And it started to work; we were growing rapidly. I started to get a reputation of being the "go-to" expert in direct response social media.

Well, at the time, because we had a lot more clients coming to us in our local community, I needed more staff. I had put out a post on Facebook to my friends to say, hey, do you know anybody who's looking to get into a marketing firm, or is a freelancer, or someone who would be a good match for our team? A woman in my community, a new acquaintance from volunteering on different boards with her, suggested a friend of hers who was looking to do more freelance work. So I hired this freelancer and she started to work on some of our accounts. It was going well, but my intuition and gut was telling me something was up with this. But I just kept ignoring it and told myself she's doing great work.

About a month into her working with us, we were running an event in our community. One of my big client accounts was the city where our office was located. We ran all their events. During one of the big events, the friend who recommended the freelancer asked to use my restroom. Of course I let her, but I felt weird when she walked into my office. She was looking all around and it kind of felt like she was snooping. Which again, I'm telling my instinct, "That's not weird. You're wrong, there's nothing wrong here, it's fine."

Two days later, the freelancer quit and I found out the woman who had been snooping (and had recommended the freelancer) was starting her own marketing firm. The two of them were in cahoots and she had sent this freelancer into my business to steal as much intel as she could. The freelancer had purposefully never sent back the non-disclosure and non-compete forms, and we didn't recognize that. The two of them went through my entire client list and went to every single account and offered to do work for them for free for six months to take them from my firm. Turns out she had done this to multiple people in my community. She also filed a frivolous lawsuit with someone else who I knew, liked and trusted to get cash to cover her expenses for six months, so she could work for all these accounts for free.

So, in this moment, I felt betrayed. I felt hurt. I questioned everything about myself, that I'm a giving and nice person. The worst was when one of my dearest, long standing clients left. He was a good friend of mine, and because we had such a close relationship he came to deliver the news that he was leaving in person. It was the first time that I had to leave my staff meeting to go into the bathroom to cry. I've never had that before, but it just hurt to the core. I was feeling like, "God, why is this happening to me?" So much betrayal has happened when I am just trying to take care of everybody. So, it hurt. It hurt really bad.

About a week later, Dan Kennedy came to me and asked me to co-author the *No BS Guide to Direct Response Social Media Marketing* with him, which was my first major publication. It's a book that made me a best-selling author. It brought me local, national and international client accounts that grew my firm to the point of being able to exit someday. I never would have had the bandwidth to do that if I kept these small, not profitable accounts that I was never going to get rid of on my own. Because I loved these folks so much, I was always going to do this work for them even though it wasn't profitable for my company. It was actually through that transition of reflection of being grateful in that moment, that I didn't have those small accounts anymore that I gained an understanding that I am not broken. The fact that it happened to me doesn't make me bad or wrong. I am a giving person who trusts people and I'm okay with it. It just means I have to surround myself with other people who are that way. And I made a conscious decision that I'm willing to deal with the consequences of when people don't reciprocate it because I'd rather have a life that's filled with more people like that than not. And I'm okay when those moments happen because now when they happen, I know they happened because I'm choosing to be the way that I am.

That situation literally took me from a mindset shift of things happening TO me to things happening FOR me. Everything I see is a blessing and it's my job to figure out how. It was a monumental change in my life that I never would have done myself and I have found over and over again, in my life, God has trimmed my branches for me when I refused to do it myself. Now, because of that, I'm much more likely to do it myself. And I'm much more likely to move faster and listen. Because I know my only regret when He has to do it for me was I should have done it sooner myself. I would have gotten the relief and joy and whatever was behind the next door, if I had just done it then.

But I see all of those moments in gratitude now that He's willing to help lead me to the decisions I should have been making all along.

Q&A

Jana: So, what is your coconut milk?

Kim: For me, it was the ability to grow my agency from locally known to internationally known. This attracted a buyer for my marketing firm, which allowed me to sell it and start our coaching business. So it was really a big detour I was about to make, not that far after all of these things happening. But I had to actually get on the exit ramp, and I was never going to go on my own, so God put up a detour, forcing me to the side so I could go in a completely different direction.

Jana: Did you find that you had to go inside a little deeper to make that happen?

Kim: I did, but for me, it wasn't inside. It was more connecting with my faith and trusting that the calling wasn't an accident. When I finally connected with what I knew I was being called to do, it became so much easier. And it's funny, because I look back on it and think, "How long did you struggle with listening to the voice?" Now I just listen to the voice because I'm like, duh, it's right all the time, so listen to it! And now that all of that is so much easier, I almost can't even remember what it was like to argue with it.

Jana: I am sure there will be readers of this book who can resonate with a business or personal life situation similar to yours, where there is betrayal and sometimes that betrayal can actually freeze you, where you don't know what the next step is. What advice would you give those readers?

Kim: Oftentimes, when those moments happen, we're typically holding on to something so tight that we can't let go a little bit, which would allow ourselves to be open to the opportunities that exist…if we would just let go. If something is taken away from you, think of it as a gift. Instead of thinking, "this happened to me," think, "why is this happening FOR me?" This opens ourselves to opportunities and incredible blessings.

I was just talking with a client earlier this week, and he was sharing that there was a major referral source that would bring him to all of the events and have him speak, and he would get all these clients from this group. He had a very strong relationship with this individual. He just found out (by seeing the promotion for the conference), that he's no longer the person, but his partner didn't even discuss this with him. It hurt him to the core, which makes sense, but I challenged him to look at it differently…as a gift. We are actually working on his lead generation now, which he wouldn't have done if this would have continued on and he never would have set up his company to be able to sell it because no one is going to buy his company if he just has one source for all leads.

So, I believe it's a gift that this happened and I could see that. Sometimes you need somebody else to see it for you if you're stuck right now. In these moments if you can't see how this is a blessing, that's when you need a coach, a friend, a mentor, someone you can trust to say, "Can you help me see how this is a blessing?" Because sometimes they can see that when we can't.

KIM WALSH PHILLIPS is the founder of Powerful Professionals, a business coaching and education company. She went from 32 clients to over 11,000 in less than a year and was recently named #475 in the Inc 5000 and is an MBA-free self-made millionaire.

Named "a must to read by those in business" by *Forbes Magazine*, she is the best-selling author of multiple books including *The Ultimate Guide to Instagram for Business* and *The No BS Guide To Direct Response Social Media Marketing*.

She's the behind-the-scenes secret weapon of some of the biggest names in business including Kevin O'Leary from *Shark Tank*, Dan Kennedy, Profit First Author Mike Michalowicz, Harley-Davidson, Hilton Hotels and High Point University and has spoken on stages beside some of the world's leading thought leaders including Tony Robbins, Grant Cardone, Barbara Corcoran and Gary Vaynerchuk.

She resides just outside of Atlanta, GA with her very tall husband and glitter obsessed girls and is fueled by faith, love, laughter and lots, and lots (and lots) of coffee.

GINA

All right. Let's do this. When I thought about this invitation, I thought about the word dreams. My 10-year-old client gave me a card that said, "My dreams are important and worth pursuing."

This got me thinking of "The Greatest Showman" movie and the song "A Million Dreams." When I was a young girl, I didn't even know what a dream was until my Aunt Lourdes asked me, "What do you dream?"

At the time, it was a question I had never received. And I thought, I have a dream? Yeah, you have a dream. She says, "What do you want in your life? What are you dreaming of?"

I said, "Well, I love to dance. And I don't know what my dream is, but I just love dance right now."

She said, "Maybe your dream is to be a dancer someday."

And I said, "I don't know."

I just remember being so excited about the question….and the attention she gave me in asking.

When I returned to school after seeing my Aunt, I started asking this question to my friends: What do you dream? Many of them dreamt about getting married and having kids and as they shared this, I started judging my own dream, yet getting married wasn't really in my heart. At that time, I didn't really desire to get married, I never saw a marriage, I saw myself dancing on stage and that is what lit me up at that time.

I remember going through life as a young girl with dance training being everything for me. That was my talent, that was my gift, that was my discipline, that was my everyday journey that lit me up. It was also what was helping me overcome scoliosis. I called dance, my love, my passion, yet I questioned whether this dream was right or wrong? I didn't feel my dream fit in and therefore almost compared it to others and then after a while I just knew.. dance was it, no matter what anyone else said or thought. I knew...

Fast Forward, I chose to go college for dance and follow my passion. And then one day, I had another dream. This idea of being in an intimate relationship. I began thinking of being in love someday. One day a gentleman showed up, and there I thought this is it, this is my new dream, this is love. It was challenging, it was complicated. It was hard, it made me nervous, it gave me anxiety, I felt out of my body, and felt like my head was spinning.

People say when you're nervous, you're right on point, you should be nervous, but I felt uncomfortable, uneasy, and at some point even inauthentic. And then, I thought of all the taglines out there, like "move into the uncomfortable." "If it's hard, push through it." "Go get it." "If you fall, get back up." "It's normal to feel nervous." "Relationships are supposed to be hard."

Those outside taglines and words I heard from others, made me feel like I was doing the right thing. So because it was hard, because it was challenging, because I was nervous, because I was out of my body, I must be in love, right? This is what being in love is supposed to be, right? I saw myself shifting from my dance dream a bit, and began obsessing over this love. Or at least the idea of being in love, or the idea of Prince Charming or the idea that relationships are supposed to be tough.

I graduated college in 2002, with my BFA and I went to Las Vegas with my dreams to be a professional dancer. I was so excited to have auditioned for a show and made it. During the transition of moving, I knew in my gut that this person I was with was not supposed to come with me. I knew in my gut this was not in alignment and I knew knew knew knew knew that....and didn't know how to choose that. So I declined 'the offer of my intuition' that was guiding me, and did what I knew how to instead. I pushed, I made it work, I kept the struggle going.

Four years go by, and I am in this cycle of hardship, challenge, abuse, and fear. I felt very uncomfortable and was living in what I would call complete darkness. And I didn't know how to get out. Dance was still very present in my life, thank God, and that kept me moving and going and auditioning and kept me out of my home at times and away from this relationship, however I didn't know "why" I was choosing this life of abuse and of fear. My belief systems in my head were so strong, that I felt I was supposed to make it work in everything I did.

So many people hear that you're supposed to make it work. If it's challenging, you can push through it. Give it another try. Well, maybe if you try this, then that. This circle of an idea that maybe just maybe someone will change or this will work out eventually kept playing in my mind again and again. As a creative artist, I became so infatuated with this idea of what love was supposed to be that I was actually living and choosing fear again and again and again in my mind, my body, my soul, my relationships, my career, my home, etc. This led to a lot of anxiety, pressure, outside influence, and unhealthy habits.

Here is when it shifted: I call these 'angelic offers'. My dear friend shared, "Gina, you're not yourself." "Gina, this isn't what a relationship is supposed to be about." Or "G, what do you want with your life because this doesn't have to be it?" All of these angelic messages and/or questions kept coming to me and I still kept declining the offers. Until…

My family was going through a hardship when my cousin Michael, 7 years old, was diagnosed with a rare form of leukemia. I began watching my family deal with hardship and pain from a distance as I was living in Las Vegas and they were in New York. I kept thinking about them and wishing there was something I could do from afar that could help them. I remember my grandmother teaching me about prayer and so I began to pray. As I began talking to God and asking for help, I also began to ask God to help me help myself and be able to get out of this relationship. I needed a sign.

The day my cousin ascended, something shifted inside my spirit. There was a new strength and a new sense of courage that I felt that I had never felt before. I flew home to see my family and my Aunt Lourdes, the same Aunt that asked me about my dreams, handed me a check for $2,500. She had put it in my hands, looked me in the eyes, and said, you know exactly what to do with this, and I did.

I landed back in Vegas, and I went and put a deposit down on my own apartment. I finally accepted the "angelic offer." I made a choice I had never made before and I felt so grateful that my intuitive Aunt was a guide for me in this lifetime helping remember my dream, and why I was here.

One month later, I booked a dance agent in NYC and moved across the country to pursue my dance dreams in the big apple. I became a Radio City Rockette and more, and then moved on to becoming an ICF Professional Coach. I wanted to help others pursue their dreams and yet I knew I was also meant to do this. Throughout my journey of becoming a coach, I knew I had to first look within my own being and heal and love the parts of me on all levels before I felt I would be able to coach others. I had to look back and see all the times I declined the many 'angelic offers' that were showing up as messages and messengers. I began to wonder how many others were declining these offers too.

What I learned is that the 'angelic offers', also known as 'God whispers' are like the universe's messages that are coming to us in a variety of ways 24/7. They come in all forms and in ways that we can receive. Sometimes they are through a person, on a license plate, a billboard, through a text, maybe even in a book, through animals, nature, feelings, our ancestors, magazines, and more. I am wondering what angelic messages you as the reader are declining and/or receiving right now? Are you listening and taking action or are you declining them like I did for years and years until a trauma experience woke me up to change?

What I didn't mention to you before was that when I moved to NYC to live my dance dreams my body broke out in a rash that no doctor was able to help me with. I had it for a year until the angelic message came in three times, to see this woman named Karen who was a constitutional homeopath. My first session with her completely changed the way I saw my past. She said you are not here to heal who you are today, rather you are here to heal from what happened to you in the past. As we began exploring my past relationship in Las Vegas, she went on to share that my body needed a homeopathic remedy that is given to people who are "raped" emotionally, physically, spiritually, and mentally. When I heard these words, I began to cry. I started blaming myself and being angry that I lived with such abuse for so many years. And then the angelic message appeared: you are safe and loved, and what you learn here is part of your purpose in teaching and helping others. The day after I took my remedy, the rash went away and never came back. I don't know about you, but I was SOLD! This inner discovery stuff, holistic approach, past healing journey is worth every penny in my pocket. I knew then I was on my way to learn more and dream bigger.

I thought I would be single for the rest of my life after that experience and I clearly was not interested in dating ever again until in my coaching program we began to create a vision and learn ways to build one that was in alignment with my soul. I was fascinated by this process and fully stepped into the unknown which meant I was open to receiving new information that had proven to be successful. Shout out to Leadership That Works, Coaching for Transformation in 2011.

What had been a dream of my young friends in grade school, was now becoming a part of my vision. I desired a soul partner and knew it was time to include that desire in my life. For so many years, dance was it and the only vision I could see, and when I learned how to create a whole vision, I was applauding or in show mode we call that a standing ovation. I felt so alive, connected, and inspired seeing what my soul really desired. I could recall that moment right now so well. It's as if my entire being did a 360.

So, fast forward to 2016 when a friend says, what would it feel like to go on a date with Dr. Stella? I knew right then and there that this angelic message felt different. I didn't know how, I just felt right now. I was in the moment of what this message felt like versus the idea of what it was going to be like.

Our first hug was that touch when you know, you know. My Aunt Mickey had shared with me one day that I would know by the way I felt his touch. It was the most calming, loving, present, and secure feeling I had ever felt from another human being. I can recall that moment in my body right now and I can feel that same sense of pure hearted love. Some call that a "match made in heaven." I can say in reference to this book that David is my coconut milk. LOL.

You know, each one of us has our own journey. I share with people all the time, especially my youth clients, that each one of us has dreams that are planted inside of us, some call it our souls calling and it's unique to each one of us. I've lived a lot of my dreams, and I am 42 years old as I write this. I have also declined many many angelic offers along the way that would have helped me live these dreams with a lot more ease, joy and fun, however I am now a teacher to many on how we can live our dreams and purpose, the ones that are for us, with more ease, joy and fun too. You see, I have turned my pain into a purposeful lifestyle and help others do the same too if this is what they are dreaming.

Learning about myself on all levels has been the greatest gift.

For me, this has been the key to being able to see and embrace my coconut milk being David, because it wasn't something I was able to imagine for my life right away and it showed up. There are times in life when we know things and times in life we do not.

What I knew after living my dance dreams was that my soul was here for transformation. It was here to help others and the world. I knew knew knew my soul was here for that. That is why I am here right now on this planet. I am sure of it.

What has happened at times in my life is this tug of war between ego and soul. It's the fear versus love. Pain is the resistance to love, so when I experience pain, I know somewhere I am creating excuses around love, loving myself, and loving others.

Q&A

Jana: That was amazing. Amazing. Thank you for sharing that. So why this story now?

Gina: I love love love loving David. People comment all of the time on our soulful partnership, seeing this pure hearted unconditional love. We know we are being the example of what's possible for others in their conscious relationships. Both David and I did not see this example growing up, so we both discovered this possibility along our journey. We know the universe has gifted us this sacred love so we can share it with the world.

Before I came to share my story with you, I asked David. "Babe, if you heard the title *When Life Gives You Lemons . . . Drink Coconut Milk*, what story would I share?

He said right away, I am getting for you to share your journey about being in an abusive relationship, and then meeting me. And I said, "oh babe, so you're my coconut milk, huh!? And he said, "that's right."

David is so intuitive, and he is so present with everything and everyone, that when I ask him something, I know it's exactly what I need to hear at that moment. I trust it, I know it, and it is a gift that I am grateful for each day.

Jana: How did you find yourself? Did you have an eat, pray, love journey where you traveled? What are some things you did in that phase of your life?

Gina: I mentioned a brief part of this earlier however it was the beginning of me loving myself.

When I left my previous relationship and moved to New York City, I ended up having a rash on my body that was not going away for a full year. I told you about Karen earlier. I started working with her in 2008 and she is still a part of my personal well being each month. She was the catalyst in my choice to walk the holistic pathway.

After that, I enrolled into a life coaching program in New York City through the ICF. It was called Leadership That Works. An embodiment program and very heart-centered and on the first day they said, you think you're here to coach others, however you're here to personally transform yourself so you can then be able to coach others. I knew I was exactly where I needed to be.

Fast forward 11 months later after I graduated, I did have my eat, pray, love moment. I bumped into my old ballet teacher in NYC and she was looking for a teacher to teach dance in Sardinia, Italy. The angelic message was crystal clear, and off I went on a one way ticket to Italy.

I really am so grateful for everything in my life. I thank God and the Universe each day and like they taught me in Italian, *grazie mille*, a million thanks. It's like the song I mentioned above, A Million Dreams. Imagine if every person walking the planet gave a million thanks each day. What else is possible!?

Along my journey I know I have shown up on purpose. I know that what's for me will not pass me by. I know that as I continue to learn about me on all levels, I will continue to love more of myself and others. I have a team of people I work with monthly to keep my wellness in mind, body and soul at its peak performance.

Jana: It's interesting how by design of the environment and the society we've grown up in, if you get a trainer, that trainer helps you with your physical health. If you have a coach, that coach helps you with your mental fitness, the emotionality and then maybe you access a spiritual guide. So you have these specific people for specific parts of your life. But what I've heard you so beautifully put together is that it's a mix and match for you. You found a way to go multi-dimensional with these people, no matter if it was the physicality of a trainer or bringing that holistic health of your homeopath together. Can you talk to us a little bit about that?

Gina: Thanks for being aware of that. I say, "My body of work has been my body of work." What I have learned and experienced in my life has become my way of contributing to others. As I sit here today, and I look at my clients and my programs, or the workbooks I've created for people, I know I am capable of walking people home to themselves on all levels. Coaching taught me about wholeness and when I began hiring many people for myself, I was inspired to become that one coach that was able to help others on all levels, not just one level. I LOVE LOVE LOVE being able to offer that.

To choose to be the one-stop shop for people is rewarding and also helps them financially. When I began my inner journey, I didn't know how I was going to afford it, I mean it paid off. I wanted to create a business that was accessible for people especially our youth, since youth is a huge part of my passion. Whether it's mental, physical, emotional, or spiritual, I can teach them. I love teaching!!

For those of you reading this, when you're choosing a mentor, or a coach or a teacher, and they haven't done it yet themselves, be mindful of your choice. In business and coaching, we get all these offers all the time. You scroll on Instagram, and you scroll on Google, and there's offers everywhere. However, what's the angelic offer, or God whisper offer you are called to receive? I encourage you to trust in the angelic messages or offers that are showing up for you and are for YOU. When we know ourselves on all levels, it is easier to know the exact offer that's now or next. I love teaching my clients how to know how to discern the many choices out there.

Jana: You frame them as these angelic offers, because not every offer that comes your way is wrapped in that angelic energy. There's contrast in our life. These distractions are purposefully put in front of us, so that maybe we don't make those shifts to something new.

What are those belief systems that don't serve us, or the ones that bubble up from the past? Like, do I have the time? Do I have the money? Do I have the support? I've never succeeded in this before, what's different now? Gina, one of the things that I've taken away from our time today is just how you've shown over and over through your story how this wasn't your fastest path to happiness. There was lots of meandering and there had to be. So thank you for all of that.

Gina: In my past, I didn't know how to feel happiness quickly or get to my purpose path with ease and joy and NOW I do. It's easy and I love love love that it is easy and fun and loving.

Wellness Educator GINA PERO teaches the art of life mastery in mind, body and soul. Through her extensive education, and her own life-altering experiences, Gina has inspired audiences worldwide for the past 20 years. At a young age and with determination and a fiery spirit, Gina overcame debilitating scoliosis to live her dreams as a professional dancer. During the height of her illustrious dance career as a Radio City Rockette, Gina suffered a brain and spinal injury in 2009, giving her yet another obstacle to overcome. By embarking on her recovery, Gina was on a mission to learn about the brain and body on all levels. Through her extensive education, certifications, and soul business, her holistic approach to life and wellness inspire the world. She currently resides in Las Vegas, has a full time coaching and speaking business, leads The Peroettes Personal Development Dance Community with a mission to turn the light up in the world, and is the Director of The Las Vegas Holistic Center alongside her soul partner Dr. David Stella. To know more about Gina, visit ginapero.com.

DR. ANITA

I was on this path of really believing that I would be a Marriage and Family Therapist and an Organizational Psychologist for the rest of my life. I had no plans of ever becoming a speaker, or an author, or publisher or a TV producer. That was nowhere near a dream, a fantasy, or desire in my life. However, there's this quote that says, "When you make plans, God laughs." I had all these different types of plans for my life. I had planned on being a minister's wife, I had planned on being a mother, I had planned on traveling the world and maybe having my own private practice as a therapist. I had no other intentions for anything else.

In 2011, I got promoted at a state university. Then, within six months of my promotion, I got laid off. So, instead of being able to go back to my old job that had been filled with someone else, I was released. Now, my first thought was, oh, no problem, because I've always been blessed with being able to get a job. And, I didn't really want to go back to the old one anyways. Well, three months turned into six months, turned into one year, turned into three years, turned into five years. By that time, I began to panic. Because the dream that I had for myself, the goals that I had set for myself, had now changed dramatically.

As you can imagine, I was living my life, making really good money, in the process of buying a brand new home, and planning on getting married to the man of my dreams. Then, suddenly everything crashed and burned all at the same time. It was very difficult because I didn't understand. I've been a good little Christian girl following all the "rules" doing what was expected of me. Firstly, as a black woman,

I had to work a little bit harder than most. Then it all disappeared. When I lost my job, my money started to disappear. I lost my home, I ended up having to move back home with my mother. How embarrassing is that? I was 42 years old when I had to move back home with my mom.

Then it got worse. I ended up having to move away because my mom had started to develop onset dementia, and that was a huge shock. Then my father died. Then the love of my life disappeared. Then I got really, really sick. So, it was just loss after loss, and trauma after trauma. By 2017, I was so confused. I had no idea who I was anymore, where I was going, what kind of life I was supposed to live. All the dreams and goals and my desires that I had for myself, had just dissolved and disappeared. There's a passage in the Bible that says a "hope deferred makes the heart sick." I had lost all hope. Because, at that point, here I am, a highly spiritual, highly ambitious, highly driven person who has accomplished so much in my life. And then, all of a sudden, the dreams and the goals that I had disappeared, and I didn't know what else to do. The reason being was, I had built so much of my worth and my identity on what I did, and not necessarily on who I was or am now.

My value had come from my accomplishments and didn't know it because in my mind and environment had basically convinced me that that's the only way I would be accepted and maybe even unconsciously, loved.

In 2019, things started to turn around. I had another major loss at that time that actually put me in the position where I was homeless. When people look at my life and what I've accomplished they have truly no clue that behind the scenes it's been hell. Meaning, I was homeless, I didn't have a home. I was living from one friend's couch to the next, and even staying at a few hotels for a while trying to figure out, how did I get here and how am I going to make it? I couldn't go tell my mom this because she wasn't doing well. As I said before, she had just started to develop onset dementia. My brother had just lost his wife, so he was just disconnected and he didn't have the energy or the space for what I was going through. And, it was weird asking for help when I was always the person that people came to. It was in these experiences that I learned and realized that I'm not good at asking for help, and I definitely wasn't good at receiving.

So, over time, I began to learn the power of surrendering. I think so often people believe that surrendering is just about letting go, and just throwing up your hands and saying, whatever. However, what I learned about surrendering is that it's really about faith. Surrendering for me was and still is all about truly trusting in God, source, spirit, in the universe, whatever word you want to use. I'm going to use the word God. Learning a deep lesson in trusting in God and truly even trusting in myself that I am worthy of more is a lesson that so many of us have to be willing to learn. Now, it took me a long time to get this because it's one thing to know it in your head, and understand the meaning of the words, but it's a whole other truth to embody the understanding of surrendering so that it resonates in your whole being.

I had to go through this journey of being broken, my own death and dying process in order to learn how to give myself permission to feel. With a background as a psychologist, I was so used to handling everyone else's feelings, so much so that I didn't realize how much I wasn't handling my own. I always thought of myself as being very intuitive, very discerning, even psychic, if you will. And yet, I had no clue how disconnected I was from myself. Despite having a background in ministry, as a therapist, and an organizational psychologist, I lost myself in just focusing on everybody else. Especially, as a woman of color, most often we are raised to think that it's not about you and/ or you are here for everyone but yourself. I grew up in a single family home where my mother had that belief system, so of course I learned that from her. In truth, I learned that from all the aunts in my family that believed if anything was going to get done, it had to be done by you.

2011 to 2018 were the most painful years of my life because I literally experienced back-to-back losses. Now I realize it was more of a metamorphosis process. I was actually being transformed from the inside out during that time. Old belief systems, old ideals, the way I had been raised, my value systems were all being challenged and transformed. In the process, I realized that I had been living someone else's dream for me. I'd been living what my family expected of me, even teachers who saw something in me and said, oh, you should do this or that. I unconsciously agreed because I didn't have enough real sense of my own self of my own power to go fully after what I really desired. Now, hear me clearly, it's not that I didn't have dreams and desires of what I wanted to be, I did. But, I also had certain words communicated to me in my environment that said, as a black woman, I would never be successful doing A, B and C. I was told I just needed to trust God, serve in the church, and that's it. And I unconsciously followed and believed it. It has served me well but has also created unconscious limitations.

During this time I kept receiving divine intuitive hits that confirmed that there was more. I was/am designed for so much more. This is the truth that I feel so many women are missing as part of them stepping into their divine feminine power. Those bigger dreams, goals, and desires inside every person were placed there, I believe, by God but do you really believe it? I believe God was allowing me to be challenged and saying, "Anita, do you really believe that all those dreams and all those desires, and all those big visions you have are just there just because? I put them in you, because that's what I created you for." When that finally clicked, and it took a while for it to click, I started to pursue my bigger dreams and goals and desires. Those bigger dreams, goals or desires lead me to becoming a co-author in a book called "Bold is Beautiful". My chapter was about "I

Am Enough" because my whole entire journey was really teaching me that I am enough, not based on someone else's description of my enoughness but based on my own. THIS means everything.

Those particular lessons really taught me the power of making the decision for your own worth. Decision is my favorite word. It means to reach a definite conclusion. That lesson and that experience started to really push me to make some powerful decisions about who Anita is. What is she on this planet to do? And how is she going to do it? Well, in that I discovered that I'm big, bold, and powerful. I like intense things. The bigger the mission, vision, goals, dreams and desires are, the better. That's how I tend to go after things. But I think I have convinced myself and shied away from it for a while.

Around 2019, I started to really pursue the things that I wanted. As I said earlier, I became an international best-selling author of several books. I started to become a guest speaker on several live radio shows, podcasts, and summits. I also started my own podcast that eventually opened the door for me to have my own TV channel on a major network with VoiceAmerica. And then I launched into my own digital magazines. Despite the fact that I had accomplished all these bigger things in my business, and they looked great on my resume, on my media kit, however, I was still hiding. One of the phrases that really dropped into my life or what I believed God was telling me was, "Anita, you're hiding in plain sight. You're very visible. People see you, they know you, they connect to you. But are you really showing up?"

By that time I was beginning to realize this, I was in the midst of experiencing another loss. I lost a second job. This happened twice now which meant I was missing something; I'm not learning the lesson that needed to be learned. Now, I really believe the lesson that I'm learning is, the more I believe in myself, the more I fall in love with myself, the more I deeply own my authentic truth, the greater my opportunity I will have to make a difference in the lives of others.

I'm finding that things just show up in my life so much easier than me having to make it happen. Because, for the longest time, I have been one who has made things happen. In that process you end up thinking, I have to continue to work hard, I have to be the one to do it. But when you are positioned, when you are called, when you are designed to make an impact in the lives of others, you will have experiences that cause you to surrender to God asking to be used in a way that makes a bigger impact. When we, as women, become convinced that our own worth is based on others' approval, and acceptance of us, we burn out quickly. We become overwhelmed. However, when a woman decides that she is truly enough, others will follow her lead. That's been another powerful lesson that I learned. Others will follow me or respond to me based on how I treat myself, whether I'm conscious of it or not.

If I were to break everything I've shared into points, I would say that the number one point that you really need to focus on is understanding your worth and value as a woman, and understanding it from a spiritual perspective, understanding it from an energetic perspective, and understanding it mentally and emotionally. Number two, you definitely have to have a community. You've got to have a sisterhood who will unconditionally and absolutely love you for who you are and will hold you accountable to your own stuff, your own shift, your own challenges and won't allow you to settle for less. Because I think too many of us as women have settled for less for far too long, especially as we've gotten older. We've just allowed things to be as they are. Well, they don't have to be. It's never too late to make a new decision to show up in your boldness, to walk in your audacity, to claim your queendom, to share your voice and to say that this year is all about me. And the third point is, you've got to be strategic. I am one who really believes in having a plan. Now, at the same time, as I said earlier, that quote of when you make plans, God laughs, I think there's something beautiful about having a plan, but also surrendering it and saying, here's the goal, here's the direction I want to go in. However, I also know that God, source, spirit, the universe, has something bigger for me. If you've got faith and you're working towards it, it's going to grow, it's going to expand, it's going to increase and it's going to change your life. So, those are the three things that I now live my life by.

This is the year, this is the season, and the time that we as women have an opportunity to be positioned to show up in a more powerful and in a dynamic way to live our highest and best life. No matter what experience we've gone through, it has all served a purpose to help us come to the fullness of who we are now, and who were called to be, and the impact on the legacy we're here to make in our own right, and for our family, for our community, and for the world. As hard as it has been, I wouldn't change anything. I am so grateful for every loss that I've gone through. I'm so grateful for every lesson that I've had to learn. I'm so grateful for the tears that I cried, for the friends who showed up and supported me, for the ones whom I was able to speak into their life when they had some sort of a major loss, and say, "This is not the end of your story. This is just another stepping stone to help you become stronger, more powerful, bold, and more ready to show up in your greatness as a woman. This is your opportunity to take your life back and live full-on for yourself.

Q&A

Jana: Anita, you offered our readers so much goodness by way of lessons learned. But I want to ask you, what is the coconut milk for you?

Anita: The coconut milk for me, and for every woman I hope reads my story is that you must know that You Are Enough…You Always Have Bee…and You ALWAYS Will Be. You just have to decide that this is true. Once you decide that that's true, everything else around you will follow your lead. That is the foundation that I absolutely believe in.

Jana: In those moments where you feel like you are back in elementary school playing freeze tag and your arms are out and you're calling for someone to come and 'unfreeze' you because you want to run around again, what is one actionable item that a woman could actually do today, as she's reading your chapter?

Anita: The psychologist in me loves the idea of always telling my clients to journal. Write it out. There is power in writing it out, power in how it affects your brain, power in how it affects your emotions. And again, if you're looking at the good book, the Bible even tells you that when you write the vision down, or the dream down, it causes the angels to see what you really want and will bring it to pass, if you will. And yet, I wasn't one to journal. I talked about it a lot, shared it all the time in my sessions, but didn't do it myself. Then, when I actually started to learn the power of journaling, or scripting for myself and my future, and writing the words "I am enough" over and over again, and it became my tagline, it started to change the way my brain's neurological pathway was geared towards understanding and deepening that truth.

I am a firm believer of journaling right before you go to bed. Now, if you have to journal something negative, release it in journaling during the day. That way, right before you go to bed, you can journal what's been positive, filled with gratitude, and surround it with love. Or if the only thing that you can journal right now is, ``I am enough", or say with your name, "I, Anita Michelle Jackson, am enough," once you write that over and over again, trust me, within 60 to 90 days you will feel dramatically different.

Jana: Is there anything left unsaid that is just waiting to get out before we end this chapter?

Anita: The image that came to my mind when you were asking that question was a burning phoenix. When a phoenix is going through a rebirthing process, it burns to ashes and then it goes through a rebirth itself. It brings itself back to life as this new and more empowered creature. I want to say to every woman, regardless of whatever experience you've gone through in your life, even the experience that you thought would take you out, the beautiful thing is you're not out yet. You're still here. You're reading this book, and you're a part of this community. This is your time to rise like the phoenix, to be transformed into something glorious and beautiful and powerful.

Every time you make a decision, reach a conclusion, on the inside, your heart says this year, this season, this time, this day, this hour, this minute, this second, I can do and be and have everything God created me to have. This is POWERFUL. Every woman has power, it's always been inside of her. Now it's just time for her to realize it and release it fully without fear but with faith in God and herself...for such a time as this!

DR. ANITA M. JACKSON is the founder and CEO of The Unlimited Woman and AMJ Productions and Publications. She is fast becoming a sought-after feminie transformational mentor, speaker, leader, and success coach within the feminie empowerment movement.

With over 26 years of experience in mental health, personal, spiritual, and business development that includes leadership, organization, and strategic planning. Dr. Anita works with women internationally in helping them become limitless and successful in life, business, wealth and so much more.

DEBBIE

A few years ago, I ended a 14-year relationship. Ah, my heart was broken. And I entered into what we all know as the dark night of the soul. What am I going to do with myself? Here I am, I'm almost 50 years old, and I'm alone. So I went to live with my kids. I have two grown boys and a granddaughter. And their father.

We were married when I was 19 years old, and had my first son at 20. So I was really young. We hadn't been together since I was 25. And we are not together now, either. But I went ahead and moved in, knowing that he was really, really sick. My youngest son had put aside his life at the age of 21 to take care of him. I was able to dig deep into the work and start looking at my life and gratitude and how that really functions in my life. It was when I first started learning about spirit, or so I thought I first started learning about spirit.

I'm going to give you the most life-altering experience I can share. That is the moment that you watch somebody take their last breath. On that fateful night, we knew he was not doing well. He had to go to the emergency room and they admitted him. We had to have that conversation with the doctors that it was done. We knew this time was coming. So I sat up all night with him, and we listened to his favorite music - Led Zeppelin. And it was spectacular. Because I promised him that he wouldn't be left there alone. It's pretty neat to be best friends with a person you have children with, even when you're not together. I highly encourage conscious parenting.

The next morning, my sons and I knew that we had to take him off life support, which we did. We put on our wedding song, which is "All Of My Love" by Led Zeppelin. He gently took his last breath as we stood with him. When I think about this, this moment in time, and its preciousness that my children and I experienced together, the one thing I can say is, you never realize how important and precious life is until you help somebody leave.

Gratitude and grief come when you look at your own life. The gift that he left me was not just my children and my granddaughter, but it was the essence of life. It was to breathe, it was to pull out of that dark night of the soul and quit feeling sorry for myself like I'm some victim and this life happened to me and not for me because that was wrong. Well, it wasn't wrong because there is no right or wrong - let me scratch that - but to appreciate the essence of all that is for what it is, and the preciousness of it. Look at life as being what it truly is, the moment, the present, the beingness. We are human beings, not doings. And that's what he gave me at that moment.

What I took away from this experience was the appreciation of life, of the planet, of everything that is living. Everything has a beautiful meaning. It is working for us and not against us. That's what I took away from it. I will always be eternally grateful for that experience.

Being a single, older female coming out of a long relationship, getting back on my feet was quite a journey. This journey took me into a place where I was getting ready, I knew I was going to need to move again. I remember I was driving in the car and I was listening to a song. I thought to myself, it's time to do things differently. If I continue doing things the same way, it won't change in the direction that I needed to change into. This came into the unknown. I have to trust the unknown, trust these facts that I'm going to step out and I don't know where I'm going, I don't know how it's going to be done. I don't know a thing, but I know I'm gonna have to trust that.

My boys were having a tough time with everything that had happened. They were in Europe at this point. They were not around, and it's really just me. I'm all I have. I just have me. That's it. There's nothing else. It's just me. I literally was stripped of everything so that I could sit with myself. Now, sitting with yourself is a really good thing, especially when you've got to trust the unknown because the only thing that I have to look at is me. This allowed me to stop pointing my fingers at anybody for being the cause of the creation that I had made. I was responsible now for everything because accountability is huge when you're stepping into the unknown. The unknown requires that you strip everything from you that you've ever known, and be willing to trust that, take that step and take it boldly.

I was driving in my car and I lived near the beach. I opened the sunroof on my car, and this song by Christopher Cross comes on and it's called "Sailing." I love music and there's always something about music. In fact, this is an insight to whoever's reading this right now. When a song is playing, if you hear a song and it means something to your heart, go read the words because I call that 'spirit DJ is in the house'. So, go and listen. Listen to the message that is coming through and mine was Christopher Cross' "Sailing."

This was the first time this overwhelming emotion came through me. And that was the God's spark that said, ahh, and I was just here. I just sat with it and listened to the message, and listened to God singing a love song to me. And that, wow, oh, he/she energy, whatever you want to call it. God sang this love song to me and it wasn't even a love song. It was just freedom. The essence of the song meant to me was freedom.

I kept following on this journey, this journey of trusting the universe. And it was some wild stuff. It was some wild, wild stuff. I'd wind up in the desert, because one morning I woke up and I heard spirits say you need to go meet Joan of Angels out in the desert. Okay, Joan, I'm going to come out and meet you in person off the cuff. That led to another beautiful relationship. That just kept happening over and over. I would meet these incredible people, including my best friend. So much incredible stuff was happening. And I was trusting it, and I was just in this space where I knew that every possibility could happen. I didn't believe that I had to stop living in order to survive. I said I'd rather live and thrive, however that's going to look, but it required trusting and having no answers.

That's the other thing. There are no answers. My life has no answers. I can't tell you from one minute to the next what that's going to be. But I do trust it. I trust whatever I'm stepping into. So, here I am listening to this song, and it carries me on and I go meet all these wonderful people. And I love that. But my being is not done with the bigger challenges. I had one more to go through. The reason that I go through experiences, I don't know about you, but this is what happens for me, I need to be empathetic and compassionate for every human being on the planet. At this point in my life, I have experienced virtually everything that we could call trauma. If you want to start from childhood, or you want to move it all the way forward, I could guarantee there's virtually hardly anything that I haven't yet experienced. I'm just really grateful that I have had all of the experiences that I've had because it has truly taught me empathy.

But I wasn't done. You already know I can't be done. I'm never gonna be done. Well, this time was a stinker. I found myself living on a ranch at a cabin while I was working and doing my thing. My kids, like I said, weren't having a really great time. I got a phone call from one of them. I've always told my children, I don't care what it is that's going on, if it gets tough, you need to call me. I don't care what it is, we will figure it out together. So I get the phone call, and my youngest had attempted suicide with drug use.

Spirit just kept plucking me. Plucking me. If you've ever been plucked before, if you've ever been plucked out of somewhere and transplanted, it's because you need to be transplanted. It's because where you're at is not where you're supposed to be. Stop thinking you need to hold onto it so hard because it's going to just get harder.

It's not going to get any easier the more you fight it. This is how you also learn to get into the unknown and go with the flow. I had a conversation with my son and I said, well, my best friend owns a treatment center. You can make a choice. I'll give you the bus tickets and you can come here and get it together. So that's what he did.

People have huge things happen, natural disasters, fires and earthquakes and tornadoes, talk about devastation. It's not devastation. Sometimes you have to have everything undone in order to rebuild it properly, the way that suits the life that you're wanting to live. Me losing everything allowed for me to understand what that meant to have compassion and to be able to look at somebody and say, now we get to rebuild it. But to understand heart to heart what that feels like, you can't know something until you know it. That's pretty much what it was. I always say without your dark, you wouldn't know your spark. Without any of this, how would you know? So here, my son and I are asking, what are we going to do?

People were asking me, Hey, how are you doing this right now? And I'm like, what do you mean, how am I doing this? What's my option? You do it with joy, gratitude and faith and love and trust and all of that knowing the universe is transporting you right now. You're being transported and allow the shift to happen. Just allow it. Allow the flow. I stopped being attached to the outcomes. I stopped interfering with the process and allowing that to happen. Where other people are looking in, going, oh, this is so horrible, while I'm in there going, it's life, however we choose it. And apparently I'm choosing this, to restart it. But all of that stuff didn't matter. What mattered was that my son was okay. He actually went into conscious recovery with TJ Woodward, which really changed everything. And today, he's thriving. That was three years ago.

We didn't know where we're going next, but we wound up on a ranch in San Diego with horses. More healing is happening. Then we get plucked up again and we wind up north, near Napa

Valley. More healing is happening, more healing is happening. I'm working on my stuff. That's all I care about at this point is learning, compassionate communication, which I've been doing for about five years. All I care about is healing. That's all we're doing is healing and trusting. About eight months after that, we came back to visit Southern California, where I'm from, and where we wanted to be. Sure enough, I bought a car. The process was easy peasy lemon squeezy, there was no issue. It was the easiest thing I've ever done. The house that we got, and where I live now, easy peasy lemon squeezy. There was no effort. The benefit of trusting the universe is that the fruits of the tree keep nurturing the soil. You are the soil. Keep nurturing you. Keep nurturing that which you are. Quit worrying about what it should look like because what I've discovered is, it's never what you think it's going to look like. It's never what you think it's going to be. It's never that. It's better. It's better than anything you could have ever imagined. Anything you could have ever thought of, it's better. Sometimes we have that part where we have this thing, and we see the grandiosity of it, we're like, oh, yeah, we could do that. But we still don't know how good it can actually be.

In my case, I didn't have enough faith in myself, and I didn't trust myself. I also looked at myself and went, I'm not worthy. There was that underlying piece. The only way to get rid of that was to change it. Now, there was something I discovered along the way. One, there's not anything I actually need. If I want it, I'm gonna have it. But there's not anything I actually need. What I know is that the only thing that has ever been important is people. It's you. It's me. It's our children. It's people. It's the human. There's nothing else in this world that matters. Cars, the houses, the things, the stuff, and I've got stuff now, I'm even buying a house now. I'm married now. Doesn't matter. Only the people matter.

I woke up this morning and I started thinking about, who can I reach out and tell them I'm grateful for them? I started picking people to reach out to say, I'm so grateful for you. Gratitude is a life changer. I'm going to promise anybody, if you practice gratitude for 30 days, you will see a shift in your life. If you don't believe me, go read the book by Dr. Robert Emmons, "Thanks." He studied gratitude for 35 years, and in 35 years has proven scientifically that it alters the chemistry of our brain. It also alters productivity in businesses. It alters productivity in your own life. Gratitude is the ooey, gooey essence of everything. It's what holds stuff together. It's what moves things along. Gratitude is a vibration. It's a frequency. It's a state of being. It's not just a word, but an actual feeling that comes up. It's a wow, thank you.

The one thing I had to learn was, no matter what I went through in the last five years, no matter what I've gone through in the last seven years since we broke up, not in one of those cases did the world do this to me. Learning to be accountable was the best thing I've ever done in my entire life. It's accountability, it's truly sitting there and owning you. I don't mean accountability where you beat yourself up. That's ridiculous. You've done enough of that. Stop it already. Stop it. Just quit it. Accountability means, I see this, I think I want to change it. I'll give you an example. I could have an argument with somebody, and in that argument, all of a sudden, I realize we are arguing because of my approach from the very beginning. I started this conversation and it requires stepping away from my ego.

All of these things I learned during this process of everything coming undone. I see so many when everything's coming undone and they start freaking out. I'm going to encourage you to stop. Just stop it. You've done that long enough and it's not working. The only thing that's going to change it is getting grateful for what's happening in your life right now. It's just as simple as that. I swear to God, it's that simple. It's so simple to get into gratitude. It's so simple to appreciate somebody or something. I have the best hack for getting out of your victim, and feeling sorry for yourself and sitting there crying because your boyfriend broke up with you, your husband or wife cheated on you. So here's the hack. Be of service. Do something for somebody else, period. It takes no money to do something for someone. Back when my children were little, I created a group called The Circle of Friends. We took 25 sixth-graders one mile every Friday to the convalescent home. I went to the convalescent home, got approval from the district, so everything was just awesome. We even went to a bird farm and on the way we'd have this conversation about how your time is the most expensive commodity you've got and how you spend it is extremely important. The fact is, you can give your time to somebody. That is what it's about.

I have pictures of my kids learning to play poker from an older gentleman from the convalescent home. It was precious, they loved it. But the idea is that if you are really feeling it, and you think life is beating me up, and oh my God, all these things have happened, I'm going to suggest and encourage finding somebody you could do something for. The reason for this is that it shifts the energy. It shifts what's going on. It shifts the neuroplasticity in your brain from being back here in the reptile area up into the frontal lobes and connecting our heart conscious space. That's where the energy flows. It isn't back here in the past, in the ego. Things that are happening presently aren't happening back there. They're happening here in front of us. But we spend so much time looking behind and living from that space that we forget that right here in front of us is the only thing that matters. It's the only thing that's important. When we are of service to somebody else, that right there is all you need to do. Your life will shift. Because it's the law of reciprocity. The Law of Reciprocity is the ebb and flow of life, give and take, give and take, and it just goes just like that. So, what do you want to give? What do you want to give out there? Don't tell me you don't have anything to give. We just talked about that. That's an excuse.

Let's talk about your excuses now. Anybody out there have any excuses? Because excuses are beautiful. All it is is fear. Because it's fear that holds us back. That's false illusions appearing real. And what is a false illusion period real? It is a trigger that hits from something that happens that makes us think that the thing is the way it is when it's actually not. Now, what I do is, I ask myself, is that true? Is that true? It's how I made it through all those nights and all those things. If a trigger hits and I'm by myself, is it true that I'm lonely? Or is it true that I'm alone? I found out that if you've made a habit, if you've created one, you can change it.

Go figure. There are a couple of other really big things too that I have to give all of you. Because I love giving away the things that I used, and I use today, to change everything. Another one was, there's no WIN in WHEN. There is no win in when, period. When I get this, I'm gonna do this. That doesn't mean you need to go out and start doing massive, massive things to make that happen. You do small, little steps every single day that build. You get momentum, you get flow. Procrastination is just the wife of when. That's all. That's it.

Our mind is so powerful. You want to know how I quit smoking? I'm gonna tell you how I quit smoking. First off, smoking was one of my crutches, it was one of my things back in the day. And I had to break up with my cigarettes. I broke up with them. I said, thank you for serving me. Thank you for being there for me. I really liked you. In fact, you know what, I really love you. I owned it, Why am I smoking? Because I dig it. Is it good for me? No. Should you probably quit? Yeah. So I was getting honest with myself. This is something called NLP, Neuro Linguistic Programming. It's repatterning our brain. I would thank them every single time I was puffing on a cigarette, looking ugly. I would tell them, thank you for being there for me, but we are really toxic for one another. We're going to need to stop. Then the beautiful day came, I put them down, and that was the end of the story. That literally happened just like that.

The key in all of these things here is that I'm appreciating, or

I'm grateful for everything that I'm looking at. The thing that we call bad, the thing that we judge, the thing that we read, or say, oh, we shouldn't have it that way, I look at it and say oh, yes, we should and here's how we can appreciate it in the most insane ways because that's not what we were taught. We were taught a behavioral pattern that was different from this. To own our stuff is the hardest thing anybody wants to do because everybody wants to hold onto their stories, and their stories are squat. Now, I told a story and it's always emotional for me.

Though I don't believe in death, I believe that it's just an exit out of our body into another energy form. That's not, I'm human. How can we love the imperfectly perfect human we are? How can you love more? How can you love and appreciate yourself to the nth degree because you are you? We're all perfectly imperfect. That's the point of being human. That's the point of feeling emotion. What's most interesting about what I've been sharing is that it's pretty consistent with letting go, not interfering, allowing flow, not interfering with life, and just letting things happen. Stepping into life rather than resisting life. Allowing that flow, that gentleness. Sometimes I can get hard on myself and I've caught myself. I've got an online business, I've got this going on and that going on and I did get my degree and I finished. But that human part will sneak up every once in a while and go, but you could do better. And I sit back and I hear that voice. I'm doing absolutely the best I can with what I've got.

About six months ago, I noticed I started getting really tired. I figured it was because I don't have a thyroid because I've had radiation, and I figured that's probably it. I was going through this physical thing that was happening. Then I had an emergency surgery and came out of that fine, except that I was still really, really tired. I found myself getting on myself because I was exhausted. I was getting things done, but at a snail's pace. And even before I realized what was going on, I remember sitting there and saying, I'm doing the best I can with what I've got, and that just has to be okay. It just has to be okay. Why? Because life is too short to waste your minutes and your time feeling like you aren't doing enough or you're not good enough, or you're not this enough, or you're not that enough. Especially if you're going through something physically that is tough.

I needed iron, I didn't have any iron. That's not new for me. I was born this way. It's something I've dealt with here and there. And now I'm feeling great. But now, I'm appreciating the fact that I went through this opportunity to see myself as perfectly imperfect, and love myself the way I was, and love me for who I am, even the 20 pounds I gained because I wasn't out walking. I am good the way I sit right now. I don't know and you don't know, we don't know if this is going to be anybody's last breath, last day. Nobody knows anything. We don't know that which is the unknown. So why are we not appreciating to the fullest nth degree the day that we're living in, the day that's in front of us, the day that we are in?

It's either going to be as simple as we make it or as hard as we make it. The choice is up to each individual based upon the individual, not on somebody else. I was a major people pleaser, so the hardest thing for me to see is when people are people pleasing. Don't do anything. Don't say yes when you mean no. Because if you say yes when you mean no, then you're going to possibly be at an outcome you don't want to be in. And that's when it's required for you to get real with yourself. Because every time I've said yes when I meant no, I didn't honor me, and I ended up in a situation where I would become fault-finding, grumbling, complaining, judging and a royal bitch.

I said yes and I really meant no, I don't want to do this. I don't want to do this, but I'm so afraid of telling them no because they won't like me. This goes back to your childhood trigger memory stuff. They won't like me, they won't be my friend, they won't whatever. Think back to your childhood. When I was six and seven, I was tall. I'm five-foot-ten. And I was taller than every child in my class and I got made fun of or whatever. I used to make up stories so they would like me. I hated not being liked. That trigger when you say yes, and you mean no, that trigger comes in and that is simply, I don't want to be not liked or I don't want to upset them.

Empathy and compassion in life teaches us that we can create a healthy boundary with the person who is asking you for something. The words "I am so appreciative that you have asked me to participate in an opportunity like this, but I cannot do that right now" are powerful. With no excuses, no anything. Just owning your own power, owning your own truth, that's all you need to do. But if you don't stop saying yes when you mean no, you're going to constantly be thinking the world is working against you and you're creating it. That's the thing. I created every aspect of everything in my life. Nobody did it for me, I did it. All of it. And people say to me, yeah, but what about my abusive husband? I've had one of those, a couple of those too. I understand. I created it. I created it because I said yes from the beginning. We're in everything because we said yes at some point. We said yes. I encourage looking at your yes, and really evaluate, does this honor me? Is this honoring me to that next level?

Start with the decisions you make that are private about yourself. Are you honoring yourself? Are you saying yes to yourself? Are you going to put something in your mouth today that's toxic? Are you going to honor the yes for you? Learn how to start telling yourself no, gently and passionately, so if it's necessary you can tell others no, gently and compassionately. I didn't learn all of this overnight, I learned it slowly over time. I've had a lot of experiences to pull from in order to experiment with other things because life is an experiment. I teach gratitude, Alchemy life experiments. It's all about that. But you don't have to take a course to do this. They're just kind of fun. The fun part you can do is just practice every single day. And the practice is the things you're grateful for, the people you're grateful for and what you're grateful for about yourself. How do you show up?

This journey of life has taught me to love myself fully, my imperfections, my wants to be perfection, but to love myself the way that I sit, to embrace the Goddess within me, the goddess of nature. The human that I am, but the spirit that I am, who chose to come here at this time, one of the most extraordinary times in human history. Well, at least the human history we know about so far. There are so many grand opportunities that are in front of you, in front of me, in front of all of us to live life compassionately, and empathetically. I can't stress enough how important other people are.

If we are too busy judging the human, we can't show up. Remember the Law of Reciprocity? The Law of Reciprocity is give and take. The Law of Reciprocity is what you put out will come back to you. Some people want to call that karma. It's just Universal Law. It's the way it is, it is the ebb and flow of life. What is it that you want to do? How are you going to show up for people? Showing up for yourself first, but then how are you going to show up for others? In everything I've ever been through, there's never been one experience I've had that didn't require some sort of compassionate empathy for me to either give to myself or to the people around me. And that's what it boils down to.

How do we choose to see our struggles? The struggle is because we're struggling, actually. When we allow it to start going, when we allow life to not be the struggle, when we just go with it, it's amazing how it flows. That includes me letting go of what I think somebody else needs to be doing. That includes my judgment of anything external, and I'm human, so I can get judgy. I'm getting better. In fact, I've noticed that I get judgy less and less, and when I do judge, it doesn't feel comfortable anymore.

I want to talk about curiosity. Curiosity is how you get out of judgment. When you become curious, what's real for another human being? This set of tools that I use, and it's one of my favorites, is the willingness to be curious. Are you willing to be curious? Ask yourself that when you see yourself judging another human being, and you see yourself wanting to think about whatever it might be, be curious. Remember that at one time, they were an innocent child who was just born into this world. How can you not be curious about them? How can you not be curious about the breath they take, the life they live, rather than judging it from an external viewpoint?

My son now has tattoos on his head. I see people stare at him a lot. He's also six-foot-seven. He looks like a Viking. He looks extraordinary. This is the same son we were talking about earlier. He has evolved by leaps and bounds. The same son who went through the tough stuff, he's just glowing up. It's spectacular. But now he's created the element of curiosity within him.

These are Marshall Rosenberg's tools, they are not mine. Marshall Rosenberg's nonviolent communication simply is the willingness to be empathetic. But, how do we get there by curiosity? By asking authentically curious questions. Are you willing to be accepting of whatever it is that somebody says? Because remember, that is their reality. Everybody's right, nobody's wrong. Because that's how they see it, it's not my job to change it. So, am I willing to be accepting of that, no matter what it looks like? And I have been challenged on this even recently.

In the long run, the only thing that matters is the breath that's coming out of another human being. It's not about anything else. Can I appreciate, not just accept? Go to the next level. Can I appreciate this person with whatever their opinion is, reality is, can I appreciate that person? Well, sure I can. They're human just like me. That's the only thing we need to know. Nothing else. That's it as far as I'm concerned.

Going further, we all just want to be loved. And that's really what this is about. All the things I've been through. Grief is love with no home to go to. You can't love so deeply and don't think you're not going to grieve. Everything is temporary. Believe me, I'm almost 55 years old. It's temporary. Nothing's forever or permanent except the love that you can hold within your heart conscious space. That's what you get to take. Everything else, forget it. So, why not start having fun?

On the list of things that you can do, and I challenge everybody, is also to acknowledge and recognize others for their accomplishments by using celebration. Let's celebrate each other, let's celebrate right now. Who could we celebrate? Think about that. Who can you celebrate today just for something they've accomplished rather than feeling envious because you aren't doing what you know you need to be doing? So you want to judge that as being envious because you're not stepping up to the plate. That's truth. Own it. Or whatever your truth might be, own whatever that is.

The true essence of the human being we can see during the most tragic events in the world. I am old enough to remember when 9/11 happened. My kids were in school. Parents like me took our kids out of school because we're like, whoa, we don't know what's happening. When you sit in there, you watch the human beings come out. There's not a question of separation any longer. We are one, we are not separated, we are always connected. My granddaughter, when she was four, recorded it on Facebook, she said, we are all connected by an invisible string. And we are. All of the experiences I've gone through, I share them because my hope is a person on the other side, the receiver of the messages I have, is going to be inspired to understand that there is another way to do this, that if what you're doing is not working, you can change it. You do not have to stay where you're at, you do not have to think you're stuck, you do not have to say, but I have a block. The block is you. There is no block, there is no stuckness if that's a word. There is not any of that. It's just a belief system. And as I have proven to myself, still a non-smoker, I can change a belief system, I can change a pattern, I can change a habit, I can change anything I so desire, because I am in control of myself. I control my brain, it does not control me. My body and me, we are in sync, we're jiving. I tell it what's up. It doesn't tell me what's up. Now, when it is telling me what's up, I have to learn to listen. Just like when I wasn't feeling well, and I had to have iron.

My first big awakening part of this was in 2003, when I had a hysterectomy and almost died and spent four weeks in the ICU. I came out of that about six months later, going, it's really as simple as nature. And that's what I'm feeling right now is to share about nature. To give you another simple tool that I love, I did this yesterday. I went outside and I put my feet into the grass and I just stood there and was just breathing. That's it. That's it. Nature is the harmony, it's the essence, it's the frequency of what we truly are, it's the essence of us. We all have a melody. In order to be in attunement with that melody, we must step out into nature. We must step out and become one with this universe because that's what we are. We must find the ground and touch Gaia and let it permeate through our soul, let it permeate through our being.

Remember the melody that is within you, because if you remember, and we all remember our melody, we are then singing in harmony. That harmonic flow is what allows life to truly grow. It's beautiful and it's amazing. You can make anything out of it. This book is all about making coconut milk out of lemons. We can make anything out of anything we choose. You are the most powerful being because you are you.

Q&A

Jana: Beautiful. You've given us so many sparks, as you call them. Through this, we are taking women through stories of turning lemons to coconut milk. What is the essence of coconut milk for you?

Debbie: Love. Love is the essence of everything. It's the ebb and flow of life.

Jana: Pretty simple.

Debbie: Actually, everything is really simple. We just like to overcomplicate it because we humans get bored. We would get bored in the house. Let me tell you, we get bored. If we had everything that we ever wanted, and we were sitting on that beach every day, looking at those waves, at some point, we're going to need to do something to keep expanding and to keep growing. Even if it's to get up and go on a walk, it doesn't matter. We don't just sit. We have to create. We're creators. That's what we do. Women are creators so go and create!

DEBBIE G. is a 6+ year veteran in the world of livestreaming and podcasts. She has interviewed people doing extraordinary work from the farthest reaches of the world. Her passion is teaching gratitude intelligence and compassionate communication skills to those seeking better relationships, first with themselves and then others. In conjunction with extensive studies in communications, which is never-ending (one cannot learn too much), there are her extensive years of personal work, experiences, and knowledge base of life. As her soon-to-be-released book says, "Without your dark, you wouldn't know your spark." She teaches from the heart of what life has taught, to reach the heart of her students, audience, readers, and you.

She is the founder of the explosive and forward-thinking Spirituality Gone Wild online platform. She is a Self-Love Breakthrough Coach who uses customized methods in the most loving way possible to produce results for her clients through the practice of Gratitude

Intelligence. She is the host and co-founder of Unify Women Rising and the popular Self Love Fest program.

As a trained energy worker, Debbie also provides unique experiences for her clients that are seeking a deeper spiritual connection within.

www.spiritualitygonewild.com and debbie@unify.org

REV. CARRIE-ANN

With my Angel Guide Oracle cards in hand, I asked my guides and higher self, "What story am I meant to share in this book?" The answer was crystal clear. "Talk about the past 10 years." Then I asked, "What lessons do we want to share with the readers?" I was inspired to pull three cards from the deck. The first one came out with "transformation," the second one was "self-acceptance" and the third one was "take charge and action." A very aligned card pull, considering that the past 10 years have been all about transformation, and what made the transformation possible was self-acceptance and taking charge of my life through action.

Sitting at my desk, I found myself staring off into space and saying, "How the hell did I end up here? How the hell did I find myself in this situation?" It was April of 2012, I was 40 years old and had spent the last 23 years of my life on a career path that hadn't brought me joy. I kept coming across blocks at work because I was focusing on making everyone else happy while I sacrificed my own happiness. I had been exerting all my time and effort into my job, which for the most part left me no time for a relationship or a life outside of work. I didn't know another way.

A couple of years earlier, I had begun to get my fitness and health under control. Prior to that, when I was happy, I would celebrate with food, and when I was upset or depressed, I would go through the drive-thru to get some fast food, or go to 7-Eleven and buy seven chocolate bars. Then, I'd hide in the car while I gorged myself, and then I'd throw the garbage in the dumpster before going inside. I had this belief that calories consumed in the car "don't count." I was also figuring out what emotional fears were holding me back because I thought once I knew that, that I would be happy. I was also trying breathing techniques and yoga to try to connect my mind and body with my soul. The only thing remaining that needed to change was my career.

I said to myself, "If I don't change now, I'll either be dead at 55 OR I'm going to be extremely overweight, miserable and I'm going to be alone." And I knew, from the depth of my soul, that if I didn't make a change, I was going to be a very unhappy person for the rest of my life. I didn't know what I wanted out of life, but I knew I didn't want that. In that moment, I realized the devil I knew was way worse than the devil I didn't know. I had to accept that where I was, I didn't want to be, and try to figure out where I wanted to take my life.

I found myself at that crossroads. What do I do? Where do I go? How do I deal with this? How am I going to take care of myself?

Answer: I left my job, moved all my belongings into a storage unit, put my condo up for sale, packed my car and moved to Penticton, where I trained on the Ironman course for three months. Here is the fun part! When I made the decision to sell my condo... I also made a decision to not have a permanent residence, aka I decided to live a gyspy-like lifestyle and nurture the gypsy within me.

My triathlon coach actually told me, based on where I was mentally and physically, that I would not cross the finish line because I was so beat up. "Statistically," he said, "you don't have the stamina or the strength to finish the race." He was probably right, statistically, but I did it. I fought through so many self-defeating thoughts and moments, and I made it – I crossed the finish line.

On August 26th, I finished Ironman Canada in 16 hours, 52 minutes and 10 seconds. The rules allow 17 hours to complete it. I finished the course with less than eight minutes to spare. I crossed that finish line with a smile on my face and my body in one piece... and quite honestly, I felt proud of what I had accomplished, and grateful that my mind and body carried me to the finish line. I knew that if I could do this, I could do anything. I could rebuild my life from the ground up.

In the months that followed, I really started to take charge of my own life. I followed no one else's rules. I did what was best for me. I had no income, I didn't know how I was going to pay rent if that's what I wanted to do, but I knew that I could do it. I didn't know how, I didn't know why, I didn't know any of that, but I knew that the life I was living wasn't one that I wanted, it wasn't possible for me to have and it wasn't one that I was willing to return to.

When I look back now, I realize my strength and my courage and my desire really pushed me through that timeframe, and that what made it all possible was self-acceptance.

One of the songs on my running playlist was "Truth Will Set You Free" by Corey Hart. This song, to me, is all about self-acceptance. In order for my life to change, I had to accept that I really "wasn't happy when I should have been" and I chose to believe, have faith and fully accept that I AM strong enough to believe that I could do this on my own terms and in my own way.

About two days after finishing Ironman Canada, I found out that my condo sold! So, to celebrate, I decided to rent a hotel room and just process everything. I was asking myself, where's my next step? What am I going to do? What do I see myself doing at this moment?

While I was at Ironman, my friends had been collecting mail from my condo and watching over the place to ensure the showings went smoothly. They came to watch me compete at Ironman and gave me a stack of mail after the race. I was sitting there opening up my mail and saw an envelope. It was an inheritance check from my grandmother's estate. And I'm like, "Okay, what am I gonna do?" I have this lump sum from my inheritance, and I'll have the payout from my condo, so I have just enough money to live over the next six months to try to figure out what it is that I want to do. I heard

Grandma say, "go live your life, figure things out, you will be okay. You are strong and can do this." I felt a warm embrace come over me, tears welled up in my eyes and I just knew that I was going to be okay.

About a year before all this happened, "when life was good," I purchased a GOLD ticket to go to the Supernatural convention in Dallas, Texas and then on to New York City for 10 days with a friend from New Zealand. And then I was like, well, can I afford to go now even though I don't have a job, I don't have a place to live? So, we had this all planned out a year prior to all of this stuff going down in my life, and I didn't know if I would actually be able to afford it. But, with the grace of everything, I was able to keep my plan. My thought was, "I have this money, so, f*ck it." I went on Expedia and I found the cheapest flight to Dallas. It had three stops and was 36 hours in total, but I didn't care. I had nowhere else to go, nowhere else to be and no one to answer to. I took charge and took action – I bought the plane ticket.

My friend in Red Deer was willing to hold my car for me while I was "searching for myself." He drove me to the bus station in Red Deer, where I boarded the bus that would take me to the airport in Calgary. From Calgary, I flew to Seattle, then Chicago, and then from Chicago to Vegas. I had a seven-hour layover in Vegas. I had always wanted to go to Vegas. It was the perfect time to stroke it off my bucket list, and I was ready to explore. This layover gave me a chance to check out the sites on the Vegas Strip. Midnight to 4:00 am equals the perfect time to see the city.

It was September of 2012. I had no idea where I was, and no idea what I was doing, but I had breakfast in Seattle, I had lunch in Chicago and now I was having late-night supper in Vegas before I flew into Dallas for the Supernatural convention. I hailed a cab and I said, "Take me to the Strip."

The driver asked me, "Where on the Strip?"

I said, "I don't care, just take me to the Strip. I've got three hours to kill." So, he dropped me off in front of the MGM Grand. Awesome, that's where they filmed "Ocean's Eleven," so I was like, I know this place.

It was two in the morning, and I was just wandering the strip. It was nothing like I expected it to be because it was so quiet. But, I found a place to have a burger. I wandered around some of the casinos. I walked by Madame Tussaud's wax museum so I could say I saw it. And then I hailed a cab, and it turned out to be the same driver. He goes, "You're the only one who's ever visited Vegas for three hours, and you're not even drunk. You didn't have a single drink." We both chuckled.

I landed in Dallas on September 26th and spent the weekend with my friends at the Supernatural convention. Then we scooted off to New York for 10 days. When I was in New York, I paid attention to the foods that I was interested in eating, the smells, the taste. I was testing all the senses, noticing what I was attracted to as far as colors, books, movies and even architecture. I just really paid attention to the world from a place of clear vision, with no expectations on myself and no expectations from anyone else. I had the strength and the courage to try something new and to try something different, to really experience this transformation of self-acceptance and taking charge of where I wanted my life to go, not where anyone else was telling me to go.

It was an amazing 10 days in New York. My friend was going back to Seattle, so I said, "Well, that's where I will go too," because I didn't really know what else to do. I went to Priceline.com and I bundled my hotel and air for October 7th. It was actually one of the Priceline packages including a hotel stay where you only know the departure and arrival time and you take a chance at everything else they offer in the package. I didn't even know what hotel it was going to be at until after I bought the tickets. So there I am, taking another risk, taking another chance, I'm trusting in the universe. I'm having faith and I'm having courage to go through life and just let things be the way they are.

When I arrived at the hotel, it was rated 5-star and they upgraded me (at no cost) from a basic room to a one-bedroom suite. Even my backpack had its own room! AMAZING! As I was celebrating my good fortune, and feeling gratitude for the upgrade, I also found myself contemplating more questions: "I've completed the Ironman, I went to a Supernatural convention, I stayed in New York, NOW WHAT? Where do I see myself going? Do I want to go back to Manitoba where my family is? Do I want to go back to Calgary? Do I want to go somewhere else? If I could manifest this beautiful room, what else could I manifest?" I didn't really know the answers, but I had faith that they would come.

Then I got an email from my friend, Michelle. She wrote, "We're having a three-day weekend event, called 'Discovery' and I'd like to gift it to you." Michelle was one of my friends from my old job. She knew I was struggling and didn't know what I was going to do with my life. She also wrote, "You can stay at my place for the time being, a couple of weeks, till you figure things out."

And I said "YES." I booked my flight back to Calgary and attended this personal transformation weekend called Discovery Training. It was a true gift. When the three days were over, the answers I had been searching for came. I decided that I didn't want to buy a new condo, I didn't want to have rent to pay. I actually just wanted to live life on what I would call God's good grace, trusting the universe and having faith that it will all work out.

Mid-October, I chose to live without a permanent address and just go where I found myself with no hidden agendas or expectations over the next six years. I house-sat, I pet sat, I visited my parents in Arizona every winter. I was the youngest Snowbird they've ever seen. I was an honorary Snowbird in Tucson, Arizona. Near the end of 2013, I also launched an internet radio station and podcast network, interviewed more than 100 personal success experts, produced close to 500 podcasts and helped many clients figure out "how to live life and do business in a way that works for you and comes from your truth."

Right after the Discovery weekend, Carolyn, part of the Discovery group, mentioned she had a room available for me and this is where I first met The Angels. Carolyn became my teacher for Integrated Energy Therapy (IET) and in November 2012, I took the "Meet the Healing Angels" course. I took the intensive program two weeks later. By the end of November, I had reached the advanced level of IET and developed a relationship with The Angels.

Also, during the Discovery Training weekend, I met Darcy, who realized that I was looking for a place to belong. He introduced me to his family, friends and neighbors who asked me to house-sit and dog-sit when they needed to go away. He recommended me to half a dozen other people in the neighborhood, which resulted in recurring house-sitting gigs, where I was getting paid to live in their house.

Looking back at it now, I see that this was me saying YES to the universe, YES to possibilities, YES to opportunities that were never really in my realm of thought before. During my gypsy years, I found myself needing assistance from others to live my life and the universe answered my needs by providing me with so many opportunities to house- and pet-sit. I was given the opportunity to figure out what I wanted to do with my life, and they were gifted the opportunity to travel the world, knowing that their house and pets were well taken care of. So, it really became a win-win scenario. I was learning how to help others while taking care of my own needs as well – what a gift!

Another friend, Christina, who was yet another amazing person from the Discovery weekend, allowed me to use her address as my permanent mailing address on my driver's license and on all of my legal paperwork. Once every three months, I would meet up with her to pick up my stack of mail and go through it.

Being gifted the Discovery Training provided me a place to land and people who allowed me to tap into a different skill set – a skill set that I had forgotten I had. When I was a child, I connected with nature, had psychic abilities and connected with the non-physical world, but I had long buried those skills when I entered the corporate world. That weekend, I had once again found those skills, as well as my ability to express kindness, courage, bravery, strength, trusting others, trusting myself and giving and accepting unconditional love. But most importantly, it gave me the strength to believe that I could do more than what I was told I could do.

Throughout my time of house- and pet-sitting, I made a lot of elderly, furry friends who all taught me an important life lesson. This one dog, Loki, who is blind and deaf, still trusted the people around him. I could take him into the middle of an intersection with his leash, and he just happily walked in circles in the middle of the street, not even caring what direction he was going in. He was just happy to be in the moment. I saw that as a sign of strength.

Another dog named Chubbs would walk out of his house every day and would never take the same path two days in a row. He would just trust in his connection, trusting where he wanted to go. But he would never take himself further than what he could do. He knew his limitations, he knew his capacity. He knew what he was capable of. I saw that as a sign of courage.

My friend Daphne is a gifted animal communicator, so I asked her to connect with these two amazing dogs. She said, "Each one of them feels like you are their soulmate, that they were your boyfriends and that they are here to help you move through this part of your life." That comforted me. These furry friends taught me about strength. They taught me about courage. They taught me about having faith, the power of now, as well as the power of the pause - stopping in the moment, assessing what I know to be true and then making a decision that feels right for me.

Both Chubbs and Loki passed away within a year of each other. I heard them say to me, "It is time for you to move forward. You are ready to commit to your future. You know what you want." They were right. It was time for me to move into the next part of my life.

I didn't know what that looked like – yet. So, I reached out to my dear friend Lorna, who had offered me regular pet-sitting gigs in the past. This time, she let me stay at her home on a more permanent basis. In exchange for rent, I would take her dog, Pepper, for walks every day. I felt so stable, so settled and so grateful for my life, and I was beginning to feel the call to do something more. I didn't know what that was – yet. But I knew it was going to be big.

I've discovered that when you decide to make a major life decision, you can always expect some emotional turmoil to happen. There will be doubts that surface, and old self-sabotaging patterns pop up to help you recognize that you are strong enough to move forward in your life. I now realize this is to help you recognize you have the strength to succeed regardless of the obstacles in your way. However, when I received the news about my business bank account, I thought life was going to be hard again. I had found myself in an unexpected predicament and had 30 days to manifest thousands of dollars. But, once again, I took time to connect with my higher self and ask, "What is next?"

Answer: I found a buyer for my podcast network, sold the platform and took care of my financial issues. Lorna was astounded at how quickly I could turn around a "bad" situation and make "something good of it."

Around 60 days later, while still staying with Lorna and Pepper, I actually landed a very lucrative contract that provided me the opportunity to shift the focus of my business from podcasting to spiritual teaching and counseling. The contract afforded me the ability to go to Long Island and get my Master Instructor Integrated Energy Therapy Certificate, which had been a dream of mine for a while.

The whole time I was living the gypsy-life, I was building my own business, my spiritual business, and this was the next evolutionary step in that process.

I had lived without a permanent residence for six years. In March 2018, when I came back from Long Island, I decided to start looking for a place to rent. I was open to all cities and provinces. I saw a Facebook post from Curtis, the guy who shared the apartment where my mail was going this whole time. He had actually moved out and into another condo to be closer to his work, he happened to be looking for a roommate in the inner city. The one place I had never lived in before was the inner city in Calgary. And I'm like, you know what, I'm gonna go live in the inner city of Calgary so I can say that I did, then I won't regret when I decided to move out of the city.

When I moved into my inner city condo, two things happened. My lucrative contract ended and I had to find a new source of income. I was sharing this with my friend Elizabeth, and she suggested that I apply at the jewelry store that she worked at. I would be a personal vibration consultant who "helps you determine what stones are most important to empower your life. As your life unfolds you can select pieces that will be specific to managing your vibration for your current needs." I thought it was super cool, submitted my application and started working the following week.

This job was the stepping stone to something much greater. I stayed in this position for three months. However, it became clear it wasn't my final destination. When I accepted this truth, I received a call from the woman who had purchased my podcast network and asked if I was willing to be her business manager/consultant. This was another amazing opportunity for me to support myself as I built up my spiritual business over the next two years. I also started to offer workshops and training based on my IET Master-Instructor Certification and was looking for a place to hold those workshops. This is when SolePath, and the love of my life, Sheldon, came into my world.

In August of 2018, I drove from Alberta to Manitoba to see family and go to a birthday party for my great-niece, who was turning two. The party was being held at my parents' house, and relatives from both sides of the family were invited. I made this trip with the sole intention of spending time and strengthening my relationship with my family. I walked into that party with an open heart, unconditional love and definitely had no expectations of attracting love.

I was on the ground, building sand castles and searching for dino eggs in the sandbox with the birthday girl, and we were waiting for her family to arrive from Winnipeg. When we heard a vehicle drive up, everyone rushed into the house to get the cake ready. I was still sitting on the ground trying to figure out how to get up, when I heard a man's voice say, "Can I help you?" Out of the corner of my eye, I saw this man extending his hand to help me. I had no idea who he was, or how he fit into the family, but I do recall thinking, "he is very nice and polite and cute too! He sure looked good in that blue shirt!"

After the gentleman helped me up, I was introduced to the rest of the family and he was introduced to me as my great niece's grandfather, Sheldon! I think his kids knew we were going to be a couple before we realized it. At the end of the party, he asked for my number. The next day he gave me a call and I couldn't stop smiling. That is when I knew I had met the love of my life.

Ok, so now you know how I met my husband. Now I'll tell you how SolePath came into my life. I had my SolePath ID energy analysis done and discovered that my key metaphysical life experience was to trust my connection with the non-physical. I was given the affirmation statement, "I am strong, steady, and wise, and I choose to relax and trust and have faith in the process of life."

Simply put - Mind Blown! I did not know any of this when I decided the life I was living was not the life I wanted. I did not know this when I decided to live without a permanent home for six years.

I went from having a vision of being a life coach who helped people escape emotional chaos to becoming an ordained Metaphysical Minister specializing in helping others find the meaning in life. My mission is to help others embrace that there's more to life than what they think there is, more than what we've been conditioned to believe, more than societal conditioning.

Through this journey of mine, I found out that my entire soul's journey, my life's purpose, was about relaxing and trusting in the process of life. The life experience that I was meant to have was one of trusting my connection, trusting source and trusting the non-physical world to get me to where I want to go. I discovered that I AM a metaphysical and spiritual explorer.

The moment I was able to be comfortable with myself and accept myself for who I really was is when I started to take charge and action of my own life. And I call it my own life, because up until I left my job and went on this journey, it didn't really feel like my life. It felt like the life that everyone else was expecting me to live.

When I left my job in 2012, I had no idea that I was on a spiritual journey. I was simply on a mission to create a sustainable future for myself. My entire life, and especially these past 10 years, have been my soul's evolution. It was me going through my life at a very unconscious level, becoming aware of the moments of dark as well as the moments of light. I thought I was relying on the universe and God's good graces, but it was actually me relying on my own connection with universal source and infinite intelligence. And I was taking the time to have those Vision Quests to nourish my soul, and nourish my connection, so that I could find myself in this space that I had never thought would be possible.

The Result: I've manifested a life that is much greater, more empowering and more powerful than I could ever have imagined.

When I was rebuilding my life, I truly thought I was alone on the journey. I was so disconnected, but looking back, I realize how many earth angels had actually helped me along the way. I am truly grateful for everyone who helped me along my spiritual journey.

I've trained in the best methods for uncovering our soul's sacred plan. I've opened myself up to communicate with non-physical guides. I'm an ordained Metaphysical minister, and founder of the WhiteLight Metaphysical Centre, where I teach and counsel individuals on how to discover the meaning in life and discover universal truths. And for those who are called, I train individuals on their path of becoming internationally certified, spiritual practitioners so they can guide others along their own spiritual paths.

I've also attracted an amazing life partner who accepts and loves me unconditionally. We have been together for four years and have recently purchased our forever home, adopted the most amazing puppy from a rescue shelter and got married. I'm surrounded by people who love me, celebrate me and support me in my greatness. I've created a reality that allows me to live a beautiful expansive life, where I show up as I truly am — in alignment with my sacred soul plan.

When I was dealing with administrative work in that corporate world, none of this was even in my realm of understanding. But because I allowed myself to take these steps, I didn't turn my lemons into lemonade. Instead, I completely extracted myself from that life, I started to believe that I could be something that no one else ever thought possible, and I started to drink coconut milk.

Q&A

Jana: I think that is great. You've given our readers a lot to contemplate, think about and absorb. There's a lot of experiences you had throughout that story that could be your coconut milk. What would you say is the one commonality that defines that concept for you?

Rev. Carrie-Ann: The commonality is the faith to pursue spiritual growth. Having faith to know that whatever you are reaching for, in this case the coconut milk, will be exactly what you need, and you can receive it with gratitude and grace. The universe will provide. You don't have to keep trying to make lemonade out of the lemons you've been handed.

Jana: For the women reading this book who might not have the clarity they need to feel like they can identify what their coconut milk is, how do you start? How do you start to trust when maybe that has not been part of who you are for a long time because maybe lots of lemons took that concept of trust or that idea of trust out of your realm? How do you bring it back?

Rev. Carrie-Ann: To me, the very first step is recognizing that this is not where you want to be. In all the modalities I have studied, the first step in getting to where you want to be is really being honest about where you don't want to be. That's all about self-acceptance. You have to be willing to admit that you don't like what you're experiencing, you're not happy where you are. This is not what you want anymore. I didn't have hacks, or a formula, or a way to figure it out. I stumbled across different modalities and different mindset teachings to get me to where I am today.

But I'll tell you the number one thing that steered me in all of those explorations was understanding that where I was is not where I wanted to be. I was tired of feeling frustrated, I was tired of feeling doubtful, I was tired of feeling taken advantage of, feeling abused, feeling used. I was helping everyone else get ahead except myself. Self-acceptance to me is not, oh, I've got love handles, but I love myself anyway. Self-acceptance at the core, at a soul level, is saying I am no longer in alignment with the life that I'm living. I want something different than this.

I went through a whole bunch of counselors and psychologists, all that stuff because everyone was trying to fix me. One of my counselors asked me, do you want your life to end? I said I want the life I'm living to be over so that I can experience a new life. What I'm experiencing right now, I want to stop. It doesn't mean I want to stop breathing, it just means I want to stop experiencing this. And she said, no one's ever answered that question that way before. But that was my reality. I don't want to be this person, I don't want to live this way, I'm tired of this happening to me, I want it to stop.

Until you hit that emotional rock bottom, no matter what you do isn't going to change your position in life. I tried changing cities, relationships and workplaces. I reclaimed my health three times, I lost 100 pounds the first time, 80 pounds the second time. I started training for triathlons. I went from being totally sedentary to learning to run three times a week, to then adding a spin class in there, to then adding swimming lessons and losing weight. I went from living a very sedentary life to being active six days a week. But you can't get there if you don't know where you don't want to be anymore.

Jana: That was beautifully put. Is there anything that you feel is left unsaid in this experience?

Rev. Carrie-Ann: Yes. What I know to be true from my experience is this… your reality is an outcome of your input, approach and energetic attitude. That's what I think "when life hands you lemons… drink coconut milk" is all about.

REV. CARRIE-ANN, founder of WhiteLight Metaphysical Centre and Tenacious Living Consulting, believes that living life with ease and happiness is absolutely attainable! She helps people achieve this through connecting with their higher selves, the spirit of others, and the non-physical elements of this world.

From an early age, Rev. Carrie-Ann had a hunger for personal success and a desire to break through any obstacles she encountered. These qualities allowed her to unearth her power and find the truth within herself to overcome any barrier in life.

Based on her life experiences, she has collected and developed effective strategies to guide others through their own obstacles, emotions and roadblocks so they can live their best life. Over the past 15 years, she has worked with many private clients and stood in front of countless groups as a teacher and trainer. She invests in others, helping them to find inspiration and purpose.

Rev. Carrie-Ann is an expert at guiding others along their self-empowerment and spiritual journeys and teaching them how to trust their intuition, embrace their gifts, and discover their greatness. Rev. Carrie-Ann dreams and lives big and she wants to help you find the power and possibilities within yourself to do the same.

Rev. Carrie-Ann's professional development and diverse work experience in the corporate world have given her a broad insight on the world and she is grateful for what each experience has taught her. Through all those years of hard work, she has garnered many insights, and from her point of view, there is nothing better in life than to be able to give back.

Rev. Carrie-Ann's passion is to help you discover your potential and lift your doubts from your mind. Her hope is you will discover why your purpose is bigger than your objections and help you see your path to success and happiness more clearly.

Contact Information:
Ph: 204 720 6688
Email: office@whitelightmetaphysical.com
Website: www.whitelightmetaphysical.com
Facebook Page: https://www.facebook.com/revcarrieann
Facebook Group: https://www.facebook.com/groups/sacredsoulplan
Instagram: https://www.instagram.com/revcarrieann/
LinkedIn: https://www.linkedin.com/in/revcarrieannbaron/
Vimeo: https://vimeo.com/whitelightmetaphysical
Amazon Author Page: https://www.amazon.com/Carrie-Ann-Baron/e/B00H2FLB4U

DR. MAYA

I think my life is full of "when life hands you lemons . . . drink coconut milk" kinds of stories. For me, that is very much what I would call the spiritual path. To always be making meaning and looking for the signs, symbols and synchronicities that present themselves in any kind of situation. Because life is very much about how we navigate challenging moments. We cannot guarantee ourselves only smooth experiences.

The story that stands out the most in this moment is about my son, who already had health issues in his first year of life. That experience took me into a deep dive around food and neurological conditions and it ended up being the inspiration for my book, "The Dirt Cure." Ultimately, he got healthier. We got him on a good diet, we got him out in nature, we were doing all the things. He was around seven, and we were living in an apartment in New York City at that time and he was exposed to mold. We had a mold issue in the apartment.

He was having such significant breathing problems that ultimately we had to move out of the apartment for five months. I had threatened to sue the co-op that we lived in, and we had to have a huge remediation that ripped out the bathrooms down to the studs, and got rid of all of our upholstered furniture and all the stuffed animals and even all the clothing of all three of my kids. Everyone had to have everything cleaned, and we had to do a huge purge and live outside of our home for five months.

We finally moved back in. We had cleaners come in, they cleaned the frames of the doors with actual toothbrushes, everything was cleaned and tested. There was no mold, there was no dust. It was pristine. The leak had been fixed. Everything had been done. About two weeks in, my son went to go take a shower, my youngest son, who was the one who had been having health issues. In those five months, interim five months, he'd been on a special diet, we'd been doing detoxification, we'd really gotten him into a great place. He goes to take a shower, and I'm on the phone with a friend. And a certain amount of time goes by and my middle son comes running in and says, "Mommy, Erez is lying on the floor of the bathroom and I think he's unconscious.

I go running in there, I look under the door because the door is locked. The shower is running. Luckily, he's not in the shower. But he's on the floor, and he is not responsive. I'm trying to figure out how to break in. I'm ready to break down the door, I'm ready to call the police. I'm banging on the door and he finally gets up, I don't know how many minutes it was. So he opens the door and comes out. He had wet himself, and it turned out he had a seizure. Here I am, a pediatric integrative neurologist. It felt like a moment outside of time, if that makes sense, when your son is having a seizure. And he's already on all the remedies, he's on all of the different approaches.

I was holding him so tightly in that moment, and I was thinking to myself, this is not a physical problem, this is like a spiritual problem, an energetic problem, a soul problem. There's something about this space that is causing him to be sick. And I always call Erez my cosmic magnet. Because if something's going to happen, he is like the sentinel. He is the one who's going to fall if there's a thing to trip over. I also call him my muse, especially after this experience.

I was one of the only, if not the only, pediatric neurologists in the world that did all these integrative approaches and conventional approaches. I had a certain amount of pride at that time, and I thought, I can help anybody. Did I think I could cure anybody? Not necessarily, but I knew that anybody who comes to me is going to at least get better, significantly better. But holding him in my arms, I realized this is something I don't know how to do. I am going to have to go on a journey to find someone who's going to be able to do this sort of energetic spiritual soul work. At that time, it wasn't that I didn't know people, I knew people who did Reiki and who did craniosacral. I did have some community of people, but not for what he needed. And that was so clear to me.

Thankfully, that was his only seizure. Yet moving forward I had people placed in front of me, it was one experience after another. I was talking to a friend of mine, and she said, oh, you should really talk to this woman. And I was like, well, what does she do? She said, well, I don't know exactly, but my friend thinks she's the most amazing person in the world, and I think you should talk to her.

So I reached out to her and she said, "I can't take anybody right now."

As a desperate mom I persisted. I emailed her every once in a while. I didn't even know what she did. But I told her what was going on with my son and I continuously checked in and finally, she said, Okay, let's have a session. She ended up becoming a really profound spiritual teacher and guide for me.

Then there was another person that I had met at an herbal conference who was a fourth generation shaman and a PhD in ethnobotany. She also ended up becoming one of his healers and became my teacher for a time. And I ended up the following year flying to Ecuador, and studying with different indigenous elders and healers, learning from the plants, and ultimately becoming a real student of many different indigenous elders from around the world.

So, how did this story go from the lemons to the coconut milk? I couldn't have imagined in that moment, when I was holding him, that level of crisis and disorientation you have when not only is someone you love in danger, but also your own constructs about yourself and your life and what you believe are crumbling in front of your eyes. I was very open to a lot of integrative things, but I had not yet really embraced my own spiritual path yet.

It was this ego death moment for me, where I was so uncertain, so scared. I didn't know who, what, where. I just knew that the conventional thing is not really going to be the right approach. I knew the integrative thing would not be enough. And I knew that I had to go in this other direction.

The coconut milk of my journey has been that I've become a medicine woman. And I have embraced my own indigenous lineage. I ended up breaking out of a lot of things in my life that were maybe not healthy for me anymore. I changed the work that I do, I do a lot of work with plants, more so now with psychedelics, I do a lot of spiritual guidance. I actually trained and became an ancient astrologer. So I do numerology and astrology, in addition to doing physical, mental, emotional, spiritual healing work, using all different kinds of approaches that I've learned from my teachers and the lineage that I've been initiated in.

I emerged from the experience a new person, and much more authentically who I was here to be, personally and professionally. It really taught me that it's important to feel all the things that you feel in those pattern-interrupted moments or those ego-death kinds of moments. It's not to say that you just bypass the difficulty, or the grief. There's real grief in those kinds of moments, and sometimes fear. But it's really important to have this bigger perspective, at least for a few seconds, or moments here and there, to remember that you can make meaning, and that sometimes these death periods precede birth periods. You might enter into a phase of your life or your career or your relationship that is so much more profoundly authentic and satisfying, and allows you to embody your purpose in a whole new way.

Q&A

Jana: What do you say to those thoughts or beliefs of our readers where they might be thinking, well, Dr. Maya is a neurologist, so of course she's going to have more confidence around looking outside of the traditional medical system. What do you say to those voices who are the "Yeah, but..." And I think as women, sometimes we can really easily fall into that frozen state.

Dr. Maya: As a neurologist, it was in some ways probably more stigmatized for me to go into something spiritual, or energetic or soul related than for someone else. That was actually one of the scariest transitions of my life. Not as much going into integrative medicine, where I felt like, oh, I have scientific papers I can show people. When I went into integrative medicine, the gut-brain connection was not something that was plastered all over the New York Times. It was not being talked about, and it was still very controversial. Giving vitamin D to people when I first started out was very controversial. But that I felt comfortable with because I could show scientific papers and scientific studies.

What I moved into and evolved into really didn't have that kind of scientific foundation yet or that sense of respectability, that I felt was becoming of a doctor. So with my colleagues, if they thought I was wackadoo, if they thought I was off the rails by looking at diet and herbs and supplements and becoming an herbalist, as a neurologist and treating neurological issues. I was thinking what they would say when I'm doing shamanic work, or when I'm talking about astrology. It really took a tremendous amount of courage that I don't think I could have accessed if I hadn't been catapulted into this journey against my will.

Some people definitely challenged my credibility because of it. But the key that I've experienced is feeling that sense of knowing in your whole body. It's something that I train people to tune into, and to listen to, to recognize those sensations in the body or that sense of intuition, or those signs or symbols or synchronicities that we've been taught to discount. Because that is a kind of knowing that I think everybody has, and I think women truly and deeply have been taught to disbelieve. Yet it's as valid as all the rational linear information that we are taught is acceptable.

Jana: Okay, I love that and can you tell us, how is Erez today?

Dr. Maya: Erez today is a over six feet tall, tallest person in the family, 17-year-old strapping guy who runs Spartan Races. He is an athlete, he is active, he's bright, he's healthy. And I really consider him a spiritual teacher in a way because although he has taught me in these very intense moments and experiences. It always takes me on my own professional and personal journey. I think we have a sort of karmic relationship where I care for him and he guides me.

Jana: Oh, that's so amazing. One last question, do you think there's anything that's been left unsaid before we wrap this chapter?

Dr. Maya: The one thing I'll say is that it's really important to remember in those death moments, that there are always birth moments and new beginnings to come. And not to fall into that place of despair, but to surrender and then pick yourself back up and find your courage. Because it's very possible that what will come next will be so much better than you could possibly imagine.

Jana: Well, with that, I feel like the lights go out and the curtain comes down. Thank you so much Dr. Maya for your wisdom and opening up your family story to us to help us learn and really connect with that deeper inner wisdom that's all within us. Thank you.

MAYA SHETREAT, MD, is a neurologist, herbalist, urban farmer, and author of *The Dirt Cure* which has been translated into 10 languages. She has been featured in the *New York Times*, *The Telegraph*, *NPR*, *Sky News*, *The Dr. Oz Show* and more. Dr. Maya is the founder of the Terrain Institute, where she teaches earth-based programs for transformational healing, including professional training programs for psychedelic-assisted approaches. She works and studies with indigenous communities and healers from around the world, and is a lifelong student of ethnobotany, plant healing, and the sacred.

MICHELLE

Friday, April the 13th, 2012, was the day I received a stage 3 breast cancer diagnosis!

After a whole lot of testing and a whole lot of medical procedures, this was the day, I finally got the official diagnosis. The medical assistant calling on the phone said, well, I guess you know, you have invasive lobular carcinoma. I didn't actually know until that moment, but she thought the doctor had called me the night before and told me. Truth be told, he was hesitant to tell me because he thought waiting until morning would prevent me from having a sleepless night.

I'd had a sleepless night anyway.

The call from his assistant was how I got the news that I had invasive lobular carcinoma.

This type of breast cancer is harder to detect because it doesn't typically form a lump.

It grows more like a spiderweb in more of a diffused manner. By the time it was diagnosed, this cancer was more than six inches, not centimeters, but six inches!

That diagnosis led me through an over two-year journey of all different types of treatments, and pretty much everything you can imagine that can go along with a breast cancer experience. Needless to say, getting a diagnosis like that can certainly feel daunting.

It's such a shock!

As with most people who are diagnosed with cancer, you don't necessarily see it coming. It can literally turn your life upside down and can change the trajectory of your whole life. It's like getting hit by a fast-moving train! You feel like life as you know it has come to a screeching halt and the rest of the world goes on without you.

It's such a strange feeling!

This diagnosis put me on a very challenging and difficult soul-stretching journey. It was indescribably painful at times. There were so many times when I would cry, and cry, and cry. I would cry out of pain, out of fear, out of sadness, out of the feeling of loss, and because of the feeling that I was losing my identity. I cried at least once a day for a year or more. In addition to having cancer, I was losing all of my feminine parts due to the cancer treatments. It was an assault on my identity as a woman. As part of the medical treatments, they removed my ovaries, I had a double mastectomy, I lost my hair, my eyebrows, and my eyelashes.

When I looked in the mirror it felt like I didn't know who I was any more.

I never really thought that I would be able to say there were many gifts in the experience, as painful and daunting as it was. But now, after some time, after some perspective, I can tell you that there were many gifts in the experience. Those are some of the things I'm going to share with you today.

Before I begin sharing more of the journey, and some of the gifts that came out of this experience, I want to just share a little bit more of what transpired before the diagnosis. I feel it might be really valuable to someone out there. I believe one of the things we have as women is a divine gift of inner guidance, inner wisdom, intuition and trusting that our souls really know what is best for us.

Our bodies will often tell us what is best for us or warn us when something is wrong.

About a year before I had this breast cancer diagnosis, I was working in the business world. I had a 20-year corporate career. This was prior to doing what I do now, helping women meet and find love with the right man. Unfortunately, I was working in a corporate position I hated! I hated this particular job so badly that when Sunday nights came each week and a new work week was about to begin, I would feel sick! I would get a big knot in my stomach because it made me feel so awful to have to face another week in this job. However, I was very well-compensated. It felt like the invisible financial handcuffs were holding me there. They were also talking about giving me another raise. This raise would represent a higher level of compensation I'd ever made in my 20-year corporate career. Yet, I hated this job with a passion. Coincidentally, at the same time, I was also offered a position to work for a nonprofit organization. I felt very much aligned with and very much attracted to the opportunity with the non-profit organization, but it was at a much, much lower salary.

One night I was on the bed talking with my husband and we were having a conversation about my work. More or less, it was me speaking my thoughts and sharing my feelings about the dilemma I was going through. I was telling my husband how much I hated the current job, but how they were planning to give me this additional raise. I was telling him I was already making a lot more than I would be making at this nonprofit, but I felt drawn to the new opportunity. My soul was giving me a clear message already, but I needed to verbalize these thoughts and feelings and say it all out loud.

I wanted to get some feedback or confirmation on what my soul was already telling me. My husband patiently listened to me share all the pros and cons. When I finally asked him what he thought I should do, he said only three words.

Those three words are three words that I've tried to live by since that time.

The three words were simply, increase the peace.

That's what he said to me! Increase the peace!

So, what does this have to do with this breast cancer journey?

Well, I did end up taking the position with the nonprofit. I ended up loving the position for the time that I worked there. Those three words of advice turned out to be very significant!

If I had not taken this advice, if I had not listened to my soul, and this confirmation from my husband, I don't believe I would be here today! I wouldn't have been going to doctor's appointments for checkups. I felt so much pressure in the corporate role I didn't even feel like I could leave work long enough to go to a doctor appointment. The cancer would not have been found. It would have progressed further and I would likely have died.

What I'm telling you is that choice, that message from my soul (and the three words from my husband) a year before I was even diagnosed, literally saved my life! It saved my life!

Because had I not been having regular checkups and going to the doctor, there's no way the cancer would have been found when it was. I would not be here today.

I feel that's a really important preface to this story, and a reminder to listen to our souls, our bodies and those who truly love us.

As women, I believe we have this gift of divine intuition, feminine intuition.

It's so important for us to pay attention to this, because I think it's a God-given gift.

In this case, it was life-saving.

Shortly after I left that earlier position and started the new job, I did go in for a physical to get a mammogram. At that time, I was already feeling a little different in my body. I couldn't really describe it because, like I said, this kind of cancer didn't form a lump. Yet I was already feeling like my breast felt strange. I expressed this to my doctor and he said, well, we'll have you get a diagnostic mammogram. This is where they take an ultrasound wand and go over and over the breast to take an even closer look. This is done in addition to a regular mammogram. |I had an excellent radiologist and he said, everything's fine. However, I still felt uncomfortable. So, then I went to a surgeon. He took a look at the imaging, and said, everything's fine.

I still didn't feel like everything was fine!

Fast forward another six months. I went back to my doctor because my body was now feeling even more different to me. My breast felt different to me. There was something I couldn't quite describe. It was like my breast felt heavier! Physiologically, my breast felt different. We know our own bodies; we have the best knowledge of our own bodies. So, I went back to the doctor and told him I needed to have another mammogram. It had only been six months since the last one. He said the insurance won't pay for it. I said, I don't care, I need to have another mammogram. This time he set me up with a radiologist who is very renowned. He's in our area, and is known for being very good at catching tricky cases of cancer. He is often asked to look at tough breast cancer cases. My doctor said, whatever you do when you go in for this next mammogram, make sure he's the one who takes a look at your mammogram.

I went in for the second mammogram in less than 6 months, and they wanted to hand me off to another doctor because the radiologist was very busy. He is very much in demand. I said, no, no, no, I have to wait, I have to wait. Well, this time I have the mammogram and I have the diagnostic mammogram. He's going over and over and over my breast with the ultrasound wand. The radiologist has a concerned look on his face. Then he says, I have a very bad feeling about this!

Well, at this point, I have a very bad feeling about this too. Even with that, though, it still took a variety of tests, a breast MRI, and a surgical procedure to take big swaths of breast tissue out before they could finally diagnosis the cancer.

Now we're back to the Friday the 13th when I got the diagnosis.

My point in sharing this is if I hadn't been listening to my soul's intuition, and my body's messages, I don't believe that I would be here today.

I'm certainly not here to give anybody medical advice. I'm not qualified to do that. However, what I am here to tell you is, listening to my soul's intuition, and listening to my body was essential. I feel this is an important piece to the story and I think it is important to remind other women about this.

When I was diagnosed and got the news from my doctor's assistant on the phone, she assumed I already knew about the diagnosis, but I didn't. Once she realized this, she said, let me see if the doctor can see you today. He agreed to meet with me that day. My husband and I set up an appointment to go in right away.

Normally, we leave our house through the garage. But, for some reason, this morning, my husband pulled the car out of the garage, and I walked out the front door.

As I walked out the front door, something caught my eye. I thought, I have to go look at that. I'm looking at my garden. It's early April. None of the flowers had bloomed up to that point, but something white caught my eye. I went out to the garden where I have three little rocks in my garden. One says love, one says joy, and one says hope. I'm in my garden and I can now see that what caught my eye is the very first flower of the spring. I took a picture of this flower coming out from under the rock. The very first flower of my garden for the spring was a crocus that has come up underneath a rock that says hope. It was the only flower in my garden at this point, and this is the first time I'd see it, on the morning of this very day.

I felt that it was a divine message to give me hope for what was to come.

That diagnosis sent me off on a new trajectory. I decided to go the full medical route because I felt like it was my very best chance of survival. I supplemented with a lot of natural healing and spiritual healing practices as well. I thought this combination was my best chance to preserve my life. I felt the right decision was to do everything and anything I possibly could because I really, really wanted to live! I wanted to give myself the very best chance.

This cancer diagnosis was very serious, because of the size of the tumor and how advanced it was. The doctors were telling me, we're going to do what we can, we're going to throw everything we've got at it, but no guarantees.

It's not what you want to hear, but that's what they were telling me.

However, the experience with the flower and the hope rock helped me believe in my heart that there was hope.

I felt like it was a little gift of divine grace to give me hope to face what was to come with courage!

I met with a big board of various medical doctors with different specialties. This is called a tumor board and it included surgeons, oncologists for chemo, oncologists for radiation, etc. All of these doctors were looking at my case and providing their recommended treatment path.

Those medical recommendations included a lot of things. It started out with six months of very intense, very hard chemo. They wanted to do the chemo first. This is different from how they often treat breast cancer. A lot of times they do surgery first, but because of the size of this tumor, they were hoping that the chemo would shrink it down and give us a better chance of getting clean margins when they did the mastectomy.

I had six months of chemo. I lost my hair first, which felt like a really big deal. Initially, it felt even like a bigger deal than losing my breasts. That wasn't necessarily the case in the long run, but it felt like a really big deal at that time. Because it was hormone sensitive cancer, they also wanted to remove my ovaries to prevent my body from producing more estrogen. When they removed my ovaries, I got slammed into menopause.

Along with feeling awful from the chemo, I now have these brutal hot flashes because I was now in menopause. There's no way to mitigate this with hormone therapy or even natural supplements for menopause support because the breast cancer is hormone sensitive. To say this was a difficult and challenging experience is definitely an understatement. My emotions were a wreck. I would cry and cry and cry out of fear, pain, sadness, and loss.

I can remember saying to my husband (on more than one occasion), I can never imagine feeling joy again. And I meant it! I could never imagine feeling joy, again because of the depth of sadness and sorrow I was feeling at that time. My husband would reassure me I would feel joy again. But at that time, it was very, very hard for me to believe it.

I also had people tell me, you'll never feel so loved as you feel when you're going through cancer. That was an interesting side-benefit because I did feel loved. I truly felt like I had angels surrounding me. Both the heavenly kind and the earthly kind of angels!

What was interesting though, is the angels who showed up weren't always necessarily the ones I would be expecting. One thing I feel like I've learned about angels, both the heavenly and earthly kind, is they have their own timing and they have their own ways of showing up.

I experienced love like I've never experienced in my life. Random people showed such incredible kindness and love for me! It was so moving. People showing up for me in such beautiful ways frequently brought me to tears.

At one point, after the double mastectomy, I looked in the mirror and felt so pathetic. Imagine me here - I'm completely bald, no eyebrows, no eyelashes, looking sickly, and recovery from double mastectomy. I'm looking in the mirror and I'm thinking, I don't even know who I am. I was having an identity crisis. I felt like I was losing so much, including all of my feminine parts.

I'm looking in the mirror and saying, I don't even know who I am anymore. I was having this major identity crisis.

During this time, my husband was so wonderful. I was not looking beautiful! Believe me when I tell you this! However, he would kiss my bald head, and he would tell me how much he loved me and how beautiful I was.

This was such an incredible gift. I got love from him in a way that I never even could have imagined. He really loved me, but it wasn't because of how I looked. It wasn't because of what I was accomplishing. It wasn't because I was so much fun to be around. It wasn't because I was such a great wife. I was just trying to survive. I was just trying to get through all of this, moment by moment, hour by hour, day by day. What I got in a deep and profound way is he loves the true me, the essence of who I am, for my soul, for my spirit, for who I am.

This was incredibly moving because I knew he loved me in a deeper way than I had understood up to this point in our marriage. I experienced love in a way that I never could have imagined before.

For women in particular, we often think we're loved, because of how we look, or what we're doing, or what we're accomplishing. In reality, so much of real love it is about who we are, on a much deeper level. I experienced love in a whole different way as a result of how my husband showed up for me.

There were many acts of kindness from so many people. People would show up, some who I didn't even know, on my doorstep with a gift or a flower or a prayer. I even heard about some people who were on a humanitarian mission over in Africa. When they heard about me, they asked this whole African tribe to pray for me. And they did! Things like that were just so incredibly moving and overwhelming.

One of the insights I gained through this experience is there is an abundance of love and goodness out there. That's not always what we see though. The media doesn't necessarily portray the best of humanity.

I believe there is so much love and so much kindness in the world.

Sometimes people say that cancer can be the ultimate clarifier. I believe that can be true. I'm not saying cancer is the only clarifier. However, I certainly believe it can be one of the ultimate clarifiers in life though. One of the things that became very clear was what was truly important to me and what wasn't so important to me. While I was there in my bed during those days when I was so ill, I would look around at the things in my house. I would think about the money or the time or the energy I'd expended on acquiring those things. It became so clear those things were not what really mattered. I knew if I wasn't going to be here, none of those things mattered anymore. I didn't know if I would live at that time, but I knew for sure none of those things were coming with me if I left this world.

I got clearer about how I wanted to spend my time and how I wanted to prioritize my life.

It became very clear to me that some of those things I'd been spending my time on weren't so important any more, and other things were much becoming more important to me. As I began to progress through this journey, I started to have more and more hope that I would not only survive, but that I would have a good quality of life after this. It was at least couple of years to get to that point where I really felt this way.

I began to think more deeply about what I really wanted to do with my life.

One piece of the story that I haven't shared yet, is I met and married my husband and became a first-time bride at age 43. I used to joke and say I was going to write a book called "dating for decades", chronicling all my dating misadventures out there. It was a long journey to find and meet my husband. I only been married to him for a short time with him when I was diagnosed with this cancer. Even before I met my husband, I also had this desire, this hope, this dream to become a relationship coach. I believed I could help other women to bypass some of the speed bumps and potholes on the road to the right man. I wanted to be able to help women meet and attract someone whom they could have a loving partnership relationship with because I understood how meaningful this was for me!

Until I had met and married my husband and figured out some things for myself, l didn't necessarily feel like I could put myself out there in integrity as a mentor for other people. But, now I felt ready! One of the things that became clear as I was coming through this cancer journey is that my life, and the life of every person out there, is incredibly precious. We cannot take life for granted. The preciousness of life was thing that was clear, but also, how do I want to spend my life?

It became very clear to me that I no longer wanted to spend my life working for some corporation, or even this nonprofit I had a deep affection for. I wanted to go out there and live my life's mission of helping other women. It was a desire, but I also felt like it was a calling for me. In addition to having more time with my husband, I wanted to live so I could embark on this journey to help other women meet and attract the right person and find love.

This deep desire gave me clarity and a sense of my own mission. It felt like an important priority for the rest of my life. I felt a new sense of urgency too! One thing that I learned by facing my own mortality, is we can't take for granted the time we have on this planet.

However, we can choose what we do with the time we have. I had a new sense of urgency about my own life and my own life mission.

Even while still trying to recover from the cancer and treatments, I started gradually taking steps toward really establishing and growing my business. I began to see new ways to reach more people and to find my tribe, those people who were going to resonate with who I was and my message. I felt an urgency for myself, but also for other people out there. I wanted to convey, not in a panicky way, but in a way that honored the preciousness of life, that it's really important how we use our life's energy and our precious time. We want to use the time we're given in the best possible way. Time is the most precious commodity, the most precious thing that we can never get back. We can't take life for granted. This kind of clarity was something that came through strongly in this cancer journey. It is a very profound part of what I discovered, learned and gained from this experience.

I'm not sure I'm totally there 100% yet, but when I'm really feeling like I'm at my peak and my strongest spiritually, I can get to the place where I believe all the experiences we have, no matter how difficult or how traumatic, can lead to something good, to something beautiful. Everything we experience can ultimately be a blessing. I'm now in a situation where I can say I believe this chapter in the book of my life, was a divinely given gift. It helped me to understand, grow and clarify things about my own life and my own mission in ways that I don't know any other thing could have done.

It was like a very condensed and intense, learning experience.

When we're growing, it can be incredibly painful.

I can see it was actually a gift now, and perhaps it was even necessary. I also believe when we experience times of sorrow, sadness, suffering, pain, there's an excavation going on in our soul so we will be able to receive additional joy. It's a strange thing when we've experienced the extreme of one side of the equation, it also seems to expands our capacity to receive more on the other side of the equation. I certainly felt the capacity to feel joy before all of this happened, but I feel like my capacity to feel joy has increased as a result of this experience. Great joy is often on the other side of deep suffering and sorrow and pain. I've come to believe in the abundance of love in the world and that we can each be force for love in the world in how we show up.

I've come to believe that our lives really do matter. I believe we need to use our time and our gifts in ways that are meaningful. This is really important for us to think about and remember. We can't take our most precious gift, our time on this planet, for granted.

We just can't take it for granted.

I can now say that despite this being a very difficult and painful experience, and not one that I would wish on anyone, it was a blessing. I can now say this very, very sour, bitter lemon has definitely turned into some sweet coconut milk for me. I can actually say I'm grateful for it now. I'm grateful for the experience. I hope that's helpful. I hope that's helpful for someone out there.

Q&A

Jana: You've offered so much to our audience, Michelle, with your story. And there have been these little nuggets of what I would call coconut milk moments. But if I were to ask you, what is the essence of your coconut milk in your life right now, what would you say?

Michelle: The essence for my coconut milk would be to be very clear about what your life is all about. For me, that is summed up in one word, and that's love. Not only because I'm a teacher of love, and I'm a mentor for people to find love, but also because I believe being a force and a presence for love on the planet is one of the most powerful things that we can do. I also believe following the path of love is something that can bring us the most joy and satisfaction and clarity about our life's purpose. When we're operating from that place of love and knowing what our purpose really is, it can make the difference in the choices we make in our lives and how we choose to invest our time and energy. I believe that's so essential and so important for everyone out there.

Jana: It's beautiful. I want to just thank you for the way you showed up today. When I got this idea for this project, I visualized a woman with her reading light on by her bedside table with this book, going through each chapter of these amazing women who have shown all the resilience and the understanding and the love. The list could go on and on and on, and I just want to thank you for showing up in that way because I know that for that person or those thousands of women, this could be the answered prayer that they were waiting for, or maybe they didn't even know they needed. So, thank you so much for sharing.

MICHELLE MARCHANT JOHN-SON is a professional relationship coach, author and speaker. In her business LoveLifeCoaching.com she works with women around the world who want to enjoy a loving, passionate, committed relationship with an extraordinary man. She works with a very select number of private and group coaching clients as their virtual wing woman to 1) help identify what may be blocking love, 2) walk through the potential landmines of dating and 3) provides support on the journey to the relationship of your dreams.

DatingAdvice.com has named Michelle as one of the Top Ten Midlife Relationship Experts for her popular advice. After decades of career success, but frustration, heartache and disappointment in her love life, Michelle got support, uncovered her own inner blocks to love and discovered the secrets that allowed her to meet her Mr. Right. She became an ecstatic first time bride at age 43 and has been married to the man of her dreams for over 10 years.

As a breast cancer survivor, she believes life is precious and is meant to be lived with purpose, love, and joy. She is thrilled to see her amazing clients meet/attract/and find love with the right guy and enjoy happy, loving, passionate relationships. If you are a woman who wants to meet and attract the right man, improve your confidence with men or increase your feminine presence, then you'll love what Michelle will share with you!

With her proprietary system, she'll help you attract your man with Grace, Ease and Elegance. Please visit https://mrrightacademy.com/join/ for more information.

KRISTI

I love life. I enjoy the wonders of this earth, especially mystical human beings. For most of my early years, I lived in magic and wonder. Through my own life experience, I now know that I learned the value of joy, love, and peace through my shadow and the dark times. I remembered who I truly am and what it means to love.

My husband and I got married and moved to Las Vegas for the next five years. We bought our first home and had two beautiful young children during this time. Outside looking in, life is better than we could have imagined. Perfect marriage, home, toys, etc. We experienced some of the greatest joys in our early years. I also sensed some deeper "issues" both Ryan and I keep suppressing that reared their ugly heads every so often. Feelings of depression, unworthiness, and doubt with patterns of alcohol and avoidance.

In 2011, my husband had an excellent corporate job. He was at the top of his game and doing very well working for a large worldwide corporation. Unfortunately, it started changing dramatically, with less satisfaction, appreciation, and pay. Ryan began to get uncomfortable with the demands it put on him. He was in an atmosphere he did not want to be in. The demand and expectation of his job were slowly killing his joy, dimming his light. Drinking became part of his day with lingering depression. As a result, we started to plan the transition of leaving this corporate job and leaving Las Vegas.

We were able to move to St. George, Utah, and get out of the low vibe of Vegas; however, he kept making the trip back and forth. Oh, how he dreaded the days of making the drive from our family to the low vibration of Las Vegas work. As we planned his exit strategy, he was let go unexpectedly. His corporate job was over. It was difficult, frustrating, and felt like a betrayal. This began a decade of hard shadow work and deep healing.

We were ready to start our new solar company. We quickly learned what I'm good at, what he is good at, and what we are not good at together. He excelled in the corporate space because it is very structured. He knew what to expect, he knew exactly what to do, and he learned how to do it. He was always at the top of the leaderboard, crushing his competition. But in the startup world, that is not how business works. There were many twists and turns, creating as you go, pivoting often. I had experienced it quite a few times before this, so I was way more fluid in it.

Our business was doing well and required us to move to Salt Lake to expand and grow. We picked up our now four kids and moved. It was the right decision. We tripled our revenue, and our company was booming. We bought a building, and everything seemed to be going better.

In my avoidance of our personal life, I became wholly addicted to business. Something about the move triggered Ryan into a tough place. Ryan could not avoid his trauma anymore: the trauma of leaving the corporate, leaving his identity, leaving the financial success, and the accolades in the business. The loss of his identity resulted in severe trauma. It stole his soul. He went into an intense, dark depression and masked it with alcohol. Feelings of depression existed before this happened, but this just triggered a deeper, darker level.

I was running our company quietly, suffering, and very concerned about our future together. It was scary and very different from anything I could relate to or experience. At the time, my mentality with depression was to snap out of it and be happier. What are you doing? Get out of bed. Why are you doing it this way? He tried to hide and mask his depression with alcohol. Now we were focusing on drinking versus depression. It felt very chaotic.

My husband was experiencing depression, and I was a workaholic. His drinking became a huge problem. I do not like the word *addiction* because of its labels, even though I know some people need to call it something to heal. But for me, it seemed more like binge drinking when you could not handle something. It became daily. The drinking part of it was confusing for me. I felt like my entire world was falling apart. I was not as present with my kids because I was always working. I didn't feel safe leaving them home. My mother-in-law had stepped in and been helping us, but I hid it from everyone I knew because it carried so much shame towards me, towards him. I was scared. I kept asking what my self-worth was and why am I not doing it differently.

By the grace of God is how we made it through this time. Every day, I asked and prayed," Is this the day I can leave"? And every day, I got a "No, not yet, there is more for you to learn." Even today, that still makes me cry with gratitude for listening to this inner knowing.

I had felt Ryan's soul, the true essence of HIM. I knew this phase was for both of us. I knew who Ryan really was, not the version we were experiencing. I knew ME! I had known and felt HER, not this scared, workaholic woman trying to prove her worth. Through this time, I learned to ask better questions. Empowering questions about who I am, my purpose, and how this happened FOR me?

In 2017, a prayer was answered. A friend asked me if I needed help. I took my first job in 20 years, and we sold the business.

I had been running so hard, so fast, for so long. It was the most significant release of a breath when I felt like someone had permitted me to change it. The breath released all the tension and pain in my body I had been holding on to so tightly. For me, that was a gentleman handing me a coconut. At that moment, it was just permission to think differently and make changes. His advice was to "Focus on what you want." I took a job at a wealth management firm. That one decision was probably the scariest, but I knew it was the right step for me to the core of my being. This was perhaps one of my most significant transitions of faith in changing where I was. I reflected on my life and marriage. I began to take accountability for everything I was experiencing. I learned in that lesson to stop pointing my finger at other people.

I needed to take accountability for how I was feeling. Stop blaming others when life is not going as I wanted it to. Stop blaming my husband for not being healthy, not stepping up, and not providing me with what I wanted. I started to empower myself to make choices for myself. It was the way I was raised. I just forgot. I had just forgotten how to stay in my power. This would be one of the most significant transitions. This was one of my most life-changing experiences where someone offered that coconut and said, "If you take it, your life can be what you want it to be." I took it, and it was compelling.

My job was to bring people to the wealth management firm. I got super creative with how I was going to do that. I started meeting many people and talking to everyone in business and CEO positions. The luxury of my job is that I get to speak to many people, meet many different types of businesses, and start building my network. I was in my dream job. Unfortunately, I am not a great employee. So I talked to the CEO and said, "Hey, I have some ideas that I think would be amazing. Would you be interested in hearing them? Because I want to stay working for you, but I also need to feed this entrepreneurship spirit in me."

I brought some ideas, and we created some companies! We started a funding company for subprime auto lending. We manufactured CBD and started a magazine telling CEO stories about giving back to the community. I was very proud of the businesses we started.

I began to feel that I had a choice in how I thought and felt. My life forever changed when I went to Canada and met Bob Proctor at his house. Everything was exploding in my life, learning about synchronicities and healing. It came into my life in such a profound way. Everything I thought about became my reality. I started consciously participating in life. I was living such a high daily life. I learned to play with what it meant to manifest and to play with energy and move energy. I was living like a giant balloon, full of air and life. Everywhere I went was magical.

Then I would go home; my husband was still struggling at that time. I remember the day I decided I needed to let go of the resentment and blame I was holding between us. If I let go of this resentment and guilt, I would move into a thriving state. I realized that it was mine. This was a vast, profound thing for me. This was probably the biggest game changer in my marriage and my life. I feel like I have released my husband from all my energetic expectations. The most magical thing happened when I removed the shame and guilt he was receiving from me.

I released the control I thought I had and the perception of control I had in the world about the realness of my life. I decided to let go of the illusion of a life that does not exist. I accepted it to be what it is, let everyone be who they are, let everything fall where it may, and trust it. Let go of my judgment for myself and Ryan. That energetic release and the healing that came with that is what changed every single thing in my marriage and kept my life moving profoundly.

That energetic release of my shame and guilt put on Ryan every day began dissipating. I released myself and focused on love, light, peace, health, wealth, and healing. Our lives begin to radically, radically shift. And that was a game changer for me to give up the illusion of control, the blame, and the shame that I put on the things outside me for how I felt.

I learned about emotion. It started at the Metrix with Bob Proctor. He taught about what you think you can hold in your hand. When I was there, I received downloads about emotions. I did not know why I was learning all of this. I would listen to him all day, then journal at night. I wrote a whole book about emotions while there. I declared that I would teach about "emotions" globally through technology. I had no idea what that meant, but I claimed it at that event.

Everything started to shift when I cared more about my feelings than anything else. I had to let go of my resistant emotions. Feel them, heal them, and let them go. It was the most powerful thing to reclaim my feeling and then start to clean up the thinking to get out of the programming that caused those emotions, or that those emotions caused, depending on how you look at it.

I realized that all those businesses and that part of my life had served their purpose. I wanted to be in a thriving marriage with the love of my life, Ryan. I needed to reevaluate. I wanted to be more present as a mother. I started to love myself again.

We made a radical decision for me to quit. I decided to leave my day job and these companies. I knew why I built them. It was ego-based, trying to feed my ego to prove to the world I could. I did it, yea me! I wanted something more. I wanted a thriving life with my husband and family. I wanted to be with Ryan, this amazing man who had gone through his healing and transformation. He remembered his joy, connected with his soul, and let go. He was no longer held captive by old stories, depression, and alcohol abuse. It was the most beautiful thing to witness, and I wanted to be around that more. Not only did I do my work, but I also witnessed the transformation of another person I adored and cared about.

We had begun the creation of Vibeonix. Vibeonix quantifies emotional intelligence by analyzing your voice. I just felt this move through this emotional technology, self-transformation, and self-directed behavior change that came from all of this. We wanted to share that with the world. This is the business we do today.

Just weeks after leaving my corporate job and businesses, the greatest gift arrived - COVID hit. We stayed in our home with our family, and we got this extraordinary time to recalibrate with each other. For the next 18 months, we would work day and night to patent our technology and build our Algorithm, APP, and platform. Our company Vibeonix helps thousands of people increase their emotional intelligence so they too can LIVE. We know that when we feel we heal. Feeling emotions gives life meaning: the ups, the downs, the highs, and the lows. Your emotions are what you experience. They are not who you are!

In February of 2021, we got the call to move. We put our house up for sale in June, and within three months, we sold the home. But we took a massive leap of faith during this time. We moved back to southern Utah, the magical place we loved and lived once again in St. George, Utah.

My life has never been better. Taking the most out-of-control, chaotic, deepest, and darkest situation, I learned. Here's the gratitude. I am a rainbows and butterfly kind of person. So dealing with depression, alcoholism, unworthiness, being unsure, being scared, and feeling fear was a new territory I was trying to avoid. Fear has been my most challenging thing to understand and conquer daily. But to understand the depth of those very negative emotions, I know that every single one of those things that we experienced was for my healing, to understand the absolute depths of those emotions. When we teach how to live a more thriving life, we know what it feels like not to be thriving. We learn to the depths of our being what it feels like to be scared or to feel stressed, lonely, ashamed, guilty, or sad. I am grateful for those experiences; I learned so much and still do every day. I am human. I feel all emotions. I have learned how to feel, move and understand my feelings by increasing my emotional intelligence. I care about myself. I have found how to love myself, and now I know how to love others.

Q&A

Jana: I have one question. You mentioned your coconut milk a few times and have identified lemons throughout your journey. What is the ultimate coconut milk in this story for you?

Kristi: Self-love.

Jana: I wondered. I felt like it would be something around self-trust or self-love. You have shown us how to embrace the contrast in order to help people understand more about who they are. If you did not experience the dark, how could you experience the joy of the light? If you did not have fear or scarcity, how would you ever know you were in a moment of abundance? What do you say about those women reading this book, and maybe some tears are sliding down their face as they feel stuck, alone, or frozen? What is the next step?

Kristi: That what you seek is within. Everything you desire is within. I built the businesses. I had friends. I had the magazines. I had the podcasts. Yet I kept seeking the answers outside myself. The gift came when I remembered it was with me the whole time. When you feel the loneliness, or the fear, or the unworthiness, or the confusion, the peace, the love, and the connectedness is here within you. When we remember that, all the other things outside of you are just magnitudes of it. But that embodiment is within. Just remember that it is nothing you need to seek for. It is just something you need to remember. You are meant to live this life for yourself. It is not for someone else because when you put it outside of you, it's a moving target. That feels exhausting. And it is confusing, and it is hurtful, and it is fearful. It is hard to find the thing because it feels like a moving target. For me, it is just remembering daily that I am a vibrational being having a human experience. That I am not any of those experiences. But I am here to feel and move and be in this life. I am meant to experience all those things, but it is not who I am. For me, it is just to remember that who you are within and what you seek begins to seek you when you just sit in your knowledge of self. When you sit in that self-love and the depth of yourself, the life you are looking for has been with you the whole time.

KRISTI HOLT is the CEO of Vibeonix, an API platform that quantifies wellness using voice analysis AI. Kristi began her career as a young entrepreneur over 20 years ago. As a born entrepreneur, she is recognized for her leadership, community involvement, and ability to mobilize change. Before her role at Vibeonix, Kristi was involved with ten start-up companies in various industries such as E-commerce, Solar, Subprime Auto Lending, CBD Manufacturing, Media company (local magazine), and Technology. She has successfully exited 6 of her start-up companies. With each start-up, Kristi has fundraised, led an acquisition, led sales and marketing, and developed numerous successful processes.

At Vibeonix, Kristi's business strategy has radically transformed businesses and the lives of those who have used her product. In an age of various new ways to measure wellbeing, she has developed a product that is unique to the market in measuring vocal frequency as an insight into emotion. She has spent years building an innovative voice technology assessment and aims to shed light on one's genuine emotions and how to build a healthy relationship with each of them.

Although Vibeonix started as an in-depth, multifaceted assessment, it has now transformed into a simple yet revealing tool that anybody can utilize in their journey of self-awareness. Vibeonix aims to make a niche outside the diagnostic space while still being in the conversation about mental health.

Kristi recently founded The M.E.C.A Project, a non-profit foundation on a mission to raise the vibe of humanity. Being a mother of four, she has realized the importance of emotion and wants every child, parent, and adult to have access to tools and resources to increase emotional intelligence. As the Founder/CEO, Kristi is leading the organization's donor program, sponsor partnerships, user experience, and technology development.

We are the most in debt, obese, addicted, and medicated adult cohort in U.S. history! You cannot selectively numb emotion. The M.E.C.A Project closes the gap in the self-growth world by offering free physical, mental and emotional wellness resources, increasing self-awareness through voice technology, and measurable emotional frequency data for users over time. Everyone deserves the opportunity to improve their mental, emotional and physical well-being. Everyone deserves to thrive!

JANA

My lemons to coconut milk story that I'm sharing with you today is really how I came to be a wellness entrepreneur. Growing up as a farm kid, the eldest of three, my upbringing was lots of open space to run around, acres of gardens, fresh fruits and vegetables, with a small town community where the natural thing you did was lend a hand.

At this time in my life, I believed that when you weren't feeling good you went to the doctor, and the doctor figured out what was going on. And then you got better. My pain journey started in my late teens. As a very A-type personality, high achiever, it became normal for me to experience digestive pain and gut pain at certain times of my life. These times seemed to coincide with exams or different sport competitions, or back in the day, waiting for a certain boy to give me a call. And because my dad was also someone who had acid reflux, I remember he would always have Tums in his pick up truck. Some people have breath mints in their vehicles. Well, he would always have Tums, and as a farmer, it tends to be a higher stress type of profession. So I thought well, if dad eats these Tums, maybe I should, too. And I did. But they really didn't help. My stomach pain wasn't a big enough deal when I was in high school so we didn't really do anything about it. Now fast forward to when I was in university. I was in the middle of my four-year Bachelor of Commerce degree, a little more higher stress. To get into that college, you had to have high marks coming out of high school. So everyone there was the same caliber that I was used to in the top of the class back in high school. The workload was more. Not having meals cooked and having to go and pay your own bills all added to the transitional stress of moving from the safety of my family to this new city. Even though I had my then boyfriend, now husband with me, it was still stressful.

I started to experience my digestive pain a little more often. My pain was around my belly button. It was a burning sensation. I found a doctor and I went to see her. Immediately, she listened, we had some basic tests run, and before I knew it, I was on a journey in the medical system to heal my gut. Like a baton in a relay race, I would be passed from one specialist to the next to the next. I would be poked and I would be prodded. I would drink the grossest tasting stuff, the grossest smelling stuff, the grossest feeling in my mouth and throat stuff, and still no answers, no diagnosis came out of any of those tests.

I thought my goals in life were pretty simple, because I only wanted three things. I wanted to marry my high school sweetheart, I wanted to be a mom, and one day, I wanted to run my own business. Having grown up in an entrepreneurial farm family, it just felt like a lifestyle that I wanted. Yes, there were long days, and you're at the mercy of different environmental stressors as an entrepreneur, but yet there was something magical about always having my mom there at sporting events and my dad most times too unless it was seeding or harvest. But that sense of freedom, that sense of impacting through the fruits of your labor, your ideas, your manual labor, was extremely appealing to me. Yet there were some days where I could not get out of bed. By the time I was 22 years old, finishing up my degree, I was taking 11 medications a day. It got to the point where some of the medications I was taking were just to counteract the side effects of some of the medications that were higher up on the list of priority.

There were moments where if I didn't take a certain medication at a certain time, I would literally be doubled over in pain. I started to question, how will I do all these things? These three things- be a wife, be a mom and be an entrepreneur. At this time I was newly engaged, but I kept thinking, I love this man so much. Why would I ever give him what I would call his 'jail sentence'? Why would I ever give him a jail sentence to live his life with a woman who may not be able to enjoy life? Who may not be able to have kids? Who he may not be able to grow old with? Why would I even walk down that aisle knowing that? But I kept it all inside. Voices in my head asking, could my body even get pregnant? Could it even grow a baby for 40 weeks? If this is how my pain is, and it continues to manifest this way, how will I manage a newborn? Can it all be left to Jason? These questions were just going through my mind, spinning over and over and over and over. I was just praying to God that at the next doctor's appointment there would be some answers, but there were never answers. Until one day, I was sitting in my doctor's office and she said to me that on behalf of the medical team, they believed that the pain was in my head, and I was seeking attention, and I should have a nice life.

So talking about lemons, that was a big frickin' lemon that day. I was told once that if you feel like you're going to start to cry, if you look up toward the arch of your brow, the tears don't flow. I think I learned it when I was learning to do my makeup back when I was 13 or 14 years old. And that's what I did, I was trying not to cry because I felt like my lifeline to heal my body was just severed. In my mind, I was thinking if these white coats with stethoscopes believe that the pain is in my head and that I'm seeking attention, maybe that's actually what's happening. I started to question everything about me. I didn't acknowledge it then, but when I look back now, I did go into a depression. I don't know how long I was there for - three months, four months, five months, I don't know. There were days I just didn't want to get out of bed. As a very athletic, volunteer-hearted person who wanted to join everything and be a part of everything, I hid. I did only what was necessary. I didn't realize it, but my pain was literally and figuratively silencing me, taking away my voice. I was in a state of protect, protect, protect from my pain. I would pray at night I would wonder, what did I do, God? What did I do to pull the short straw? It was a moment in my life where I felt there was no way out.

One day, I was in line at the grocery store. I looked over at the magazine rack that's beside every single checkout in a grocery store. I saw Madonna on the cover of a fitness magazine. Madonna and I go back to the Tiger Beat days. I would pull posters out of that magazine. There was John Stamos and my Bon Jovi section, and there was my Madonna section. I had a Tiffany section. I loved everything about the Material Girl. So I picked up that magazine as I wondered, what's Madonna up to these days? One of the headlines in the magazine was the word Pilates. I didn't even know how to pronounce it, I thought it was 'pilots'. I really did. So I put the magazine in my cart and I went home. Without even taking the groceries out of the bags, I picked up the magazine and I sat down and I read the article. It made absolutely zero sense to me. Because the article was talking about this form of movement that healed the body from the inside out. This form of movement that focused on breath and spinal alignment, movement of the spine. It showed some of the exercises, some looked like sit-ups and most of it looked like yoga to me.

I read the article probably about 10 times that night. I thought to myself, I'm going to see if there's a Pilates class somewhere in my city. This was at a time before you could go onto your computer, let alone your phone and Google it. We had our City Leisure Guide with all the different classes offered at our city wellness facilities listed. I went to the P section and I found a Pilates class at our local civic center. It was a mat class on Tuesday and Thursday nights. I treated myself that weekend before my first class to a new water bottle, a new pair of leggings and a new Pilates mat. My husband came with me, but of course he didn't want to go to this Pilates class. He went to lift weights. So he went to lift weights and I went into the studio where the class was being taught. I walked in and immediately I surveyed the room and I made a judgment about every single person in that room. They were older than me, they were all shapes and sizes. Some more lying on their mats, already in meditation or breathing. Others were like chit chatting in groups. And in true Jana Danielson style, I took my new mat, and my new water bottle, with my new leggings that I had on that night, and I went right to the front row, center-stage, right in front of the instructor.

The class started and our instructor began talking about breathing with our diaphragm. I thought to myself, I know the diaphragm because of my fitness education, I knew it was the main muscle that helped us to breathe. The instructor was cueing this breath. She would say, inhale through your nose and fill your belly button with air and exhale out of your mouth. Make this sound like an H-A, relax your jaw, make sure the tongue is not on the roof of the mouth. And I could hear her English words. It was English she was speaking to me. But it could have been some other language because my brain was not interpreting any of those messages into anything close to what my body could create. I could not get air into my belly button, I could barely get air past my collarbones. That exhale made no sense at all to me. Then we started adding spinal movements. We were floating our hips in the air and melting down through our spine. It was a disaster, and about less than 60 seconds in, for the first time in my life, I regretted being in the front row in the center. I wanted to run out of that room. But the idea of that was more frightening to me than just sticking it out for the rest of the class. I promised myself at that moment, the next time I went to class, I would be in the back row right by the door. And that's what got me through that class.

It was a disaster. For some reason though, I lingered after the class. I didn't just roll my mat up and get out of dodge. I lingered for whatever reason. As most of my fellow Pilates classmates had left, my instructor walked up to me and she said nothing. But she just put her arms around me, and just held me. She gave me this great big hug. I melted and I sobbed. The only thing she said to me was, come back on Thursday night. I just nodded at her, and I left the studio. My husband was sitting in the hall waiting for me, and when I came out, of course I'd been crying. Do you know when you're chopping onions for dinner, and you start to cry, and your eyes get all swollen? Well, that's what my eyes were like. I walked out of class and all these people were smiling and talking, leaving that studio space. I walk out and my eyes are swollen, and my nose is running. And he's like, what happened? Are you okay? Do I need to go talk to someone? I just said to him, no, I just have to come back on Thursday. What I realized that night as I was lying in bed was that even though on the outside I looked healthy, I looked happy, on the inside I was dying. I was disconnected from my body. My mindset was not right. But instead of being more depressed and heavy about that, I was so grateful for the lesson that I learned that night. I realized that I was looking outside of myself to heal. It did not even dawn on me for a second that I actually needed to look inside to heal. That's what I started doing.

I went back the next Thursday, and the next Tuesday and Thursday, and the next Tuesday and Thursday, and each Tuesday and Thursday after that for 16 weeks, which took me right up until Christmas of that year. By Christmas I was off every single one of those 11 medications. I had no idea what was going on with my body. I didn't understand in the least. I thought it was just luck. I had all of these old wives' tales beliefs that I would cross my fingers and knock on wood and I wasn't really sharing my journey with anyone because I thought if I tell somebody this, maybe karma was going to come and get me, and my pain would come back. I didn't want that. So, I finally shared it with my husband, and he was so surprised and shocked. He said, what? How have I missed all of this?

I wondered and wondered, how did simple breathing and

movement and integration of the two heal me? Do you know how God, Spirit, the universe, angels, put opportunities in front of you, and if you're too busy you sometimes miss messages? Well, I was so intrigued (and this is years later) I wanted to do my Pilates certification. I was already a mom at that point. Every time I got pregnant, I would stop doing Pilates. I thought, oh, my gosh, when I do swan rocking, I'm going to squash that little embryo, so I would just stop. I would stop. No one told me that I could keep going.

After we had our three boys, I really wanted to learn more and be trained and understand the body in a different way. But at that point, I had to either uproot my family and go to Vancouver or Toronto. We were still farming at the time, we had our corporate jobs, and it just wasn't in the cards. But then, enter the universe, and it's magic. A woman from Phoenix was coming to my little city of Saskatoon, Canada, to do her Pilates mat and comprehensive certification. Like, what are the chances? So I signed up. Jason said to me, what are you going to do with this learning? And I said, I don't know, I don't know. If it is only for me, and you, and these three little boys, whatever I learn, that's enough. But it turned out that that wasn't all it was supposed to be.

I loved it, I fell in love with it. I fell in love with learning. I learned about that diaphragm. I learned about all the body systems. I learned about fascia, I learned about blood flow, I learned about posture and I learned about the pelvic floor. In the middle of that, I learned about mindset and motivation and how the inside out form of movement trumps the outside in form of fitness all day long. All those old belief systems that I subscribed to that you had to leave a puddle of sweat on the floor, that your body had to hurt the next day after a workout to determine if that workout was impactful enough. All of those things were left in the dust. I had a new paradigm. I had a new way of helping myself understand my body. I came to know it really well, so well that people around me were noticing that I was moving differently, that I was looking different.

I have Ukrainian roots and I always wanted a really beautiful pair of black leather high zip-up boots. For the life of me, I could never ever find a pair that I could zip up over my calves. I talked about my Baba in the intro of this book. My Baba would say to me, oh Jana, we are Ukrainian. We just have big bones. Be proud of them. You don't need fancy black boots with zippers and I was like, well, okay, maybe she's right. Maybe I'll embrace my Ukrainian calves, and I'll just stick with pull-on fuzzy boots instead of these beautiful, sexy, black, zip-up heeled boots. And you know what? Through Pilates, my body started to change more than any other time in my life. And I did finally buy a pair of black zip-up, high heeled boots that beautifully went up and over those Ukrainian calves. There were these mini miracles. Not that I'm comparing my black, high-heeled boots to the fact that I weaned myself off 11 medications and was starting to learn about this journey. This amazing journey of healing, of movement. Movement is medicine. I wanted to do more.

So I got my husband, the amazing man in my life, and he recruited six of his friends for guys' class. I got my sister and some of our friends for a girls' class twice a week. I started teaching four classes a week out of our home in the evenings, in addition to running to hockey practice and soccer practice. At that time, I was just wrapping up my corporate career and I was going to be starting my own business consulting firm while teaching Pilates. Those four classes grew into eight, and eight grew into 12, and 12 grew into 16 classes. About 16 months after I taught my first class out of my basement, I was teaching 16 classes a week, and about 20 hours of private sessions while building my business consulting practice.

I came upstairs one night from teaching my classes that night. And of course, Jason was in charge of bedtime. He had the boys sleeping and I walked upstairs. I smiled at him and he had this look on his face, and I was like, what? He said, "I wish you could hear what I hear." I was like, what do you mean? He said, "I wish you could hear what I hear when you're teaching." He said, "Jana, you become a different person when you are down there. You educate in a way that offers bite-sized pieces of information that are accessible for people. They understand you. They get connected to their body. They remember what you teach them. You inspire them with your story. They inspire each other with their own little miracles that are happening in their life. If you haven't seen it by now, this is what you're meant to do." He said, "I want to transition from my corporate job and I want to take over the business consulting practice so that you can open up a Pilates studio outside of our home." He knew that the business consulting business I was building was important to me, I had built a solid business. So that's exactly what we did. That's what we did. He left his corporate job to take over that consulting business and I opened up my first Pilates studio!

We found space for the studio in June 2010. And in September 2010, we opened our doors. My master instructor from Phoenix came back up to Canada and trained more instructors. Those instructors started working with me. It was this beautiful 2,200-square-foot facility and I loved it. I loved it. I was the front desk person, I was the janitor, I was the teacher, I was the scheduler, I was the payroll person, I did it all and I loved it, it was mine. And I was making an impact. Two and a half years into our five-year lease, we couldn't grow our clientele anymore. We were maxed out. So we started looking for new space. In July 2015, we opened the new vision, which was an integrated health therapies clinic along with the studio. I knew that I would find people in my city who believed the same thing that I do, that the body is not a one-trick pony. The body needs different things at different times. When you have experts in their field who understand the integration of wellness, they will not feel threatened if someone goes from their treatment room to another treatment room, or is in their treatment room for less time because of all the movement classes that their patient is doing. I found those people and those people found me. We have been able to impact hundreds of thousands of people, not only within the City of Saskatoon, but online as well. The gift of Covid granted us some new opportunities to think about the business in a different way. We now serve people from around the world online. It gave me the confidence to launch the Metta District, which is my online movement community.

In the meantime, when all that was happening, I fell in love with women's health and pelvic floor wellness. But I got mad. I got really mad, really pissed off, that I would teach workshops based in Pilates, which is all about the core and I would teach about the pelvic floor. No one would talk about it, and then my inbox would be full. And then there would be women meeting me after class in tears expressing that they felt like I was talking directly to them. It was that inspiration that gave me the spark to create the world's first pelvic floor fitness tool called the Cooch Ball for women in the Gooch Ball for men. I educate and inspire with all these different tools, with my team at my bricks and mortar business, with my online Pilates business, and my product. I help people understand that looking within can be absolutely critical to starting their wellness journey.

It's the simple things, the simple things like hydration, proper breathing, good sleep, moving your body. Joseph Pilates said, "Physical fitness is the first requisite of happiness." I truly believe that. Our body is meant to move. We are not born with replacement parts. Even though now in our medical system you can get them, we weren't born with them. This body is meant to last us from our first to our last breath. What are you doing in a day that takes minutes to ensure that that happens? What choices is your present self making to nurture your future self? There have been so many lemons along the way. Those lemons sometimes, in the moment, feel heavy and gross. Sometimes I felt unlucky, and asked the world, why is this happening? Until I really started to dig into the uncomfortableness and realize that these situations were happening for me, not to me.

My pain journey was gifted to me so that I could show up on this planet the way I was meant to show up.

Later in my life, I was gifted a pain journey with our middle son, Will. Then after that, I was gifted a pain journey with my mom. Had I not gone through my own pain journey, I would not have even remotely come close to supporting and serving those two very important people in my life to work through their own pain journeys and help take their lemons and turn them into their coconut milk. As you sit here reading this chapter, I want you to take a big breath in through your nose and a relaxing, calming breath out of your mouth. Whatever lemon is smack dab in front of you right now, I want to encourage you to look at it with a different set of lenses. Look at the colour of the peel. Feel the texture of the peel. If you cut that lemon open and taste the juice, it might make your eyes wince. Smell it. That lemon is multisensorial. What is it there to teach you?

My coconut milk is understanding that I have what I need within. Once I realized that, I was able to be empowered and inspired to change the path of my life. In the moments where it feels like I have this backpack that weighs hundreds of pounds and I can't take another step forward or I'm frozen in fear, I just think of that coconut milk. I go within. Sometimes I'll ask myself, what is one thing right now that I can do? And sometimes that one thing is just to take a big breath. Sometimes that one thing is to go and find Jason and ask him to hold me. Sometimes that one thing is to just go be with my boys. Go walk outside, put my hands on a tree and my feet on the ground. Sometimes that one thing is as simple as that.

Each and every one of us has a sense of resilience. One of Newton's laws states that for every action, there is an equal and opposite reaction. I am a true believer in miracles, in the good Lord, and that what is in front of us is there for a purpose. It's on purpose, for a purpose. That's my coconut milk. That's what I want to leave you with. Look within. You might be extremely surprised at what you find.

JANA DANIELSON is an award-winning wellness entrepreneur who through her own experience with physical pain turned her mess into her message which has now become her mission. She is an Amazon Best Selling Author, Founder of Lead Pilates and Lead Integrated Health Therapies and the Metta District, her online wellness community. She is the creator of the Cooch Ball, the world's first patented pelvic floor fitness tool for women. Jana has coached and consulted with tens of thousands of women from all over the world to help improve their quality of life, their confidence, and their impact in this world. You can connect with Jana on IG @janaldanielson. Also, check out coochball.com, @thecoochball on IG and mettadistrict.com, and @mettadistrict on IG.

CONCLUSION

So there you have it. Pages upon pages upon pages of the divine feminine in its most raw state. It is so easy to look outward and judge, compare and see the lives of others with a different set of lenses that we see our own lives with. I hope that you have made a connection with at least one of these twenty-one women who said 'yes' to this project and who you got to meet within the pages of this book. I know that they have educated you, inspired you and moved you to see your world in a different way.

Life is not a linear experience with tomorrow being better than today and next month being better than this month. Life is a meandering, twisting, turning journey and the contrast of the shadows and the light is a part of that. How we choose to show up on that path is up to us. What are the gifts, what are the lessons, what are the challenges, what are the celebrations?!

I invite you to connect to one of the most untapped superpowers that we have - our mindset. What are the words you use, remember your brain hears them. What are the thoughts spinning in your head, remember your body feels them. What can your current self do right now to nurture your future self?! Right now.....you can take some deep breaths, you can reach for your water bottle, you can get up and move, you can get your feet on the Earth, you can smile, you can give yourself a huge hug. Pick one.

You are amazing, you have had or maybe currently are living in the middle of being gifted with the biggest lemon of your life. What are you going to choose to do with it? My dream for you is that you turn it into the sweetest tasting coconut milk and enjoy every last drop!

Okay, my Sparkly Sisters! Let's stay in touch. You can follow me on Instagram @janaldanielson and keep up to date with all the fun @mettadistrict and @thecoochball on IG.

Now, let me leave you with this . . . we all have a story. I would love the opportunity to connect with those of you who are being called to raise your hand and say "yes" to upcoming Seasons of *When Life Gives You Lemons . . . Drink Coconut Milk*. Email me at info@mettadistrict.com, and we can jump on a call, get to know each other, and maybe you will see your name in future "lemons to coconut milk" pages!

—Jana

www.ingramcontent.com/pod-product-compliance
Lightning Source LLC
Chambersburg PA
CBHW061142120626
46546CB00005B/1894